AT THE RIGHT HAND OF LONGSTREET

RECOLLECTIONS OF A CONFEDERATE STAFF OFFICER

GENERAL G. MOXLEY SORREL

INTRODUCTION TO THE BISON BOOKS EDITION BY

Peter S. Carmichael

UNIVERSITY OF NEBRASKA PRESS
LINCOLN AND LONDON

Manufactured in the United States of America

♾

First Bison Books printing: 1999
Most recent printing indicated by the last digit below:
10 9 8 7 6 5 4 3 2 1

Library of Congress Cataloging-in-Publication Data
Sorrel, G. Moxley (Gilbert Moxley), 1838–1901.
[Recollections of a Confederate staff officer]
At the right hand of Longstreet: recollections of a Confederate staff officer / G. Moxley Sorrel; introduction to the Bison Books edition by Peter S. Carmichael.
p. cm.
Originally published: Recollections of a Confederate staff officer. New York: Neal Pub. Co., 1905. With new introd.
ISBN 0-8032-9267-8 (pbk.: alk. paper)
1. United States—History—Civil War, 1861–1865—Campaigns. 2. Sorrel, G. Moxley (Gilbert Moxley), 1838–1901. 3. United States—History—Civil War, 1861–1865 Personal narratives, Confederate. 4. Longstreet, James, 1821–1904—Friends and associates. 5. Confederate States of America. Army Biography. I. Title.
E470.S72 1999
973.7′3—dc21
99-34461 CIP

No material has been omitted in this Bison Books edition, which begins chapter 1 on arabic page 19.

BISON BOOKS

Christmas, 2016

To Nicholas —

I hope you find enjoyment in this memoir of the "late unpleasantness". May you strengthen your knowledge of our American history by its reading.

Much Love,

Dad

& Katherine (Mom)

Very truly yrs

G. M. Sorrel

TO MY WIFE

This Volume is affectionately

DEDICATED

In illness and tedious convalescence it was she who suggested these reminiscences of the past, as a solace, giving me cheerful encouragement and material assistance in their preparation, for which my grateful thanks are ever hers.

INTRODUCTION TO THE BISON BOOKS EDITION

Peter S. Carmichael

The transformation of James Longstreet's historical image from scapegoat to Confederate hero has been remarkable. Until the 1974 publication of Michael Shaara's *Killer Angels*, most Civil War enthusiasts and historians saw James Longstreet as a villain. He was disloyal, Lee's Judas, a man who lost Gettysburg because of his seditious ways, and thus the South's best chance for independence. This damning interpretation surfaced in the 1870s with the Lost Cause writings of Jubal A. Early and William N. Pendleton. Their criticisms drew not so much from Longstreet's battlefield performance, but from his postwar criticisms of Lee and his allegiance to the Republican Party. In many ways, Longstreet was his own worst enemy. He wildly exaggerated his contributions to the Army of Northern Virginia, often at the expense of Lee and his fellow officers. He even characterized Lee as a general who relished a good bloodletting on the battlefield. Once Longstreet had insulted the Confederacy's greatest chieftain, the gloves were tossed off across the South. Confederates of all ranks eagerly joined the Longstreet witch-hunt, waging a bitter and malicious campaign that ultimately destroyed the general's military record.

Only a few ex-Confederates challenged the anti-Longstreet crusade. Next to the famous First Corps artillerist Edward Porter Alexander, Gilbert Moxley Sorrel stands as Longstreet's most important defender. In *At the Right Hand of Longstreet: Recollections of a Confederate Staff Officer*, Sorrel offers a balanced view of his former superior that captures the complexity of the man, his faults and virtues, without succumbing to the popular view of the time that

Longstreet was a malevolent and conniving subordinate.

Although Sorrel would eventually receive a brigadier's commission and command a brigade in the Army of Northern Virginia, he is best known for serving as Longstreet's chief of staff. Born into a prominent Savannah, Georgia, family on February 23, 1838, Sorrel received most of his education at Chatham Academy. Just before Fort Sumter, he worked in his native city as a clerk for the Central Railroad. Although the position lacked prestige and lucrative financial rewards, he acquired the skills necessary to manage the administrative affairs of the First Corps. On June 1, 1861, Sorrel enlisted in the Georgia Hussars, but the War Department's tardiness to accept the unit for Confederate Service frustrated the young private. After thirty days he received his discharge and headed to Virginia. A short stay in Richmond preceded his arrival at his father's home in Fauquier County, not far from General P. G. T. Beauregard's army at Manassas. Through his father, who knew the adjutant of the neighboring Confederate force, Sorrel became a volunteer aide to General Longstreet. He acquitted himself well at First Manassas, impressing James Longstreet who wrote that Sorrel "came into battle as gaily as a beau, and seemed to receive orders which threw him into more exposed positions with particular delight."[1] Not wanting to lose the services of Sorrel, Longstreet became a strong advocate of the Georgian, asking for his promotion to captain and brigade assistant adjutant general. Richmond authorities granted the request on September 1, 1861.[2]

As Longstreet's stock rose in the Army of Northern Virginia, so did Sorrel's. His promotion to major and divisional adjutant became effective to date from May 5, 1862.[3] With his increased responsibilities came the politics of command, a minefield impossible to avoid. After the Seven Days' Campaign, the *Richmond Examiner* published a favorable piece on A. P. Hill's division that slighted Longstreet's men. Outraged by this perceived injustice, Longstreet contradicted the *Examiner* in a letter to the *Richmond Whig*. Instead of signing his own public defense, he asked Sorrel to merely sign the article as adjutant general. Sorrel dutifully fulfilled his superior's wish, believing the article would set the record straight without offending Hill. It proved to be a bombshell that initiated a heated, acrimonious correspondence between the two officers. At one point Hill refused to acknowledge any order or correspondence signed by Sorrel. Longstreet considered this insubordination, and requested Sorrel to place Hill under arrest. A nervous Sorrel walked into Hill's tent and told the general that he was confined to his own camp. Hill did not speak. He only saluted. "The occasion however," Sorrel recalled after the war, "was smooth, formal, and courteous—Afterwards I had nothing but kindness from poor Hill."[4] Lee eventually intervened and healed relations between Longstreet and Hill and their accompanying staffs.

Sorrel's duties extended beyond mind-numbing bureaucratic matters to the battlefield where he behaved with exceptional gallantry and effectiveness. When the Confederate center nearly collapsed at Antietam on September 17, 1862, Sorrel and other members of Longstreet's staff worked the guns of the Washington Artillery. Later in the day, when carrying some orders, a shell fragment bruised his right shoulder. At Gettysburg, on July 2, he again was hit by a shell fragment that paralyzed his right arm for ten days. He impressed his comrades with his fearlessness, his single-minded determination to execute orders regardless of his own safety. By the spring of 1863, Longstreet started to campaign for Sorrel's promotion to brigadier general, writing to a Georgia congressman that Sorrel "has had more experience probably than any Brigadier now in the Service, and is well qualified by capacity[,] experience and gallantry."[5] A wreath and three stars did not immediately follow, but a lieutenant colonel's commission arrived during the Gettysburg campaign, dated June 23, 1863. Not all members of the First Corps regarded Sorrel so favorably, however. Fellow staff officer Francis W. Dawson considered Sorrel "bad tempered and inclined to be overbearing."[6]

Sorrel's finest moment with the Army of Northern Virginia came at the Wilderness when he orchestrated a brilliant flank attack on May 6, 1864. Winfield Scott Hancock's Union Second Corps had launched a devastating attack against the Confederate right flank earlier in the morning, nearly breaking Lee's line. In the confusion of battle, Hancock had neglected his left flank. Longstreet would not let this kind of opportunity pass. He immediately called on Sorrel, telling his chief of staff that "there is a fine chance of a great attack by our right. . . . Hit hard when you start, but don't start until you have everything ready."[7] Although there is some controversy about who led the flanking party, the contemporary evidence conclusively proves that Sorrel commanded this critical mission. Using an unfinished railroad to screen his movements, Sorrel drove Hancock's surprised soldiers to the Brock Road defenses with four Confederate brigades. Longstreet followed his victorious soldiers, hoping to capitalize upon Sorrel's flank attack when a Confederate volley accidentally hit the general and a number of other officers. Sorrel rode near Longstreet when he tumbled out of his saddle, and the lieutenant general gurgled on his own blood from a grievous throat wound that nearly took his life on the field.

Longstreet's wounding ended the First Corps's offensive, but Sorrel's attack had stabilized Lee's flank, extinguishing any possibility of a Union counterattack. The army recognized the tactical ingenuity of Sorrel's movement, including one Confederate soldier who observed that "we made a brigadier of him that day."[8] Maybe so, but it probably did not hurt that Longstreet urged for Sorrel's promotion while convalescing from his Wilderness wound. In his official report, he noted that "much of the success of the movement is due to the very skillful manner in which the move was conducted by Lieutenant-Colonel Sorrel." A different Longstreet letter to Robert E. Lee asked for Sorrel's promotion to brigadier general on May 19, 1864. Not until October 31, however, did Sorrel receive his brigadiership, a commission to rank from October 27.[9] Ironically, his old adversary, A. P. Hill, secured his promotion. Hill specifically asked for Sorrel to command Wright's brigade, a disorganized and demoralized crew of Georgians who lacked capable leadership. One of his new soldiers acknowledged that Sorrel "is very brave & also very kind," but that "he is not at all handsome."[10] Sorrel revitalized his new command, and led it into battle at Hatcher's Run on February 7, 1865. In his first major battle as a brigade commander, he received a serious wound to his right lung that sidelined him for the rest of the war. While attempting to return to the Army of Northern Virginia, Sorrel learned of Lee's surrender to Appomattox. After the war Sorrel returned to Georgia and served as the manager of the Ocean Steamship Company. He also served on the Savannah city council from 1873 to 1875, and as an officer of the Georgia Historical Society. Shortly before his death on August 10, 1901, he wrote *Recollections of a Confederate Staff Officer*. The book was published posthumously in 1905. He is buried in his native Savannah.

Sorrel's written legacy, *At the Right Hand of Longstreet*, ranks above most postwar memoirs because it is not overly burdened by Lost Cause ideas and rhetoric. Unlike most ex-Confederates, Sorrel stepped outside the dominant opinion of the time, delivering a mild but deliberate critique of Lost Cause orthodoxy. Such a bold move might have resulted in social ostracism if he had been alive when the book was published. His wariness of Lost Cause dogma originated, in part, from his recognition that historical memory could sidetrack the pursuit of truth. With disturbing regularity he had witnessed his old comrades twist the past for their own purposes. "The memory alone is called on," Sorrel admitted in writing his book, "and as the events go back forty years it is something of a test; but I hope I am rather strong on that point" (41). His earnest pursuit of objectivity translated into a rich volume, chock-full of perceptive sketches and critical analysis of Lee's officer corps.

Like Douglas Southall Freeman in his masterpiece, *Lee's Lieutenants: A Study in Command* (1934–35), Sorrel tells the story of the Army of Northern Virginia by using a group biography approach. This is not a tactical rehash of the army's movements. Such originality impressed Freeman who wrote in 1959 that Sorrel's book possessed an "easy style," only surpassed by Richard Taylor's *Destruction and Reconstruction* (1879). Freeman thought Sorrel's volume "deserved a larger circulation than it has enjoyed."[11] Although Sorrel's book reads like a tabloid at times, full of intriguing gossip, he gives honest assessments of his fellow officers, never afraid to expose their weaknesses. In the case of George Pickett, widely recognized throughout the army as a perpetual adolescent and an unreliable officer, Sorrel writes that "taking Longstreet's orders in emergencies, I could always see how he looked after Pickett, and made us give him things very fully; indeed, sometimes stay with him to make sure he did not get astray" (54).

What is particularly striking about *At the Right Hand of Longstreet* is that it never succumbs to the Lee worshiping or the Longstreet bashing so widely practiced by Sorrel's peers. He is careful, however, not to elevate Longstreet at the expense of Lee. He admits that Longstreet sulked at Gettysburg and displayed a curious lethargy that nearly incapacitated Lee's army. "As Longstreet was not to be made willing and Lee refused to change or could not change," Sorrel wrote of Gettysburg, "the former failed to conceal some anger. There was apparent apathy in his movements. They lacked the fire and point of his usual bearing on the battlefield" (167). Lee also does not escape Sorrel's critical eye. After Ambrose E. Burnside's 1862 debacle at Fredericksburg, he believed the commanding general squandered a great opportunity by not counterattacking. Sorrel even echoed the controversial sentiments of Longstreet, when he unequivocally stated that "to succeed, he [Lee] knew battles were to be won, and battles cost blood, and blood he did not mind in his general's work" (80).

Instead of a strident defense of Longstreet, which some might expect from a confirmed First Corps man, Sorrel provides a more sympathetic, human view of the general. He emphasizes the light-hearted, spontaneous side of "Old Pete," a man who loved to sing with his fellow officers, play a quick game of cards, or stay up late enjoying some fine whiskey. The relaxed, jocular tone around First Corps headquarters reflected the demeanor of its commander. No wonder Sorrel developed such a lasting bond and deep affection for Longstreet and his fellow staff members. At the end of his book, he imagined the time when he would "cross the river like the others." When death came, Sorrel planned to ask: "Where is the Army of Northern Virginia? For there I make my camp" (292). If there is any justice in the afterlife, greeting Sorrel at the pearly gates would be the outstretched arm of "Lee's Old War Horse."

NOTES

1. William A. Blair, "Gilbert Moxley Sorrel," in *The Confederate General*, ed. William C. Davis (Harrisburg PA: National Historical Society, 1991), 5: 192.

2. Compiled Service Record of Gilbert Moxley Sorrel (hereaf-

ter cited as CSR), M331, roll 233, National Archives, Washington DC (repository hereafter cited as NA).

3. CSR, NA.

4. Gilbert Moxley Sorrel to Thomas Jewett Goree, 5 March 1888, *Longstreet's Aide: The Civil War Letters of Major Thomas Goree*, ed. Thomas W. Cutrer (Charlottesville: The University Press of Virginia, 1995), 169.

5. James Longstreet to Julian Hartridge, 28 February 1863, CSR, NA.

6. Francis W. Dawson, *Reminiscences of Confederate Service, 1861–1865* (Baton Rouge: Louisiana State University Press, 1980), 128.

7. Robert E. L. Krick, "Like a Duck on a June Bug: James Longstreet's Flank Attack, May 6, 1864," in *The Wilderness Campaign*, ed. Gary W. Gallagher (Chapel Hill: University Press of North Carolina, 1997), 242.

8. Blair, "Gilbert Moxley Sorrel," 193.

9. U.S. War Department, *The War of the Rebellion: A Compilation of the Official Records of the Union and Confederate Armies*, 127 vols., index, and atlas (Washington DC: Government Printing Office, 1880–1901), ser. 1, 36(1): 1055; James Longstreet to R. E. Lee, 19 May 1864, CSR, NA.

10. Letter from James P. Verdery, addressee unknown, 9 November 1864, James P. Verdery Papers, William R. Perkins Library, Manuscript Department, Duke University, Durham NC.

11. Douglas Southall Freeman, *The South To Posterity: An Introduction to the Writing of Confederate History* (New York: Charles Scribner's Sons, 1939), 176–77.

CONTENTS

CONTENTS

INTRODUCTION

BY

JOHN W. DANIEL

Formerly Major and Assistant Adjutant-General
Early's Division, Second Corps, A. N. V.

A few months ago I entered a room where a group of five or six gentlemen were seated around a table in conversation. As I took my seat to join them, one of the number, a distinguished Northern Senator, of high cultivation and who is a great reader of history, made this remark to his companions: "The Army of Northern Virginia was in my opinion the strongest body of men of equal numbers that ever stood together upon the earth." As an ex-Confederate soldier I could not feel otherwise than pleased to hear such an observation from a gentleman of the North who was a student of military history. As the conversation continued there seemed to be a general concurrence in the opinion he stated, and I doubt if any man of intelligence who would give sedate consideration to the subject, would express a different sentiment.

The Army of the Potomac, the valiant and powerful antagonist of the Army of Northern Virginia, was indeed of much larger numbers, and better equipped and fed; but it would have nevertheless failed but for its high qualities of soldiership which are by none more respected than by their former foes. Both armies were worthy of any steel that was ever forged for the business of war, and when General Grant in his "Memoirs" describes the meeting after the surrender of the officers of both sides around the McLean House, he says that they seemed to "enjoy the meeting as much as though they had been friends separated for a long time while fighting battles under the same flag." He prophesied in his last illness that "we are on the eve of a new era when there is to be great harmony between the Federal and Confederate."

That era came to meridian when the Federal Government magnanimously returned to the States of the South the captured battle-flags of their regiments. The story of the war will be told no longer at soldiers' camp-fires with the feelings of bygone years, or with even stifled reproach, but solely with a design to cultivate friendship and to unfold the truth as to one of the most stupendous conflicts of arms that ever evoked the heroism of the human race.

"Recollections of a Confederate Staff Officer," by Brigadier-General G. Moxley Sorrel, of the Army of Northern Virginia, is a valuable contribution to this great history. Its author received his "baptism of fire" in the First Battle of Manassas, July 21, 1861, while serving on the staff of Brigadier-General James Longstreet as a volunteer aid, with the complimentary rank of captain.

The forces under General Beauregard at Bull Run were known at that time as "The Army of the Potomac." The name of the antagonist of the Federal "Army of the Potomac" was soon changed to the "Army of Northern Virginia"; and Longstreet, the senior brigadier, became major-general and then lieutenant-general.

Sorrel followed the fortunes of his chief, serving as adjutant-general of his brigade, division, and corps, with rank successively as captain, major, and lieutenant-colonel, and distinguished himself many times by his gallantry and efficiency. During the siege of Petersburg the tardy promotion which he had long deserved and for which he had been time and again recommended, came to him and he succeeded Brigadier-General Girardey, a gallant soldier who had been killed in battle, as commander of a brigade in Mahone's division, A. P. Hill's Third Corps.

When promoted he showed the right spirit by making a faithful and brave courier his aide-de-camp. As a general, as well as while on the staff, Sorrel often had his "place in the picture by the flashing of the guns." At Sharpsburg he leaped from his horse, with Fairfax, Goree, Manning, and Walton, of Longstreet's staff, to serve as cannoneers at the guns of the Washington Artillery, whose soldiers had been struck down. While he was carrying a message to a brigade commander his horse was shot under him, and still later on the same field a fragment of a shell struck him senseless and he was for a while disabled. He passed through the maelstrom of Gettysburg, here and there upon that field of blood; the hind legs of his horse were swept away by a cannon ball, and at the same time he and Latrobe, of Longstreet's staff, were carrying in their arms saddles taken from horses slain under them.

At the Wilderness, May 6, 1864, he was at the side of his chief when that officer was badly wounded, and when General Jenkins, of South Carolina, and Captain Dobie of the staff were killed. He won his general's wreath that day, although it was some time before it reached him. At the crisis when Longstreet's corps was going to the rescue he was entrusted with marshalling three brigades to flank the advancing forces of General Hancock. Moving forward with the line of the Twelfth Virginia Infantry, of Mahone's brigade, he endeavored to take its colors as it advanced to the onset, but Ben May, the stout-hearted standard-bearer, refused him that honor and himself carried them to victory. When this battle was over General Lee saluted him as "General Sorrel."

He was wounded in the leg while commanding his brigade on the right of the Confederate line near Petersburg; and again he was shot in the lungs at Hatcher's Run in January, 1865, the same action in which fell the brave General John Pegram, then commanding Early's old division.

During the illness resulting from this wound, General Sorrel was cared for by relatives in Roanoke County, Virginia, and having recovered sufficiently returned to the field. He was in Lynchburg, Virginia, on his way back to his command when the surrender at Appomattox ended the career of the Army of Northern Virginia.

Scarcely any figure in that army was more familiar to its soldiers than that of General Sorrel, and certainly none more so to the soldiers of the First Corps. Tall, slender, and graceful, with a keen dark eye, a trim military figure, and an engaging countenance, he was a dashing and fearless rider, and he attracted attention in march and battle by his constant devotion to his duties as adjutant-general, and became as well known as any of the commanders.

General Sorrel has not attempted a military history. He has simply related the things he saw and of which he was a part. He says of his writings, "that they are rough jottings from memory without access to any data or books of reference and with little attempt at sequence." What his book will therefore lack in the precision and detail as to military strategy or movement, will be compensated for by the naturalness and freshness which are found in the free, picturesque, and salient character of his work.

General Sorrel was of French descent on his father's side. His grandfather, Antoine Sorrel Des Revieres, had been a colonel of engineers in the French Army, and afterwards held estates in San Domingo, from which he was driven by the insurrection of the negroes in the early part of the nineteenth century. He then moved to Louisiana.

His father, Francis Sorrel, became a successful business man in Savannah, Georgia, and his mother was a lady of Virginia. If he inherited from one those distinctively American qualities which were so attractive in his character, we can but fancy that he inherited in some degree at least from his sire the delicate touch with the pen which is so characteristic of the French. They have written more entertaining memoirs than any other people, and this memoir of General Sorrel is full of sketches, incidents, anecdotes, and of vivid portraitures and scenes which remind the reader no little of the military literature of the French.

No military writer has yet undertaken to produce a complete history of either the Army of the Potomac or the Army of Northern Virginia. Indeed, it has scarce been practicable to write such a history. The rolls of the two armies have not yet been published, and while the War Records have furnished a great body of most valuable matter and there are many volumes of biography and autobiography which shed light on campaigns and battles, the deposit of historical material will not be finished before the whole generation who fought the war has passed from earth. This volume will be useful to the historian in giving him an insight to the very image and body of the times. It will carry him to the general's headquarters and from there to the picket-line; from the kitchen camp-fire and baking-oven to the hospital and ordnance wagon; from the devices of the commissary and quartermaster to the trenches in the battlefield; from the long march to the marshalled battle line; from the anxieties of the rear-guard of the retreat to the stern array of the charging columns. He will find some graphic accounts of leading characters, such as Longstreet, Ewell, D. H. Hill, A. P. Hill, Jeb Stuart, Early, Anderson, Mahone, Van Dorn, Polk, Bragg, and many others who shone in the lists of the great tourney. The private soldier is justly recognized, and appears in his true light all along the line, of which he was the enduring figure. Lee, great and incomparable, shines as he always does, in the endearing majesty of his matchless character and genius.

General Sorrel's book is written in the temper and spirit which we might expect of the accomplished and gallant soldier that he was. It is without rancor, as he himself declares, and it is without disposition unduly to exalt one personage or belittle another. It bespeaks the catholic mind of an honest man. It tells things as he saw them, and he was one who did his deed from the highest and purest motives.

The staff of the Army of Northern Virginia (of which G. M. Sorrel, assistant adjutant-general, was a bright, particular star) was for the most part an improvised affair, as for the most part was the whole Confederate Army, and indeed the Federal Army was almost as much so. It showed, as did the line of civilians turned quickly into soldiers, the aptitude of our American people for military service and accomplishment. Even the younger officers of military training were needed in armies of raw and inexperienced recruits for many commands.

The staff had to be made up for the most part of alert young men, some of them yet in their teens, and it is remarkable that they were so readily found and so well performed their duties.

At twenty-two years of age Sorrel was a clerk in a Savannah bank, and a private in a volunteer company of Savannah. He slipped away from his business to see the bombardment of Fort Sumter in April, 1861, and a little later we then find him at his father's country estate some ten miles from Manassas Junction, looking forward to a second lieutenancy as the fulfilment of his then ambition.

An introduction from Col. Thomas Jordan, the adjutant-general of Beauregard, to General Longstreet fixed his career with that officer, and he was by his side transacting his business and carrying his orders from the start to well-nigh the finish. On the Peninsula, and in the trenches at Yorktown, at Williamsburg and Seven Pines, in the Seven Days Battle around Richmond, at Second Manassas and Sharpsburg, at Suffolk in southeast Virginia, at Gettysburg, Chickamauga, at Knoxville, at the Wilderness, and in many combats along the Richmond and Petersburg lines, General Sorrel shared in many adventures and was a part of many matters of great pith and moment. Like Sandy Pendleton, the adjutant of Jackson, of Ewell, and of Early as commanders of the Second Corps of the Army of Northern Virginia, and like W. H. Palmer, of Richmond, the adjutant of A. P. Hill, he had no special preparation for his military career; and all three of these valuable officers, like many others who might be mentioned, are simply illustrations of the fine inherent qualities that pertain to the scions of a free people.

I have not written this introduction in the hope that I could add anything to the attractiveness of

General Sorrell's recollections, nor have I undertaken to edit them or to pass upon the opinions which he expressed concerning men or things or battles. My part is simply that of a friend who belonged also to the staff of the Army of Northern Virginia, and of one who, from opportunities to observe General Sorrel on many occasions and to know him personally, learned to honor and admire him. I deem it fitting, however, to say that in some respects I differ from General Sorrel's opinions and would vary some of his observations respecting Ewell, Stuart, Early, and a few other conspicuous leaders.

"Fortunate indeed is the man who like General Sorrel is entitled to remind those around his deathbed that he did his best to do his duty and to serve his country with heart and soul. The records of his life tell us how well, how faithfully he did serve her, and if anything can console you and others for his loss it must be that fact."

These are the words of Field Marshal Wolseley, written to Mrs. Sorrel, the widow of the General, upon his death in New York in 1901.

They are worthy of repetition in connection with General Sorrel's name by reason of their just estimate of his worth as a patriot and a soldier, and of the high spirit which they breathe; and that they are uttered by a soldier and a man of such character and ability as Field Marshal Wolseley impresses all the more their inherent merit.

They better introduce the volume of General Sorrel's composition than anything I can say, for they reveal in short compass the nature of the man, the principle that actuated his life, and the estimate formed of him by an eminent soldier who had no partial relation to him or his deeds.

JOHN W. DANIEL.

WASHINGTON, D. C., May 1, 1905.

RECOLLECTIONS OF A CONFEDERATE STAFF OFFICER

CHAPTER I

BATTLE OF MANASSAS, JULY 21, 1861.

Forbears and Home at Savannah—Fort Sumter attacked—Hostilities begin—Leave for Virginia—Visit to my father—Beauregard's camp at Manassas—Colonel Jordan—Introduced to General Longstreet—Sketch—General Stuart—General Johnston—The battle—Enemy defeated—Pursuit stopped—March to Centerville—Stonewall Jackson—Prince Napoleon—The review—Colonel Skinner—His Exploits.

My forbears were French on my father's side, His father, Antoine Sorrel des Rivieres, Colonel du Genie (Engineer Corps) in the French Army, was on his estates in the island of St. Domingo when the bloody insurrection of the blacks broke out at the opening of the century. He had the tragic horror of witnessing the massacre of many relatives and friends. His property was destroyed, and his life barely saved by concealment and flight to Cuba, thence to Louisiana, where a refuge was found among friendly kindred. There he died at a great age.

His son Francis, my father, was saved from the rage of bloodthirsty blacks by the faithful devotion of the household slaves, and some years later succeeded in reaching Maryland, where he was educated. He married in Virginia, engaging in business in the early part of the century at Savannah, Georgia.

My maternal great-grandfather, Alvin Moxley, was from Westmoreland County, Virginia. He was one of the signers of what is known as the Richard Henry Lee Bill of Rights, 1765, the first recorded protest in America against taxation without representation, and which twelve years later led directly to the Revolutionary War. The original document is now preserved and framed in the Virginia Historical Society at Richmond.

Death bereft my father of his wife in time's flight. An eminent merchant, successful and prominent, we find him in the Civil War in health and ease, happy in the love of many children and the esteem of hosts of friends. As a child he had seen some horrors of the insurrection, but never could he be persuaded to speak of them, so deep and painful were even their distant memories. At the culmination of the political troubles in 1861 I was a young chap just twenty-two, at home in my native city, Savannah, peacefully employed with the juniors of the banking force of the Central Railroad.

When Sumter was bombarded at Charleston in April, I slipped away for a day or two and witnessed the scenes of wild excitement that attended its fall. It spread everywhere, and like all the youth of the country I was quickly drawn in. For a year or two before, like many of my associates in Savannah, I was a member, a private, of the Georgia Hussars, a fine volunteer cavalry company, with a creditable history of almost a century.

On the secession of Georgia, now soon following, Fort Pulaski was seized and the various military commands did their tour of duty there, the Hussars among them.

This was my first service. The company also immediately offered itself to the Confederate Government just organized at Montgomery, Alabama, and was eager to get into the field; but delay ensued, although it was mustered in for thirty days' service on the coast of Skidaway Island, near Savannah. There I served again as private until mustered out. A Confederate army was being collected in Virginia under Beauregard, the capital having been settled in Richmond. Becoming impatient of inaction at Savannah, our company apparently not being wanted, I decided to go to Virginia and seek employment there.

Richmond looked like a camp when I arrived, in July. It was full of officers in their smart uniforms, all busy with their duties, and the greatest efforts were made for equipping and arming the men now pouring in from the South. They were posted first in camps of instruction, where, by means of younger officers, they attained some drill before being sent to the army. How happy should I be could I get a commission as second lieutenant and plunge into work with the men.

My brother, Dr. Francis Sorrel, had just arrived from California and was gazetted to a high position in the Surgeon-General's Department. He aided me all possible, but I got nothing, and so about July 15, my cash running down, betook myself to my father's pretty country place at Greenwich, about ten miles north of Warrenton, Fauquier County. It was also about ten miles from Manassas Junction, the headquarters of General Beauregard, now in command of the army that was to fight McDowell and defend Richmond. My father said it was unfortunate I had not come a day or two earlier, because he had driven his daughters across the country for a visit to the camps, where they met many friends. Among these was Col. Thomas Jordon, the all-powerful adjutant-general of Beauregard's army, then termed the Army of the Potomac. Many years before, Jordon, when a lieutenant, had been stationed in Savannah, and enjoyed my father's generous hospitality. This was my opportunity.

I asked for just a few lines of introduction to Jordon, and a horse out of the stables. I knew them well and could get a good mount for the field. My dear father willingly acceded, and parted from me cheerfully but with moist eyes. On the way to the camp I came up with Meredith, a relation (not long ago United States Congressman from Virginia), and soon I found Colonel Jordon. He had been doing an enormous amount of work and was almost exhausted.

Jordon was considered a brilliant staff officer, and justly so; but there appeared something lacking in his make-up as a whole that disappointed his friends. At all events, his subsequent military career failed and he sank out of prominent notice. He was kind to me, read my note, said nothing could be done then; but— "Come again to-morrow."

This turned me loose in the camp. The soldiers from the Valley under J. E. Johnston and J. E. B.

Stuart began to make an appearance in small numbers, principally cavalry. We slept that night at Meredith's, about three miles from camp. Jordon, the next day, was still unable to do anything for me, and I began to be doubtful of success, but could at least go as a private with a good horse under me.

Again at Meredith's and awakened very early by cannon, we were up in a moment and galloping to Beauregard's.

There I was made happy on the 21st day of July. The adjutant-general handed me three lines of introduction to Longstreet, commanding a brigade at Blackburn's Ford several miles distant. With a good-by to Meredith I was swiftly off. Approaching the ford, shot and shell were flying close overhead; and feeling a bit nervous, my first time under fire, I began to inquire what folly had brought me into such disturbing scenes.

The feeling passed, however, and Longstreet, who had called on Beauregard for staff officers, received me cordially.

His acting adjutant-general, Lieutenant Frank Armistead, a West Point graduate and of some service in the United States Army, was ordered to announce me to the brigade as captain and volunteer aide-de-camp. Brig.-Gen. James Longstreet was then a most striking figure, about forty years of age, a soldier every inch, and very handsome, tall and well proportioned, strong and active, a superb horseman and with an unsurpassed soldierly bearing, his features and expression fairly matched; eyes, glint steel blue, deep and piercing; a full brown beard, head well shaped and poised. The worst feature was the mouth, rather coarse; it was partly hidden, however, by his ample beard. His career had not been without mark. Graduating from West Point in 1842, he was assigned to the Fourth Infantry, the regiment which Grant joined one year later. The Mexican War coming on, Longstreet had opportunity of service and distinction which he did not fail to make the most of; wounds awaited him, and brevets to console such hurts. After peace with Mexico he was in the Indian troubles, had a long tour of duty in Texas, and eventually received the appointment of major and paymaster. It was from that rank and duty that he went at the call of his State to arm and battle for the Confederacy. History will tell how well he did it. He brought to our army a high reputation as an energetic, capable, and experienced soldier. At West Point he was fast friends with Grant, and was his best man at the latter's marriage. Grant, true as steel to his friends, never in all his subsequent marvelous career failed Longstreet when there was need.

Such was the brigadier-general commanding four regiments of Virginia infantry, the First, Eleventh, Seventeenth, and Twenty-fourth, and a section of the Washington Artillery of New Orleans. The Eighteenth Virginia Infantry was afterwards added.

Three days previously, Longstreet, just joined his command, had opportunity of showing his mettle. His position at the ford was fiercely assailed by the Federals, and his coolness, good disposition, and contagious courage brought about their defeat, and was the beginning of that devotion which his men gave him up to Appomattox. His staff officers at the time were Lieutenant Armistead, Lieutenant Manning of Mississippi, ordnance officer; Captain Walton of Mississippi, aid; Captain Goree of Texas, aid; and some quartermasters and commissaries detailed from the regiments.

The army had scarcely made an attempt yet at good organization.

At Manassas Junction, while waiting on Jordon, I first saw Gen. Joseph E. Johnston and J. E. B. Stuart. The first was full bearded, dusty, and worn from long marching; a high-bred, stern-looking soldier of faultless seat and bearing in the saddle. I had the good fortune to know him well and most happily in the coming years. Once long after the close of the war I was chatting with him in his best humor. We were speaking of his varied military life and the several wounds he had received in Mexico, with Indians, and in the recent Confederate War. He had many, and as he sat in face of me the General's splendid, dome-like head was something to admire. Quite bald, it was scarred in several places, and looking at the mark of an ugly gash I inquired, "And, General, where did you get *that* one?" The smile that irradiated that strong, expressive face was brilliant and contagious as he answered, "I got *that,* sir, out of a cherry tree!" and then followed a laughing account of what a fall he had, and how he had been chased by the farmer.

Stuart, red bearded, ruddy faced, alert and ever active, was dirtier even than Johnston; but there stood the tireless cavalryman, the future right arm of the great Lee, the eyes and ears to his army. Alas! that his pure soldier's life, crowned with such splendid fame, should have ended so needlessly, late in the war, by a stray shot.

I should say here there is to be no attempt at describing battles—the military works are full of them. I shall content myself with bare outlines, and some observations of men and things, adding such incidents and personal happenings as may, I hope, prove of interest.

Longstreet's brigade had practically no part in the battle of Manassas. It sustained some desultory artillery fire, and there was a demonstration against it, but it amounted to nothing. Blackburn's Ford was on the right, where the attack was expected, but McDowell found his way to Beauregard's left and nearly smashed him until Johnston and Jackson came "ventre a terre" and turned the doubtful tide of battle into a ruinous rout of the enemy.

It was late in the afternoon, but we soon heard of it at our ford, and Longstreet, waiting for no man, was immediately in pursuit. He was halted first by Bonham, who ranked him, to permit his brigade to take the lead. Then resuming the march hot-footed, after the flying foe, we were again stopped, this time by Major Whiting, of Johnston's staff, with orders from Beauregard to attempt no pursuit. Painful was this order. We knew the Federals were in full flight, and we had only to show ourselves to bag the whole outfit.

We dismounted among some young pines to await further orders, and I saw Longstreet in a fine rage. He dashed his hat furiously on the ground, stamped, and bitter words escaped him. However, the night was on us, some food was picked up by hook or crook, and we slept well under the stars. The soundness of the order stopping pursuit has been viewed in many different ways, and I shall not add my own opinion, except to suggest that while in the condition of our army it was practically impossible to seize Washington, it was yet the proper thing to keep on the heels of those frightened soldiers until they reached the Potomac. Many thousand prisoners, and much loot and stores, ammunition, guns, colors, and other material would have fallen into our hands.

Next day the field and highways showed the terrible battle that had raged, and the ground was covered with the debris of the panic-stricken army. Our brigade moved leisurely on, and halted for some time at Centerville. The army was concentrated in the neighborhood, and about Fairfax Court House and Fairfax Station, our headquarters being for some time at the former place. About this time Longstreet was joined by two noted scouts and rangers whom he had known in Texas—the celebrated Frank Terry and Tom Lubbock, powerful men, both of them, in the prime of life. Scouting and fighting had been their part from boyhood. They were of much use to Longstreet. From Fairfax Court House and vicinity we sent regular details, called the advanced forces, to occupy Mason's and Munson's hills, only a few miles from Washington. At night the dome of the Capitol could be seen from those positions, lighted up with great splendor. There was sharp sniping in front of the hills, and Terry and Lubbock generally bagged their man apiece, each day, besides bringing in valuable information. Both men soon returned to Texas and organized a regiment of cavalry in the Confederate service under Terry. It was said to be the finest body of horsemen and fighters imaginable, and subsequently did great service in the West. Terry fell among them at their head.

It was while we lay in the neighborhood that I saw Prince Jerome Napoleon, "Plon Plon." It seems he was making a short visit of curiosity (he was no friend of the South), and was at Beauregard's headquarters some distance off.

The General sent notice to Longstreet that he was coming with his staff and guest to call on him, and suggested that he try to get up something in the way of a small review of our best-clad soldiers. Longstreet started me off at once to borrow a regiment from Stonewall Jackson and one from D. R. Jones (South Carolina), both commands being near by. The First Virginia Infantry, the Richmond regiment, was the contingent from our own brigade. I soon found myself saluting General T. J. Jackson, the first time I had seen the soldier. He was seated in a low, comfortable chair in front of his quarters, quite shabbily dressed, but neat and clean—little military ornament about him. It was the eye full of fire and the firm, set face that drew attention. His hand was held upright; a ball at the recent battle had cut off a piece of his finger, and that position eased it. He was all courtesy to the young subaltern awaiting his answer.

"Say to General Longstreet, with my compliments, that he shall have my best-looking regiment, and that immediately. The colonel will report at the point you may designate." This done, Jones gave up his best, some good-looking Carolinians, with palmetto badges, and then spurring back to meet Beauregard and party to guide them to the reviewing ground, he presented me to His Highness the Prince, who, well mounted, was riding by his side. I could not keep my eyes off the Frenchman's face. It was almost a replica of the great Napoleon, his uncle, but unpleasantly so; skin pasty and flabby, bags under the eyes, and beefy all over. A large man, tall, but without dignity of movement or attitude. The review was soon over. The three picked regiments, with a good band, looked well, although the Richmond boys were a bit out at the seat; but, as old Skinner, the Colonel, said to the Frenchman as they marched by, "The enemy won't see that part of them."

The spot was on a nice piece of turf near an old wooden church, and we had gathered a few refreshments for the occasion, but the Prince would have nothing. Coldly and impassively he raised his hat in parting salute, entered the carriage that was awaiting him, and, escorted by a lieutenant of cavalry and a half dozen men under a flag of truce, we willingly sent him back to his friends, the enemy. On returning to France he published what ill he could find to say of us, but "Plon Plon's" abuse was not to hurt or disturb honest men with brave hearts.

A word about Old Skinner, Colonel of the First Virginia. He was an old Maryland fox hunter, handsome and distinguished looking, and had lived long in France, almost domiciled there. He was connected with many of the best people of Maryland and

Virginia, and had hosts of friends. Fond of good liquor, it was almost every night that he was a bit full, and then there were wild scenes with his well-known hunter, Fox, who could do anything or go anywhere with the Colonel on him. Skinner was a fine swordsman, and had brought from France a long, straight, well-balanced double-edged cuirassier's saber. In his cups the fine old Colonel would swear he should die happy could he have one chance to use that steel on the enemy.

The chance came and Skinner was ready for it. At the second battle of Manassas a battery of six guns was mauling some of our infantry horribly. His regiment, the gallant First Virginia, was thrown at it, "Old Fred," as the men affectionately called him, leading well in advance. Out flashed the French saber, and he was among the gunners in a trice. His execution was wonderful; sabering right and left he seemed invulnerable, but down he came at last, just as his men swept over the guns in a fine charge. It was the end of the Colonel's soldiering, but although frightfully wounded in the chest and body he survived for many years. So lively was the old beau sabreur, that only a few years ago he came to New York to fight John Wise because of some fancied slight to a member of his family—Wise, too, his life-long friend! As there could be no fighting, Wise had to do some nice diplomatic work to soothe the irate Colonel and smooth over the affair.

CHAPTER II

After Manassas at Centreville

Commissioned as captain and acting adjutant-general—Pay of officers—Assigned to Longstreet's brigade—The Oglethorpe Infantry, of Savannah—Enemy preparing for winter quarters—Beauregard takes command in West—Confederate flag—Presentation of battle-flags — Starting a theatre—Georgia Hussars—A sleigh ride.

Something must now be said as to what happened to me several weeks after the Manassas battle. It will be remembered I was a volunteer aid with the rank by courtesy, but no pay. When I saw my messmates taking theirs in very comfortably, it occurred to me I should make another effort for a commission, so I wrote my application to the Secretary of War asking to be appointed a second lieutenant, C. S. A., and assigned as might be thought proper. Blushing like a girl, I asked General Longstreet if he could endorse it favorably. Glancing hastily at the paper, he said, "Certainly," and then added carelessly, "but it isn't necessary." The words made no impression at the time, but they came to mind later.

After the battle we had not been idle; at least I was set to work. There was no commissary to the brigade, and for a week or two I did the duty after a fashion until an officer of that department was assigned—Major Chichester. His papers, correspondence, and duties seemed to fall on me, naturally, by his consent, and the brigadier-general soon began to look to me for assistance.

This had been going on for some time until the official mail one fine morning brought me a commission as captain in the Adjutant-General's Department, with orders to report to Longstreet. Then his words leaped to my memory. He had a right to nominate his own adjutant-general and had applied for me while I was fishing around for a second lieutenancy. I had had no military training except some drill and tactics at school, but it seemed he thought I took to the work handily. He instructed me to relieve Armistead and take over all the duties of the office. I rose with Longstreet to be major and lieutenant-colonel in that department, and brigadier-general commanding in Hill's corps, and my affection for him is unfailing. Such efficiency on the field as I may have displayed came from association with him and the example of that undismayed warrior. He was like a rock in steadiness when sometimes in battle the world seemed flying to pieces.

Armistead left us, carrying our good wishes for his future.

I think the pay of a captain (mounted) was $140 per month and forage for two horses; a major, $162 a month; a lieutenant-colonel, $187. All general officers got $301 per month. A soldier said the $1 was for what they did, the $300 just thrown in to please them. Johnny Reb must have his little joke.

The first company to leave Savannah for Virginia was the Oglethorpe Infantry, a fine body of eager young men commanded by Captain Bartow. He was well known all through the State as an ardent Confederate, a distinguished lawyer and orator. He took his young men to Joe Johnston in the Valley, wildly enthusiastic; but Bartow could not long remain their captain. His wide reputation quickly placed him colonel of the Eighth Georgia Infantry, and with that historic regiment the company fought at Manassas, and the entire war thereafter in Longstreet's command. Bartow was commissioned a brigadier and served as such at Manassas. On July 21st many anxious eyes were fixed on it in Savannah. Then was its baptism of fire, and nobly did the young men stand it. Many were the mourners at home for the killed and wounded of these devoted youths. Their officers—West, Cooper, Butler—led them handsomely; their colonel was lost to them and to the country. Bartow was shot down at the head of the Eighth. "They have killed me, boys, but never give up the fight," was his last gasp, and his soul, with the gallant Bee's, sought its upward flight. The company became famous. It left its dead and wounded on every battlefield from Manassas to Appomattox, wherever Longstreet's corps was engaged. Revived now and honored it is at its old home, one of the leading military organizations of Georgia. Never do the men forget the memories of that day of battle on its recurring anniversaries, or fail in pride of their glorious predecessors.

As the winter approached, the enemy drew in their front and lined the fortifications and defenses on the Potomac. McClellan evidently determined not to attack and that the winter must pass idly on their part. The *gaudium certaminis* was no part of him. On ours Johnston drew in his scattered forces, concentrating about Centerville, which he fortified, and there they were, the two armies making faces at each other, and the Northern papers telling wonders about us, all believed by McClellan, whose imagination always doubled, trebled, quadrupled the fighting strength of those desperate Rebels.

While at Centerville the army underwent its first reorganization. Beauregard was sent West to important duty and J. E. Johnston assumed command of the Eastern army, to be forever known and glorious as the Army of Northern Virginia. It was then in four divisions, the second of the three brigades under Major-General Longstreet (Second Virginia and First South Carolina Brigade). First Division, also of three brigades, under Major-General Holmes (down on lower Potomac), and the district of the Valley, under Major-General T. J. Jackson (Stonewall), made up this army, besides artillery and cavalry; the latter under Stuart. The first flag of the Confederacy was the stars and bars, but it was found on the battlefield dangerously similar to the Northern stars and stripes. The battle-flag under which we fought to the finish was then substituted, and it was while we were at Centerville that the military function of presenting the new colors to the battalions was arranged.

The day for our division went off admirably. It was brilliant weather, and all were in their best outfits, and on their best mounts. The troops looked well as the colonels successively received their colors to defend.

Arrangements had been made for a generous hospitality at our division headquarters. We were occupying a dismantled old wooden farm-house well situated in the shade of fine trees. There a sumptuous repast was spread, and the principal officers of the divisions became our guests after the flag ceremonies. These arrangements were made by Major John W. Fairfax, whom Longstreet had had appointed a major and inspector on his staff. Fairfax was a rich man, owning the beautiful broad estate of President Monroe, Oak Hill, on the upper Potomac, in Loudoun County, near Aldie, also a fine property on the lower Potomac.

Major Fairfax was then of middle age, tall, courtly and rather impressive. He had attached himself at once to Longstreet, and took charge of his mess and small wants, presented him with a superb mount, and did the best he could with his new military duties. He lacked nothing in courage; was brave and would go anywhere. But Fairfax had two distinctions—he was the most pious of churchmen and was a born bon vivant, knowing and liking good things. Whiskey later was hard to get, yet he managed to have always a good supply on hand.

He is now a hale and hearty man, wonderfully well preserved.

It was Fairfax, as I said, that provided the feast, drawing the richest materials from his beautiful broad pastures in Loudoun. Everything was plentiful in that stage of the war, and much liquor and wine were consumed. Johnston, G. W. Smith, Van

Dorn, Beauregard, and others of high rank were present, and we had great merriment and singing.

Walton was quite a friend of mine and fond of me. Gifted with uncommon intellectual attainments, the favorite scholar of L. Q. C. Lamar at the University of Mississippi, he was of the most uncertain, unexpected temper and exactions; he could be dangerous at times, and only the greatest firmness held him in check until the humor passed off and then he was all lovely. When the war ended he returned to Mississippi, quarreled with a man, and killed him. Moving to Alabama he found himself in the thick of the yellow fever epidemic of 1878. Dropping all personal interests he devoted himself wholly to the sick and dying, until himself struck down by death. His memory is sweet in that part of the State.

One day, as the winter came on, Longstreet sent for me. "The men will want amusement and entertainment the long winter days," he said. "We must get them up a theater and a good company. See to it at once and lose no time. Issue such orders as may be necessary." That was all, and quite easy for the General. Draw a theater and company, properties and all out of one's pocket like a ripe apple! But it could be done with the resources of a division of infantry at one's hand, and I set about it at once. The colonels each received a note asking help and details from the ranks of actors with some experience They were sure to be found there. But more than all, I wanted a manager, and he soon came out of the First Virginia Infantry to take charge of the play. It was Theodore Hamilton, an actor of some experience. I have met him in several places acting since the peace, and he always comes to me as an old friend, although he was not to tread the boards at the "Centerville Theater."

"Now, Captain," he said, "for scenery and properties. You have the building, I have the company; what about the rest?" It was easy; painters were found in the ranks for scenery, and many of the officers chipping in, we got together enough money to send Hamilton to Richmond to get the costumes and properties. I don't think he made the most of his time there, but he got something, and after many delays we began to think we should see some acting after all. But alas! just then, Johnston, discovering McClellan's movements to the Peninsula, broke up his camp, his officers destroying needlessly an immense amount of valuable supplies, and off we marched merrily to face our old friend, the young Napoleon. Such was the beginning and the end of our first and only attempt at theatricals.

It was while we were about Centerville that a great change came over Longstreet. He was rather gay in disposition with his chums, fond of a glass, and very skilful at poker. He, Van Dorn, and G. W. Smith were accustomed to play almost every night with T. J. Rhett, General Johnston's adjutant-general, and we sometimes heard of rather wild scenes amid these old army chums—all from West Point, all having served in Mexico and against the Indians. Longstreet's wife and children were at Richmond. He was devoted to them. Suddenly scarlet fever broke out and three of the children died within one week. He was with them, and some weeks after resumed his command a changed man. He had become very serious and reserved and a consistent member of the Episcopal Church. His grief was very deep and he had all our sympathies; later years lightened the memory of his sorrow and he became rather more like his old cheerful self, but with no dissipation of any kind.

Before parting with Centerville it should be said that my old troop, the Georgia Hussars, had at last got their services accepted and were brought to Richmond under my friend Captain F. Waring, and mustered in for the war. They were thrown into a regiment known as the Jeff Davis Legion, commanded by Colonel Will T. Martin, which was to prove itself a fine body of horse.

While in quarters this winter there were several light falls of snow, a novelty to most of our Southern fellows. Not many of them were familiar with such descents from the clouds. There came, however, a storm anything but interesting. Snow was lying deep and camps were almost hidden.

My staff comrade, Peyton Manning, and myself decided it was the time for a sleigh ride of our own. No cutters were to be had, but we improvised one. Securing a stout, well-made box of good size, a plank seat in it for two made it the body of the fabric. Then the forests yielded a couple of slim saplings, which, bent at the ends over the fire, were not bad for runners. On these, braced and crossed, with shafts attached, our box, well elevated, was securely fastened, and there was our cutter. We settled that the team should be stylish and made it "tandem," in good extemporized harness. My charger was put in the shafts and Manning's in the lead, both high-spirited animals. Each horse was mounted by a small negro, postilion-fashion, good riders both, and supposed to add some safety as well as novelty to the equipage.

Manning undertook to handle the long reins from the bits, and we started, the observed of many curious, and amid the worst lot of evil prophecies of what would befall us that it was ever my fate to hear. The outfit took the road handsomely, cheered by the soldiers, our black postilions grinning with delight.

All went well for a time and then the devil himself broke loose! The spirit of the horses rising, especially that fiery brute of Manning's, they were off entirely beyond control. Over the deep-snowed roads and fields, across ditches and broken fences the gallant pair in mad race took everything on a full run, their postilions now ashy hue with terror and clinging like burs to the bounding animals. The finish came quickly. There seemed to be a sudden great fall of stars from the midday skies and Manning and I were hurled right and left into deep snow drifts, everything in pieces, horses and little niggers quite out of sight. Digging ourselves out we took a good look at each other and some ugly words were said; but although scratched and bruised no bones were broken, and we slowly trod our way back to camp, wiser if not better men from our first and last sleigh ride in old Virginia. The horses were brought back to quarters but never again were their black postilions seen in those parts.

CHAPTER III

Reminiscences and Horses.

Visit to Mr. Francis Sorrel's country-seat—Interment of Captain Tillinghast, U. S. A.—Sir William Howard Russell, *Times* correspondent—McDowell and July 21st—Seward and the French princes—Army begins to march to Peninsula.

Not long after the battle I set out on a visit to my father's country place, Ireland, fifteen miles from our camp. Hitching up two good mules to a light army ambulance, what we needed was put in, our intention being to bring back some delicacies for the messes. Captain Thompson, of Mississippi, one of the aids, accompanied me. He was an extraordinary looking person. Nature had been unkind. The son of Jacob Thompson, Buchanan's Secretary of the Interior, he had much to hope for, but for his affliction. His teeth and jaws were firmly set and locked, and no surgical ingenuity had yet succeeded in opening them. Liquids could be conveniently taken, but mechanical arrangements had to be made for solid food by the removal of some teeth.

This young officer showing a great desire to go along with me, was taken, although I could not help picturing some surprise on the part of my father and young sisters. We were made very welcome, as fresh from the glorious battlefield, and the day was a happy one. The girls had made a captain's coat for me out of homespun cloth; but such a fit! big enough for two captains of my thickness, it hung at all angles and flapped furiously in high winds. But love had prompted its making and I would never suffer any ugly remarks about it.

Something better soon came. My brother, Doctor Sorrel, in Richmond, was always mindful of his juniors in the field, and getting possession of a blockade bolt of fine gray cloth, he soon had enough snipped off to make me two good Confederate suits, suitably laced and in regulation trim, besides a long gray cape, or cloak, well lined, which was to do me good service for years.

At "Ireland" they loaded our ambulance with good things and there were shouts of joy when we reached the camp with the delicacies.

Captain Thompson was not subject to military duty and soon returned to his home.

It should be said here that these jottings are without the aid of a scrap of notes or other memoranda. The memory alone is called on, and as the events go back forty years it is something of a test; but I hope I am rather strong on that point and do not fear falling into inventions or imaginations. There were some dry notes of dates and marches, but they cannot be found, and they would be of no use with these jottings, as no attempt at dates is made. It is a lasting regret to me that as a staff officer with opportunities of seeing and knowing much, I did not keep up a careful diary or journal throughout the war. It should be made one of the duties of the staff.

This is odd. The day after the battle I came across the body of Captain Tillinghast at the Federal field infirmary near the stone bridge. The year previous I had been much in Baltimore at the Maryland Club and had there played billiards with Tillinghast, then a captain of Artillery, U. S. A., and an agreeable acquaintance; consequently there could be no mistake when I recognized his dead body. The Federal surgeon also identifying him, I set about giving him decent burial, and managed it finally by the help of some men of Bartow's Savannah company who knew me. The ground was baked hard and we could not make the grave deep, but it was enough; and with my own hands I carved his name on the bark of a tree, under which the soldier found his last bivouac—"Otis H. Tillinghast."

Some time after, a blockade-runner, passing the lines took a letter from me to my cousin, Robert Fisher, in Baltimore, a friend also of Tillinghast. It was on other matters, but I let him know that Tillinghast's body had been recognized on the field, had received decent burial, and the spot marked. I described the location and then the matter passed out of my mind.

After peace came I was with Fisher in Baltimore and learned from him that my letter had been received and the information as to Captain Tillinghast considerately conveyed to his family. Fisher was answered soon after with thanks, "but there was some mistake," Captain Tillinghast was buried by his old classmate Samuel Jones, a Confederate brigadier-general, in a different part of the field and his body later removed to the family vault. Astonishing! If they got a body from a spot not where I had laid him they got the wrong husband. Sam Jones quite likely saw Tillinghast, but he had no hand in our burial of him. Stranger things, however, have happened.

Here are some trifles of talk remembered as coming from the famous war correspondent, Sir William Howard Russell, whose letters from the Crimea broke the Aberdeen Ministry and made him one of the leading men of the Kingdom. He was not long ago knighted at great age for his service all over the world in that field of letters. I met him several years ago in New York, in the train of the notorious Colonel North, the Chilean nitrate king. Russell had always some good stories on hand, and laughed at his chase from Bull Run battlefield, whither he had gone with the Federal army to write up their victory pictures. It gave him the name of "Bull Run Russell," which stuck to him. He admitted being very far to the rear, but said there were some generals and colonels who outstripped him to Washington! Some years after the war he met in Europe General McDowell, who said, "Russell, do you know what day this is?" "No, I don't recall any special occurrence." "It is," said McDowell, "the 21st of July, and had I succeeded on that day in '61 I should have been the greatest man in America and you the most popular."

Russell also had something about the French princes come to join McClellan's army. The two young men, Comte de Paris and Duc de Chartres, were under the care and tutelage of their uncle, the Prince de Joinville, who did not follow them to the army. On landing they received their commissions as captains, and quickly equipped themselves with handsome regulation uniforms and military appointments.

They proceeded to Washington to make formal calls of ceremony before reporting to McClellan. Among their first visits was that to Seward, the Secretary of State. On that evening he was holding a large reception. Seward himself leaving the ceremony to his son Frederick, was upstairs with some cronies drinking whiskey. "Seward was screwed, you know," said Russell, "undoubtedly screwed." When the two princes entered the hall, trim in their new uniforms, erect and soldierly, they were met by Frederick Seward, who at once went to announce them. "Tell them to come right up," said the old politician; "bring them right up and they shall have some good whiskey." "That will never do," said his son. "You must come down to them; it is etiquette and strictly in rule." And down the Secretary went. "Screwed" a little, for as soon as he spied the Frenchmen, out he broke: "Captain Chatters, glad to see you; welcome to Washington. And you too, Captain Paris. I am pleased to have you in my house. Both of you come up with me. You won't dislike the whiskey you shall taste." But the watchful Frederick came to the rescue and carried off the astonished princes with all propriety.

Russell declared this to be literally true; but if not, it is at least as the Italians say, "ben trovato." Sir William was then a picturesque figure in dark blue dress coat, brass buttons, and ruffled shirt. Always interesting, he had exhaustless stores of information and adventure. A pretty young Italian wife accompanied him.

Something as to horses. I had left a good one in Savannah, in care of a member of the troop. Hearing that the horse was with him in Virginia I sent over for my property and got for answer that he was not mine; that he belonged to the man in Savannah, who not being able to enlist had contributed this fine animal to the outfit of the troop. A nice business indeed. It was easy to be patriotic with my horse, but it was soon settled. Captain Waring heard the statement, and recognizing the animal as mine had him sent to me; but the horse had been so neglected and diseased that he was no good and I was obliged to leave him by the roadside. I had, during the war, many horses, some good, some very poor. Among the best was the tough-looking clay-bank I took from my father when joining the army. He was capable of anything in speed and endurance, but with a walk so slow and a trot so bone-breaking that I had to swap him for one not so good. Many of my animals broke down from hard staff service in campaign, and a magnificent mare was killed under me in Pickett's charge at Gettysburg. A shell burst directly under her and the poor beast was instantly done for. I was not touched. In Tennessee, in 1864, I picked up a delightful little white mare, sound, fleet and enduring. I could not always get to my other horses at the outbreak of firing, and the mare's color was against us both. It was always among the soldiers, "Fire at the fellow on the white horse." She was at my brigade quarters at Appomattox and my brother rode her to Savannah. When the two appeared in front of our residence, my sisters rushed out, but could not believe that the poor, tired little mare was their brother's war horse. Their imagination had been at work.

My brother Claxton, my junior, was a fine, well set up young fellow and eager for the fray. He was also a private in the Hussars, and like myself had not waited for the company, but came on to Richmond. Here he fell in with some young Georgians from Athens, the Troop Artillery, a six-gun battery under command of Captain Carlton. Claxton joined and became a good artillerist and was a corporal when transferred. The First Georgia Regulars was organized by the State among the first, its officers being appointed by the Governor and the men enlisted anywhere. Its drill and discipline were supposed to be severer than that of other troops. This regiment was brought to Virginia and assigned to G. T. Anderson's (Tige Anderson) Georgia Brigade. With some influence and much hard work, my brother, Doctor Sorrel, succeeded in getting a commission as second lieutenant in this regiment for Claxton. Its officers were not elected; they were appointed by the Executive. Claxton's service was thenceforward with this regiment, its officers showing some of the best names in Georgia, and its reputation correspondingly high. Later I gave Captain Sorrel a temporary detail on the staff of Brigadier-General Garnett, and still later he was appointed captain in the Assistant Adjutant-General's Department and served with General John Bratton.

When we moved from Centerville my father had long since returned to Savannah with his family, and his "Ireland" place was unoccupied (it was later burned by the Union soldiers). But my cousin, Mrs. Lucy Green, and children, were at their place, "The Lawn," which would be in the enemy's territory after our withdrawal. Our first halt was near Gainesville and after getting the troops comfortably into camp I rode over to see her, about three miles. The situation was clearly described and she decided to pack her carriages and wagons and move to Richmond. I gave her a safe escort in a man from Lynchburg, Mr. Paxton, a member of Blackford's cavalry company. With farewells I rode back through the night, the better by a pair of English boots my cousin gave me. She and the children, with servants, under good Paxton's charge, made next morning a start for Richmond, where they arrived safely.

Referring again to horses, the hussar horse had been my mount at the short service on Skidaway. Henry Taylor was my messmate and rode next me on a good bay precisely the same color as mine, with considerable resemblance between them. Taylor was rich, lazy, despised discipline, and was a trial to the captain. He gave his horse no attention and the beast would have starved but for others. The captain could stand it no longer. Sending for Taylor he read him a severe lecture and promised punishment if the horse was not kept clean and tended.

Taylor was persuaded he must do something, and the next morning he was up at stable-call at the picket ropes, brush and curry comb in hand. It was very early and misty. My horse was picketed next to Taylor's and I had the satisfaction of seeing my lazy friend give him the best morning's rub he had received for many days. When Taylor woke up to what he had done and that his own horse was still to be tended he could not immediately see the joke, but soon took it in good part and had something ready for me not long after, which he thought squared us.

CHAPTER IV

Sketches

Brigadier-Generals Elzey and Early—Leaping horses—Confederate uniforms—Ladies at Fairfax Station—Colonel Stuart's Maryland line—Longstreet made Major-General—Sketches of Brigadier-Generals Ewell and Pickett—General Anderson—Major-General Van Dorn—Major-General G. W. Smith—Brigadier Early—Brigadier-General D. R. Jones.

One fine day not long after the Manassas battle, and while we were at Fairfax Court House, Longstreet called on me to ride over to the station on a visit. It was to General Elzey, who was found with General Early in a dilapidate old church. Refreshments were ordered and a good deal of whiskey consumed by the three brigadiers, some colonels and staff officers. Early had been a strong Union man until Virginia seceded, and he then took arms, devotedly and ever bravely, for his State and the Confederacy. He was, however, of a snarling, rasping disposition, and seemed to irritate Elzey, who, not a Union man, had come South without the secession of his State, Maryland. There were some hot words all around, but peace was made, however, and we all quit the drinks and adjourned to the horses and fine weather outside. Leaping fences and ditches at once began, my mount doing well and coming some daring trials. Longstreet was mounted on a fine bay not quite up to such work, with his weight, and the General turned him over to me. The bay did splendidly, surpassing all others present, and the generals were much pleased.

Colonel Duncan McRae, Fifth North Carolina, had just received from Richmond a handsome new Confederate uniform and outfit. Alas! it soon came to grief. The Colonel, in taking a high fence, lost his seat and came down very hard, splitting his fine coat in the back, from collar to waist.

A word here as to uniforms and insignia. So fast does the memory of things pass that perhaps it may be well to make a note of what was the Confederate uniform. It was designed and settled on by a board of officers of the War Department.

For all officers, a close-fitting double-breasted gray tunic.

For generals, staff and all field officers, dark blue trousers.

The arm of service was shown by collar and cuff—Generals and staff officers, buff; Cavalry, yellow; Artillery, red; Infantry, blue; Medical Department, black.

Dark blue trousers had broad gold stripes on outer seams, except generals, who wore two narrower and slightly apart.

Trousers for all line officers under rank of major were light blue with broad cloth stripe, color of service arm.

Rank was shown on collar and sleeve.

Generals wore on collar a gold wreath enclosing three stars in line, the middle one slightly larger. On their sleeves was the ornamental Hungarian knot of four braids width. They usually wore their buttons in groups of twos or threes. There was no difference in the uniform or rank mark among the several grades of general officers.

Colonels wore three stars in line, same size; lieutenant-colonels, two, and majors, one. The knot on the sleeve was three braids width for the three grades of field officers—colonel, lieutenant-colonel, and major.

For captains, rank was shown by three short bars lateral on front of collar; first lieutenant, two bars, and second lieutenant, one bar. Captains wore on sleeve Hungarian knot of two braids width, and first and second lieutenants, one braid.

For headgear the French "Kepi," color of arm of service, richly embroidered, was first provided; but the felt hat, black or any color that could be had, speedily pushed it aside almost before it had an existence.

The intention of the board of officers was to adopt the tunic like the short, close-fitting, handsome Austrian garment, but it went completely by default. The officers would none of it. They took to the familiar cut of frock coat with good length of tail.

Longstreet and two or three of us tried the tunic, but it was not popular.

Confederate uniforms were in great number at the flag presentations a little later, of which I have already spoken. We were then bravely dressed in the bright and handsome Confederate gray.

But now "place aux dames." A splendid Maryland regiment of Elzey's brigade was at Fairfax Station near by, and two lovely women, descendants of a distinguished Virginia family, were then visiting their numerous friends serving with it. They were the beautiful Carys, Hetty and her cousin Constance. The three generals, gallantly inclined, decided they must call on the ladies, and this they did, shutting out their staffs for the time. Then evening coming on dress parade was in order and Colonel George Stewart soon had his fine Marylanders in line. He insisted on the two ladies taking position by him, and when time for the manual came, handed his sword to Hetty, and stepping aside prompted her with the orders, and thus the regiment, amid much enthusiasm, was put through its manual by the prettiest woman in Virginia. They soon returned to Richmond and occupied themselves in the good work of the Southern women. Hetty, a really glorious beauty, married Brig.-Gen. John Pegram in January, 1865. Three weeks after he fell at Hatcher's Run, at the same time that I received what was thought a fatal wound. The *New York Herald* a few days later published both our obituaries. (See Appendix.)

Constance married, after the peace, my friend Burton N. Harrison, President Davis's accomplished private secretary. He began his law practice in New York, succeeding well, and his wife soon became established and admired as a woman of taste and uncommon social and literary attainments. Her books have gained deserved popularity and wide circulation.

Longstreet being now a major-general, with three brigades, the new brigadiers are to be introduced. R. S. Ewell took our old brigade. He was a distant relative of mine and one of the strangest of warriors; had served with distinction in Mexico, and all his life against Indians. He was without a superior as a cavalry captain and of the most extraordinary appearance. Bald as an eagle, he looked like one; had a piercing eye and a lisping speech. A perfect horseman and lover of horses (racers), he never tired talking of his horse "Tangent," in Texas, who appears to have never won a race and always to have lost his owner's money. But the latter's confidence never weakened and he always believed in "Tangent." General Ewell became a very distinguished soldier, and justly so. To uncommon courage and activity he added a fine military instinct, which could make him a good second in command in any army. He was not long with us. His fortunes were with Stonewall Jackson in the Valley operations, and he rose to be major-general and lieutenant-general. In the latter rank he commanded the Second Corps at Gettysburg, having previously lost a leg in the second Manassas campaign. His command suffered great loss in the slaughter of Malvern Hill. The morning after, I found him doubled up on the floor of a little shanty, his head covered up; the ground was covered with our slain. Raising himself he instantly recognized me, and lisped out, "Mather Thorrel, can you tell me why we had five hundred men killed dead on this field yesterday?" That was all; the soul of the brave General was fit to burst for the awful and useless sacrifice. It was a fearful blunder somewhere and has not yet been boldly and clearly lighted up. Kemper, a fine Virginian colonel, succeeded Ewell in command of the Fourth Brigade, and served well until he was left for dead in front of his men in Pickett's charge at Gettysburg.

Our Second Brigade was also Virginian. One evening at dark I was in my narrow office when an officer was announced. I turned and had quite a start at my visitor's appearance. It was George Pickett, just made brigadier-general, and reporting for command. A singular figure indeed! A medium-sized, well-built man, straight, erect, and in well-fitting uniform, an elegant riding-whip in hand, his appearance was distinguished and striking. But the head, the hair were extraordinary. Long ringlets flowed loosely over his shoulders, trimmed and highly perfumed; his beard likewise was curling and giving out the scents of Araby. He was soon made at home, and having already received Longstreet's instructions, was assigned to his brigade.

Pickett became very friendly, was a good fellow, a good brigadier. He had been in Longstreet's old Army regiment, and the latter was exceedingly fond of him. Taking Longstreet's orders in emergencies, I could always see how he looked after Pickett, and made us give him things very fully; indeed, sometimes stay with him to make sure he did not get astray.

Such was the man whose name calls up the most famous and heroic charge, possibly, in the annals of war. Pickett's charge at Gettysburg stirs every heart that beats for great deeds, and will forever live in song and story.

Afterwards his division was relieved to rest and recruit, and grew strong and fit. It was, however, badly mauled at Five Forks by Sheridan, although its commander is said to have made excellent dispotion of his troops and fought them gallantly.

The Third Brigade was of South Carolina regiments under command of Brig.-Gen. Richard H. Anderson, a West Point graduate and an experienced officer of the old Army. Of him and also the artillery attached to the division there is more to be said later.

At the Centerville camp Major-General Earl Van Dorn commanded a division. A small, handsome man, the very picture of a thorough light cavalryman, he enjoyed a high reputation from service in Mexico and against the Indians. Soon after he was transferred to a command in Mississippi, and there falling into a private quarrel was killed.

Maj.-Gen. G. W. Smith also had a division near Centerville. From this officer much was expected. He had left the Academy with high honors, and served many years with distinction. He resigned from the Army to become Street Commissioner in New York, a lucrative office, and thence he came South for service. There was no opportunity to show his abilities in the field until the battle of Seven Pines in May-June, 1862, and then General Lee taking command of the army, Smith withdrew, and was, I think, not again heard of in active field work. After the war he wrote a book, his "Apologies," in which he threw all the blame on his once bosom friend, James Longstreet, and upon General Johnston for field work, up to the time of his retirement.

Jubal Early, brigadier-general, was one of the ablest soldiers in the army. Intellectually he was perhaps the peer of the best for strategic combinations, but he lacked ability to handle troops effectively in the field; that is, he was deficient in tactical skill. His irritable disposition and biting tongue made him anything but popular, but he was a very brave and able commander. His appearance was quite striking, having a dark, handsome face, regular features, and deep piercing eyes. He was the victim of rheumatism, and although not old was bent almost double, like an aged man. Of high scholarly and fine political attainments, he never married, but led the life of a recluse in Virginia, entirely apart from social and public affairs.

D. R. Jones, brigadier-general, was also near us. A very agreeable, lovable man, tall and stately, he made a brave appearance, and well merited the sobriquet of "Neighbor Jones," as they pleasantly called him at West Point. His wife, a relative of President Davis, was much with him in camp, and a very decided character by the side of her indulgent husband. He could not figure with much success, his health being poor, and after Sharpsburg was transferred to some easier service elsewhere, and soon after died.

CHAPTER V

Our National Hymn

Singing among the troops—Van Dorn—Longstreet—Smith and "I Puritani" for National hymn—Surgeon Francis Sorrel, C. S. A.—Life in Richmond—Troops passing through—Toombs and his brigade—General D. H. Hill.

Among the troops at Centerville there was much singing, some of it very sweet and touching. "Lorena," set to a tender, sentimental air, was heard everywhere. "My Maryland" was a great favorite, and of course "Dixie" was always in evidence. There were, however, other sweet Southern melodies that the soldiers took up, seemingly mellowing stern hearts and bringing tender memories of home. There was constant talk of a National air, "Dixie" being thought by some as of not sufficient dignity. "My Maryland" had many advocates, but there were some that thought the noble strain of the great Liberty duet from "I Puritani" was the thing for the Confederacy. General Van Dorn was enthusiastic about it. At the banquet at Longstreet's, after the flag presentation, the talk turned on this air, and Van Dorn began to sing it. "Up on the table and show yourself; we can't see you!" said Longstreet. "Not unless you stand by me!" shouted Van Dorn; and no sooner said than Longstreet, G. W. Smith, and Van Dorn, the ranking major-generals, were clinging to each other on a narrow table and roaring out the noble bars of "I Puritani." Johnston and

Beauregard stood near with twinkling eyes of amusement and enjoyment. So much for wine and "entoosy moosy," as Byron calls it; but for all this good start, the soldiers declined the impressive air and stuck to their Dixie.

It was always gratifying to me to note the good equipment in which the troops from every State were sent to the front for the Confederacy. Governor Brown was thorough in doing the best for them that the blockade of the coast and his factories permitted. They came forward with good clothing, shoes and underwear, which, although of home make, were warm, comfortable and serviceable.

My brother, Dr. Francis Sorrel, was some years my senior. He had served in the United States Army as assistant surgeon, but had resigned and was in California when the war began. He immediately came to share the fortunes of his State. Dr. Moore, the Confederate Surgeon-General, without delay had him appointed to full rank and assigned for service as his close confidential assistant (the pair were forever rolling cigarettes). There his influence and powers were considerable and the Doctor was always helpful to his friends. He was instrumental in assigning Dr. James B. Read, of Savannah, to the officers' hospital in Richmond, and in Read's hands it became celebrated. He kept a good lookout for his two junior brothers in the field and we had many evidences of his thoughtfulness.

With a wide acquaintance in Richmond, he knew the principal members of Congress and was liked by all the Cabinet. His previous service in the United States Army put him in good touch with many high officers, and his position in all respects was enviable. Occasionally I managed to make a short visit to Richmond, and then my brother gave me introductions to pleasant men and charming women. There may be more to say of him later.

Life at Richmond at this time—January, February, March, April, 1862—seemed gay and happy, with but little outward sign of apprehension or anxieties for the future. Food supplies were abundant and the pinch for clothing and shoes was being eased by the remarkable achievement of the several States in equipping their contingents for the field.

Most of the troops passed through Richmond en route to the Peninsula, and there was much excitement and cheering. Main Street was thronged with people shouting wildly as the regiments marched down to Rocketts, where they were to take boat for part of the route.

General Toombs was quite conspicuous. Every one knows that that luminous intellect embraced no soldier's talent. It might have been so with study, but the Georgian was for once and all a politician, and in the wrong shop with a sword and uniform on.

He marched his troops down Main Street, past the crowds at Spottswood Hotel, with childlike delight. He put himself at the head of one regiment and moved it out of sight amid hurrahs, then galloping back he brought on another, ready himself for cheers, until the brigade was down the street and near the embarkation. It was somewhat amusing, but a harmless entertainment for the brilliant orator and statesman.

Being quite without notes I had almost omitted a jotting about one of Longstreet's brigadiers at Centerville—a marked and peculiar character. This was General D. H. Hill, not long with us. He was soon made major-general and sent elsewhere to command. Hill was a small, delicate man, rather bent, and cursed with dyspepsia, which seemed to give color to his whole being. He was out of West Point with a good class number, was a capable, well-read soldier, and positively about the bravest man ever seen. He seemed not to know peril and was utterly indifferent to bullets and shell, but with all these qualities was not successful. His backbone seemed a trifle weak. He would take his men into battle, fight furiously for some time and then something weakened about him. Unless there was some strong character near by, like Longstreet, for instance, on whom he leaned, his attack would be apt to fail and his first efforts go unrewarded. His speech was bitter, although a most devout Presbyterian elder. He had resigned long before from the United States Army, and had a large school in North Carolina. He was accustomed to sneer at cavalry, and once went so far as to say he had "yet to see a dead man with spurs on." It may be imagined what Stuart's gallant troopers thought of him. But Hill had brains, and rose. He was later on sent West to command in Bragg's army, was promoted to lieutenant-general, and is said to have failed grievously at Chickamauga, for which Bragg suspended him from command; and he was not, I think, restored to any service in the field. He was really a good man, but of sharp prejudice and intemperate language. If there was one department of the army well administered amid almost impossibilities, requiring most ingenious and inventive resources, it was the Ordnance, under Colonel Gorgas. Hill took a hatred to it because a gun burst in action, and his imputations on the faith of the department and its abilities were quite unworthy of him or of any good soldier.

CHAPTER VI

The Peninsula and Battle of Williamsburg, May 5, 1862

Arrival at Yorktown—Major-General Magruder—His skilful defense—Lines at Warwick River—Major-General McClellan—Retreat from Yorktown—Battle of Williamsburg, May 5—Death of Colonel Mott, Nineteenth Mississippi—Destruction of armored ram *Virginia*—Charge by Georgia Hussars—Explosives behind rearguard rebuked—Promoted major.

But I must hasten to the Peninsula, where at Yorktown and along the lines of the little Warwick River, McClellan and Johnston are frowning at each other; the former, as usual, tripling the Confederate force and bawling for more men. Persons and things I have left behind will probably come into these jottings in the loose way they fall from the pen.

Longstreet with his staff and some of his regiments were among the first arrivals to face McClellan and gave great relief to Magruder. This officer, a major-general, commanding some 10,000 to 12,000 men, had offered a most extraordinary and successful defense. It was a wonderful piece of bluff and could have won only against McClellan. Yorktown was strongly armed and well defended. Thence stretching across the Peninsula was a sluggish little stream known as the Warwick River. It was fordable in almost all places, in some nearly dry-shod.

Magruder's engineers had strengthened the defenses by some dams that gathered a good spread of water to be passed in an attack. The Warwick, of many miles extent, was necessarily thinly defended. Magruder put his whole force behind it, an attenuated line, up and down which he constantly rode in full sight of the enemy. He was known in the old Army as "Prince John," from the splendor of his appearance and his dress. Of commanding form and loving display, he had assembled a numerous staff, all, like himself, in the most showy uniforms. To these he added a fine troop of cavalry, and when the cavalcade at a full gallop inspected the thin lines of the Warwick, it was a sight for men and gods. I am persuaded he so impressed "Little Mac" that he sang out for more men and thus lost his opportunity. In very truth he was so strong and Magruder so weak that the Union ramrods should have sufficed to break the defense and gobble up the magnificent "Prince John."

Longstreet's arrival was therefore a great relief, and soon Johnston had his army in full position, making McClellan almost frantic; he more than doubled Johnston's actual strength. A strong attack should have prevailed to drive us away; and if briskly followed, eventually into the York River. But Johnston knew his man, as did indeed every Confederate leader later on. Lee, Longstreet, Jackson, the Hills all knowing his points, while serving in the U. S. Army, could now rightly measure him. McClellan was a lovable man, an admirable organizer, but with little taste for battle unless largely outnumbering his opponent. Here in the trenches occurred remarkable scenes. Many of the Southern regiments had enlisted for only twelve months and the time expired in April. Re-enlistments and elections of the officers took place under fire of the enemy! Our men were splendid, and with rare exceptions they refused home and re-enlisted, this time for the war.

Inactivity continued for some time, Longstreet commanding the center with his own and other troops, until it was soon apparent to Johnston that Richmond was too much exposed to attacks on the north side of the James River. The capital must be covered; besides, both our flanks were endangered by the enemy's immense superiority on the water. Preparations therefore began for a move, and on the night of May 3 the army was successfully drawn from its trenches and started on its deliberate, well-ordered retreat. On May 5 our rearguard was overtaken and attacked in force at Wiliamsburg, Longstreet in command, with a considerable part of the army. It was a stubborn, all-day fight, with serious losses on both sides, but the enemy was beaten off and we resumed the march that night, the Federals having enough of it. We were not again molested. This was our first severe fight, and the steadiness and order of officers and men appeared to be very satisfactory. I was promoted to be major soon afterwards, the commission dating May 5, the day of the action. There was a gruesome but affecting sight during the battle. Colonel Mott, of high reputation, had brought from his State the Nineteenth Mississippi Infantry. It was hotly engaged in a long, fierce fight, and Mott fell. His black servant in the rear immediately took a horse and went to the firing line for his master's body. I met the two coming out of the fire and smoke. The devoted negro had straddled the stiffened limbs of his master on the saddle before him, covered his face with a handkerchief, and thus rescued his beloved master's body for interment with his fathers on the old Mississippi estate.

The celebrated L. Q. C. Lamar was lieutenant-colonel of the regiment, and succeeded to the command, until forced by physical disability, he retired to Richmond for other service. The army moving on soon neared the capital and took up the several positions assigned its divisions. McClellan's huge force following, threw itself across the Chickahominy, and the siege of Richmond may be said to have begun.

On the withdrawal of the army from the Peninsula, Norfolk and Gloucester Point became indefensible and the destruction of immense quantities of material both for field use and for construction had to be submitted to. The blow was not made lighter by the loss of the famous *Virginia,* formerly the *Merrimac,* that did such havoc at Newport News. She could not be permitted to fall into the enemy's hands and was of too deep draft for service on the James River. Her commander, Admiral Josiah Tatnall, was therefore reluctantly forced to her destruction. She was blown up and disappeared. Other vessels, cruisers and gun-boats, boilers, engines, and great quantities of material for construction had to be destroyed for similar reasons. The loss was bitter to us, as so much could have been done with it all for a little fighting navy.

It was during the action at Williamsburg that I was ready to shout for joy at seeing my old troop, the Georgia Hussars, in a gallant charge. Their regiment, the Jeff Davis Legion, had been prematurely thrown at the enemy in a position he was thought about leaving. The cavalry colonel was wrong. Our Georgians went forward in fine style, expecting to carry everything, but quickly found themselves in a very hot place. The enemy was not retiring, but on the contrary gave the Legion so warm a reception as to empty many saddles. They all came back pell-mell, "the devil take the hindmost," my Hussar comrades wondering what their colonel had got them "into that galley for!" It was a severe lesson but a salutary one, and the regiment was not again caught that way. Longstreet saw them close by as they dashed forward, and said, "They must soon come back; the colonel is ahead of the right moment."

General Johnston was present on the field all day, but seeing Longstreet, the rearguard commander, carrying things very handsomely, generously forbore any interference and left the battle to his handling. He sent the latter such additional troops as he had to call for from time to time. When night came it was horrible. There were many dead and wounded and the weather nasty; the roads ankle deep in mud and slush. But the march had to be again taken up.

On the retreat from Yorktown, Brigadier-General Rains was commanding the rearguard. He was a brother of the other Rains who at Augusta, Georgia, achieved the apparently impossible task of supplying ammunition. Both brothers were given to experiments in explosives and fond of that study. When Gabriel began moving out on our march he amused himself planting shells and other explosives in the roadway after us to tickle the pursuers. Hearing this I reported the matter to Longstreet, who instantly stopped it. He caused me to write Rains a rather severe note, reminding him that such practises were not considered in the limits of legitimate warfare, and that if he would put them aside and pay some attention to his brigade his march would be better and his stragglers not so numerous. This officer did not remain long on duty in the field. His talents, like those of his more celebrated brother, lay elsewhere.

After getting into position before Richmond, less than a month intervened between the reorganization and strengthening of the army and change of its commander. I shall therefore defer any observations that I may recall as to its composition and personnel until it took its more permanent form under Lee, contenting myself with some stray reflections on the battle of Seven Pines, which by the deplorable wounding of Johnston gave us for leader Robert E. Lee.

CHAPTER VII

BATTLE OF SEVEN PINES, MAY 31, 1862.

Position taken in front of Richmond—Reception at President Davis's—Sketch—Mr. Benjamin, Secretary of State—Storm-bound—Richmond—General Johnston wounded——Von Borcke, the German volunteer—His armament.

Our positions were so near Richmond as to permit frequent visits there during the pleasant month of May.

McClellan was hugging himself in security and reinforcements beyond the Chickahominy, and the earthwork defenses of Richmond which we were guarding seemed to us then all-sufficing. Later, we could realize how little they were worth without men and guns and rifles and a leader in the field. These defenses had been scientifically constructed by the engineers headed by General Lee and Maj.-Gen. J. F. Gilmer. The latter was a distinguished officer long resigned from the United States Army, had married in Savannah in the family of dear friends of ours, and when the war broke out at once placed his unquestioned engineering abilities at the service of the government.

On one of my visits to the city I was persuaded by my brother, Dr. Sorrel, to stay the night and attend a reception at the President's. It was interesting and striking. The highest and most brilliant of the Southland were there; bright, witty, confident, carrying everything with a high hand. The men generally in full uniform and the women in finery, that seems somehow always to turn up for them under all circumstances. After presentation to Mr. and Mrs. Davis I had a good look at that remarkable man. A most interesting study, calm and self-contained, gracious with some sternness; his figure was straight, slim and elegant. A well-poised, ample head was faced with high-bred features and an expression that could be very winning and agreeable. His wife, Varina, was a rather large woman, handsome and brilliant, a bit inclined to be caustic of speech, but withal a good and gracious help to her husband.

Her devotion when he was a prisoner was later beautifully manifested. Senators and Congressmen were there in abundance. Our own representative, Julien Hartridge, characteristically indifferent to such assemblages, was taking his pleasure elsewhere.

Mr. Benjamin was a most interesting character—a short, squatty Jewish figure. His silvery speech charmed all hearers with its wit, persiflage and wisdom. His wonderful legal abilities made him *facile princeps* in equity law. His after career was extraordinary. When the collapse of the Confederate Army came he was still in Mr. Davis's Cabinet and joined his chief in flight. Separating, however, Benjamin escaped to one of the West India Islands and thence to London. It seems his nativity had actually been in a British Colony, and this fact and his great legal acquirements, with some routine attendance at the courts, quickly permitted his admittance to the bar and he was Q. C. in almost no time. He immediately took up an immense special practise and made much money.

I had the pleasure of meeting him in 1872 in Paris, at a breakfast given by Mr. Francis Corbin in his splendid hotel on the Faubourg St. Germain. Needless to say, Mr. Benjamin was delightful.

It was on one of these visits to my brother that I nearly came to trouble. I intended to ride back to camp quite early, but he had visits for me to make with him and pressed me so affectionately that I was late in starting back. Then a furious storm of rain and wind nearly drowned my good horse and myself and I was concerned for the late hour at which I finally reported to my chief. I found him provoked at my absence, because much had happened. In the afternoon a council of war had agreed with the commander-in-chief to attack McClellan the next morning. The opportunity was a good one because McClellan had posted his forces so that the Chickahominy cut them in two and they might be destroyed in detail. I was not too late, however, for the duties, and both Longstreet and myself were soon in good humor again. Orders for the dispositions of the troops were quickly gotten out and the time and line of march given. We had six strong brigades and D. H. Hill's four were to join us under Longstreet, besides a strong force of artillery and a body of cavalry on the right. When the day came (May 31) the movement began, and never was the opening for battle more unsatisfactory.

The same storm that put McClellan's army in decided peril by destroying his bridges and cutting communication between his two wings, impeded our march at every step. Little rivulets were now raging torrents.

Bridges had to be improvised and causeways made by which the column could be moved. Everything seemingly lost us time, and our attack, instead of being early in the day, was delayed until 4 P. M. There shall be no attempt to describe or discuss this battle. G. W. Smith with a large command was on our left. General Johnston with him and Major-General Huger with a strong division was expected to support our right, but for some reason we did not get it. D. H. Hill with his four brigades and our six, attacked with great fury. Smith's attack on the left was retarded and unsuccessful. We made quick progress, but with heavy losses in our ten fine brigades. The enemy could not stand before them and Casey's division, posted at Seven Points, gave way after heavy losses and was crushed. Cannon and colors fell into our hands. Darkness was then coming on and no supports, much to Longstreet's chagrin. Further attack on our part was deferred until the morning. Meantime, while Smith was making on the left his abortive attack, our gallant General Joseph E. Johnston had been struck down by a severe wound and borne from the field. The second in command was G. W. Smith, but as operations for the day had ceased there was no occasion for him to make any change in existing dispositions of the troops, and Gen. Robert E. Lee was the next day placed in command of the Army of Northern Virginia.

Seven Pines should under all circumstances have been a magnificent victory for us. It was really far from that, and while encouraging the soldiers in fighting and the belief in their ability to beat the enemy, it was waste of life and a great disappointment.

Walton, of Longstreet's staff, was wounded in the head, the bullet making a long furrow in his bald scalp. Here we saw for the first time the German Von Borcke, who, attached later to Stuart's cavalry, made some reputation. He had just arrived and could not speak a word of English; was splendidly mounted on a powerful sorrel and rode well. He was an ambulating arsenal. A double-barreled rifle was strapped across his back, a Winchester carbine hung by his hip, heavy revolvers were in his belt, right and left side; an enormous straight double-edged sharp-pointed cuirasseur's saber hung together with sabertasche to his left thigh, and a short "couteau de chasse" finished up his right. Besides, his English army saddle bore two large holsters, one for his field-glasses, the other for still another revolver, bigger and deadlier than all the others. Von Borcke was a powerful creature—a tall, blonde, active giant. When I next saw him he had discarded—taught by experience—all his arsenal except his good saber and a couple of handy revolvers. He stayed with us to the end and received an ugly wound in the throat.

CHAPTER VIII

Battles of the Chickahominy, June 26 to July 2, 1862.

General Lee in command—Sketch—Reinforced—Preparing for campaign—General Lee's staff—Longstreet second in command—His division—Artillery reorganized—Washington Artillery of New Orleans—Colonel E. P. Alexander commanding artillery—General W. W. Mackall reports—Sketch—Civilian prisoners at Fort Warren—General Miles and President Davis—The battles around Richmond—McClellan's defeat—Stonewall Jackson not on time—Ochiltree and Eastern fighting—Lord Edward St. Maur a visitor—McClellan on James River in position—Later we take again positions by Richmond.

When General Lee took command it was my first sight of him. He had been employed in the northwest Virginia mountains, on the South Atlantic Coast, and at Richmond, generally as adviser to the President. His appearance had, it seems, changed. Up to a short time before Seven Pines he had worn for beard only a well-kept moustache, soon turned from black to grizzled. When he took us in hand his full gray beard was growing, cropped close, and always well tended An unusually handsome man, he has been painted with brush and pen a hundred times, but yet there is always something to say of that noble, unostentatious figure, the perfect poise of head and shoulders and limbs, the strength that lay hidden and the activity that his fifty-five years could not repress. Withal graceful and easy, he was approachable by all; gave attention to all in the simplest manner. His eyes—sad eyes! the saddest it seems to me of all men's—beaming the highest intelligence and with unvarying kindliness, yet with command so firmly set that all knew him for the unquestioned chief. He loved horses and had good ones, and rode carefully and safely, but I never liked his seat. The General was always well dressed in gray sack-coat of Confederate cloth, matching trousers tucked into well-fitting riding-boots—the simplest emblems of his rank appearing, and a good, large black felt army hat completed the attire of our commander. He rarely wore his sword, but his binoculars were always at hand. Fond of the company of ladies, he had a good memory for pretty girls. His white teeth and winning smile were irresistible. While in Savannah and calling on my father, one of my sisters sang for him. Afterwards, in Virginia, almost as soon as he saw me he asked after his "little singing-bird."

The touch of the leader's hand was soon apparent in the reorganization of the army and its increased strength. The Administration reposing a perfect confidence in Lee, gave him all he asked for in men and material that could be furnished. It is proper to add that so moderate was the man and so fully understanding the situation and difficulties of supply, that he rarely asked for what could not be given him. His staff was small and efficient. I suppose that at this date there are some hundreds of men in the South who call themselves members of Lee's staff, and so they were if teamsters, sentry men, detailed quartermasters (commissary men), couriers and orderlies, and all the rest of the following of general headquarters of a great army are to be so considered. But by staff we usually confine ourselves to those responsible officers immediately about a general, and Lee had selected carefully. Four majors (afterwards lieutenant-colonels and colonels) did his principal work. Walter Taylor, from the Virginia Military Institute, was adjutant-general, and better could not be found for this important post.

Charles Venable, a scholar and mathematician, and with some study of strategy, together with Charles Marshall, a distinguished lawyer by inheritance from his ancestor, the Chief Justice, and his own attainments, did much of the correspondence under dictation. Talcot was the engineer officer, and Long, of the old Army, a close friend of the General, was ranked as military secretary and did various duties. At a later date Brig.-Gen. R. H. Chilton, A. A. G., was assigned to confidential duties with the General, and was sometimes called chief of staff. But Lee really had no such chief about him. The officer practically nearest its duties was his extremely efficient adjutant-general, W. H. Taylor.

Maj. H. E. Young was also attached later—an excellent officer. There were possibly one or two young lieutenants for personal aids, but this was Lee's staff, although perhaps I have made some omissions. Of course it does not include the important administrative officers like Cole, chief commissary; Corley, chief quartermaster; Doctor Guild, medical director, and his chiefs of ordnance and other organizations.

Longstreet was second in command and it soon became apparent that he was to be quite close to Lee. His camps and bivouacs were near by the General's, and thus my acquaintance with him and his staff became quite free and I was often honored by the kind interest of the Commander-in-Chief.

In the new organization Longstreet had a powerful division of six brigades, and A. P. Hill (major-general) one of six, also a fine body which Hill happily christened as the Light Division. The artillery was much improved, and loose batteries were gathered and organized into well-found battalions, generally of four batteries of six guns each, and a battalion assigned to each division. The celebrated Washington Artillery of New Orleans was given to us, and glad we were to have such gunners. E. P. Alexander commanded in reserve a fine battalion of six batteries and was to do much good service with it.

A word about this splendid fellow. He was from Georgia and a dear friend of mine. Leaving West Point with very high honors, he was immediately commissioned into the Engineers, and sent to the Pacific, whence he came South to fight. His was the happiest and most hopeful nature. He was sure of winning in everything he took up, and never did he open his guns on the enemy but that he knew he should maul him into smithereens. An accomplished engineer, he was often called on both by Lee and Longstreet for technical work and special reconnoitering. His future in peace, after Appomattox, was varied and distinguished, and he still is with us, eager, enthusiastic, most interesting, and of undiminished abilities.

The Washington Artillery was an ancient and wealthy organization of New Orleans, numbering five well-equipped, well-manned batteries. There were many men of wealth and family serving as gunners. Four batteries under Colonel Walton came to Virginia, the fifth was sent West. Walton was large and imposing in appearance, looking, as indeed did the whole battalion, rather French. This arose from their uniform, which from "kepi" to gaiters was handsomely French, and made them very fine beside our homespun infantry fellows. It was a most efficient organization, serving with Longstreet throughout the war; it always did good service and constantly distinguished itself most conspicuously.

Our own staff will not be touched on just yet, preferring to wait for the creation of the two army corps in October, when we were put in more permanent shape for the remainder of the war. At present there had been but few additions to it, since Longstreet's command was limited to a single brigade, and the staff work consequently was sometimes hard on us.

I think it was in this month, September, that I rode to one of the lower landings of the James to meet General Mackall, my brother-in-law. He had been a prisoner of war at Fort Warren near Boston, and was to land, exchanged with some others from the Federal steamer. He was quite well and I sent him on to Richmond, where Doctor Sorrel saw to his comfort. Mackall married my father's eldest daughter. He was an army man out of West Point, and an able, accomplished soldier. He should have achieved much in the Confederate war, but circumstances were against him. When it broke out he was lieutenant-colonel in the Adjutant-General's Department, considered a very enviable billet. Stationed on the Pacific, his intimates were J. E. Johnston, J. F. Gilmer, Halleck, and others of that type. A Marylander, he was under no secession compulsion; but he had a fiery old Virginia father as well as his wife's Southern family to draw him there, with the reluctance so natural to those officers of feeling—proud of their little army, no raving State's rights man, but wanting the Union, always the Union. It could not be otherwise.

The Marylander had a tedious time in Richmond waiting for active service suitable to his abilities. At last he was sent to report to A. S. Johnston at Bowling Green, Kentucky. After Shiloh, at Beauregard's earnest request, he was made brigadier-general and ordered to hold Island No. 10, a fortified position in the Mississippi, immediately to fall by reason of other combinations. In less than a week after assuming command the inevitable happened. The island was surrendered and the garrison made prisoners of war. Mackall was sent to Fort Warren, from which he was exchanged in 1863. He then took duty with Bragg's army as chief of staff; and after Bragg with J. E. Johnston, one of his dearest friends, until the General was supplanted by Hood. Mackall was afterwards given a command at Mobile, from which, however, he soon had to withdraw his force by reason of the successes of the Federal fleet. And there, I think, his active service ended. He was of a high order of mind and of the finest and nicest elevation of character; there was something supercritical, however, that would stand in his way without reason.

When General Mackall was exchanged out of Fort Warren he told me of two other prisoners, civilians, Andrew Low and Charles Green. The latter had married my cousin, and both were Englishmen of the regular holdfast, energetic type. They constituted the most important business house in Savannah, were making quantities of money, but had quarrelled and were about separating on the worst terms, when Seward's detectives, suspicious of their movements (they had both married in Savannah and were truly Southern and Confederate), clapped them in Fort Warren. There by the irony of fate they were the sole occupants of the same casemate, these quondam friends, now bitter, non-speaking enemies. The situation was difficult and rather enjoyed by some gentlemen outside who knew of the partners' troubles.

Treatment of prisoners of war at Fort Warren (Boston Harbor) appears to have been proper and unobjectionable. The governor, Colonel Dimmock, was a gentleman and knew what was due to his own reputation, as well as what his prisoners had a right to expect. There were marked contrasts elsewhere, as at Fort Johnston, but in all the four years there was yet to be found a prison commandant surpassing the brutalities of Miles. His chief distinction then appears to have been in manacling the helpless President of the Confederate States, who was advanced in years, feeble in health, with no friends near, and that in the strongest fortress in the United

States, with a large garrison and a guard literally standing over the prisoner night and day, and not a Confederate organized force in existence.

Lee was an aggressive general, a fighter. To succeed, he knew battles were to be won, and battles cost blood, and blood he did not mind in his general's work. Although always considerate and sparing of his soldiers, he would pour out their blood when necessary or when strategically advisable. His army had become much strengthened, troops filled its ranks from Georgia, South and North Carolina, being drawn from the coast, where they were doing nothing. His divisions had among them Longstreet's, A. P. Hill's, Magruder's, D. H. Hill's, McLane's, D. R. Jones's, Huger's, and Whiting's—a splendid force, nearly eighty thousand men, including Jackson's. The latter was in the Valley, soon to be with us. Lawton had just taken his immense brigade of six thousand men from Savannah to reinforce him, and the Georgians were having some lively marching and fighting in "Stonewall" Jackson's way. It was evident that the General was soon to make his great attack to crush McClellan, whose dispositions were so faulty as to offer a tempting mark. His army greatly outnumbered ours. He had thrown it across the Chickahominy and its two wings were again exposed. There were quiet but intense preparations for the important movement.

It was of great extent and covered nearly seven days. Jackson was to move secretly and swiftly from the Valley and join Lee in the attack on the Federal right. He was late, and when Lee crossed at Mechanicsville, June 26, A. P. Hill was thrown at the defenses on Beaver Dam, and was nearly sacrificed. His losses were pitiable, as were D. H. Hill's in the same attack. Had Jackson been in position the enemy would have melted before us. He had promised to be there on the morning of the 26th. On the 27th, Longstreet, A. P. Hill, Whiting, and others stormed the heights at Gaines's Mill, suffering heavy loss, but defeating the enemy badly, taking many prisoners, guns and colors, and driving him in panic after the retreating McClellan. There was great maneuvering on the 26th, and a severe combat at Savage's Station. On the 30th the enemy showed front at Fraser's Farm, and Longstreet, supported by A. P. Hill, instantly attacked with great fury. The enemy was stubborn and contested every foot. Jackson was to be with us, and had he been, our success was undoubted, but for some reason he could not get through White Oak Swamp, and denied us. Of Huger on the right we also heard nothing. The combination had failed. The enemy was thus suffered to escape, but with heavy loss. Our own was far from light.

Malvern Hill followed with its bloody fields and crest. The reckoning there was awful and apparently for no good. McClellan abandoned the hill at night and soon found himself safe at Harrison's Landing under cover of his cruisers and gun-boats. His army was beaten and dispirited and the siege of Richmond broken up; but "Little Mac" raised a faint cry of partial victory and did not fail to torment poor Mr. Lincoln for more men; "heavy reinforcements could alone save the army," etc.

Jackson's firmest friends have been obliged to admit some faults in their hero. As to these movements—either from miscalculation or something else, he was fatally late on the 26th. That he was not on hand at Fraser's Farm was also a serious disaster. Some of Munford's cavalry had got through White Oak Swamp, bad as it was with a heavy rain falling, and it would seem that a soldier so great and energetic as Jackson would have found means to push through to the help of fighting, hard-pressed comrades. It is possible that he was over-done with work and fatigue, but his men should have been there as planned.

I saw him on the 28th, and he seemed brisk enough. Longstreet had sent me after Gaines's Mill to find him and establish connections and communications. He was cheerful and pleasant. "Explain, Major, to General Longstreet where I am and how my troops are lying, and say, with my compliments, I am ready to obey any orders he may send me." When I set out to find him, Tom Ochiltree, fresh and breezy from Texas, was with us for a week as a volunteer by Longstreet's consent. Ochiltree said, that familiar with fighting in Texas, he wanted to see how we did it in the East. He had also a great desire to see the celebrated "Stonewall" before returning home. He asked permission to ride with me. We trotted off together, our route taking us by an extensive field-infirmary, where the surgeons were at their bloody work on the wounded. We halted for a few minutes. The scene was sickening and cured Ochiltree of battle sights. " Sorrel," he said very seriously, "this gives me enough; I don't want any more. It seems now I have seen everything—too much, nothing for me to do here. Better for me to ride back to Richmond and take train for Texas. Sorry not to see 'Stonewall,' but I travel the other way. Good-by and good luck to you." And off he went after just about four days' service with the Confederates in the East.

During these movements there was a young Englishman with us, our guest. He had brought letters to authorities in Richmond. It was Lord Edward St. Maur, a scion of the ducal house of Somerset. He was about twenty-one, just from the University, where he had taken high honors, and was around now with an Englishman's curiosity. A singularly handsome young man he was, with pure olive skin and beautiful features. He was always courteous, always reserved. He came as a neutral for observation, and in all the freedom of our fighting week and rough bivouacs nothing stirred him from that attitude. In truth, I don't think he approved of us. I afterwards heard he was something of a prig but destined for high political life. The battle of Fraser's Farm broke out in the afternoon with great suddenness and severity. I had given St. Maur a mount and we happened to be on the line among the men when firing began, but notwithstanding the cannonading and heavy musketry he was quite cool. "This is not my place," he said, "and with your permission I shall retire," doing so with entire deliberation; he so placed himself as to see something and we talked it over when we met at night. When McClellan took cover at Harrison's Landing, St. Maur was given an officer and flag of truce and soon landed in the home of his fathers. A very careful, neutral chap. I was sorry for his end—hunting big game in India soon after, he was mauled and eaten by a tiger.

When McClellan was safely at Harrison's Landing under cover of heavy guns (some fifteen-inch spherical shell), there was nothing to keep our army there. Besides, it left Richmond somewhat exposed from the direction of Fredericksburg. General Lee, therefore, gave the word and we were soon again in, or near, our old positions. Everything was made ship-shape, the wounded mending and returning to duty, damages repaired, and the waste of that extraordinary movement and series of battles made good as best could be. McClellan could not now see the spires of Richmond from his headquarters. Additional reinforcements were brought from the South in preparation for Lee's next move, for he was not the man to stay idly behind defenses when there was an enemy about that he might hopefully strike. Longstreet's division of six brigades was in fine condition, with filling ranks, and so was A. P. Hill's Light Division, which lay near us, and thereby hangs a tale which must be recited, I fear, at some little length.

CHAPTER IX

Rivalry and More Reminiscences.

Longstreet's and A. P. Hill's divisions—Rivalry between the two —Publications in *Richmond Examiner* and *Whig*—General Hill resentful—Refuses recognition of Longstreet's adjutant-general—Hill in arrest—Personal difficulty between the two major-generals adjusted by General Lee's influence —General Hill cherishes no rancor—Later gave me a brigade—Army busy drilling—Quartermaster Potts and Major Fairfax—Books among the troops—Gambling.

There was some rivalry between the two splendid divisions. Each had done its full share of fighting in the recent battles and each had won glory and renown. Hill had handled his men well and fought them gallantly. Needless to say how Longstreet had held his men, as it were, in the hollow of his hand (his abilities for handling large bodies under fire being remarkable), and how his never-failing valor and tenacity had supported them. The papers came out of Richmond daily, with fetching headlines and columns of description giving the events of the previous day. One of the widest read of these was *The Examiner,* very brilliantly edited. It seemed to have taken Hill's division under its special favor. Every movement was chronicled, every clash of arms, no matter how trifling, was written up, and the grand movements and actions of the division given such prominence as to dwarf all other commands. There was some feeling growing up about it, especially since it was known that a newspaper man from *The Examiner* office was serving temporarily on Hill's staff. Nothing was then done about the matter, but Longstreet's young staff officers were quite at the fighting point, as our division had come in for some animadversions in *The Examiner.*

After the short campaign, while we were occupying some of our old positions about Richmond, Hill lying near by, under command of Longstreet, the latter came one day to me with a rough draft of a short communication to *The Whig,* a Richmond paper. It flatly contradicted *The Examiner,* so far as Longstreet's division was concerned, and criticized the major-general who could suffer such reports to emanate from his own staff; it was short but positive. Longstreet asked if I objected to send such a communication to *The Whig,* signed by myself officially, as adjutant-general. He would answer for it, because I should not be expected alone to attack or criticize my superior officer. I was only too willing to carry out these wishes. The little note was prepared for the press and published in *The Whig.* It was stiff, but with military civility, and made some comment on the taste of having such correspondents along with military operations. It was not regarded as offensive, but was certainly pointed in some contradiction. To my regret I have no copy.

Such was the bomb-shell that was to burst over us in a few days. Having occasion for some routine report or information from General A. P. Hill, a note was sent him for it in the usual form. It was returned endorsed that "General Hill declined to hold further communication with Major Sorrel."

Of course I was surprised, but it was apparent that trouble was brewing and that Longstreet must show his hand. The note was handed him and he was at once on fire at such disobedience. "Write him again," said he, "and say that note was written by my command, and must be answered satisfactorily."

To this Hill insisted on holding to his refusal. The correspondence was then taken up by Longstreet personally with Hill. I did not see the letters, but several passed, until finally, a day or two later, General Longstreet came to me with, "Major, you will be good enough to put on your sword and sash, mount, and place Major-General Hill in arrest, with orders to confine himself to limits of his camp and vicinity." It was my first duty of that kind with such rank, but I was soon on my way, followed by an orderly. The General was in his tent seated in a low chair, and rose as I entered, returning stiffly my salute. Bowing, when I had communicated the orders, he resumed his chair without speech, and saluting again, I was quickly on the road to my own friendly camp. I know only by hearsay what took place afterwards. It was kept quite out of reach of the staff and confined to the two principals. Certain it is, however, that some angry letters passed and intimate friends (D. H. Hill and Toombs for Longstreet) were called in and a hostile meeting between the two generals was almost certain. General Lee, however, heard of it, and acted quickly and effectively, using his unvarying tact and great influence. He brought matters, through other friends, to an adjustment honorable to both. A few days later General Hill's division was shifted out of reach of Longstreet's command and nothing more was known of the affair. Later on Longstreet and Hill became fairly good friends, but I naturally supposed I had incurred his hatred. For a year or two we did not meet—his division being in Jackson's corps—except occasionally on the march, and then the General's manner seemed to me stiff and menacing. If so, it was only the manner, not the feeling, because in 1864 I received from General Hill the very highest evidence of his appreciation and friendliness. On several occasions previously, Longstreet recommended me for promotion to command, and it must necessarily be to a brigade of Georgians. But where a brigadier was wanted for them, there were always good colonels of long service in the brigade that properly gained the preference. This was so general that I despaired of leaving the staff for higher promotion, until one day in September, 1864, a commission of brigadier-general came to me with orders to report to Lieut.-Gen. A. P. Hill.

My preparations began at once for the change and it was necessary for me to go to the War Department, Richmond. There I found in the Adjutant-General's Office Capt. John W. Reilly, A. A. G., a fine young Virginia officer, who had once served under me.

"Did you ever see, General, the paper that brought about your promotion?" It was entirely new to me. He drew from a file a letter from Gen. A. P. Hill, commenting on the bad condition of his fine Georgia Brigade, which, left without a brigadier by the wounds of Wright and the death of Girardy, was then in the hands of a brave but incompetent colonel. He concluded by asking with great earnestness that Lieutenant-Colonel Sorrel, of Longstreet's corps, should be promoted and sent to him. The letter was referred to General Lee for his opinion and then passed between the Adjutant-General, the Secretary of War, and the President, who finally scrawled, "Make the appointment, J. D."

I tried to get the paper from Reilly as an autographic souvenir, but it was against orders and I was obliged to content myself with a certified copy. "It never rains but it pours;" some days after, Major-General Kershaw wrote me that he (Kershaw) had asked for my promotion to command one of his Georgia brigades.

Hill was a West Point man of medium height, a light, good figure, and most pleasing soldierly appearance. He surely handled his division on all occasions with great ability and courage and justly earned high reputation. When Lee created the Third Army Corps he placed him in command of it, and it was thought Hill did not realize in that high position all that was hoped of him.

His health was impaired toward the close of the war, and his noble life ended by a stray bullet at Petersburg after withdrawal of the lines. It was unnecessary and he should have had years before him. It is not necessary to say how much I appreciated his action toward myself. It proved him magnanimous and free of petty spite in that affair, and such was his nature. When I reported to him no one could have been more warmly welcomed, and thenceforward I had nothing but kindness and the most valuable support and help while with his corps.

A. P. Hill was very close to both Generals Lee and Stonewall Jackson at different times. Perhaps only a coincidence, but certainly significant it is, that, the last dying words of the two military chiefs were said to be of Hill. "Send word to A. P. Hill," whispered the expiring Jackson. "Tell Hill he must come up," were the last words on Lee's lips.

July and early August, 1862, were busy months. In front of Richmond General Lee kept the army well exercised in drill and the new men had to get into shape. Our staff work had been severe and our horses had suffered. I was obliged to keep two good mounts at least, sometimes more. It was here I fell in love with a perfect little stallion named Voltaire, and paid a round price for him; he soon proved too delicate for army work and I gave him to my brother in Richmond. There he should have thriven, but I think soon went to pieces. I succeeded in finding a handsome, powerful chestnut mare, from which I got good service until she was killed at Gettysburg. Longstreet was admirably mounted on two bays; one he had brought to the army with him, the other, a finer beast, was a present from Major Fairfax, whose horse judgment was excellent. For himself, he rode a superb gray stallion, "Saltron," widely known, which he had raised at his Loudoun estate. Fairfax lost him at Sharpsburg. A round shot struck him under the tail, fairly in the fundament, and it was at once all over with the stallion. Fairfax was excitable, and rushing to Longstreet, sitting grimly on his horse directing the battle, he broke out, "General, General, my horse is killed; Saltron is shot; shot right in the back!"

Longstreet gave the Major a queer look and consoled him with, "Never mind, Major, you ought to be glad you are not shot in your own back!"

Frank Potts, a quartermaster in the corps, tells a story of these two. Fairfax messed General Longstreet, took good care of all his wants, and kept him in whiskey and in all else that was needful. Potts says that in one of the campaigns he had parked his animals and wagons in a nice spot by the roadside at a good hour and everything was made snug for the night's bivouac until the early march next morning. Suddenly he saw a figure galloping wildly across the fields to him, taking fences and ditches as he came. "Now," grumbled Potts, "it's a move; here are the orders coming." It was Major Fairfax in full uniform. He pulled up sharply before the quartermaster, saluted, and then, "Captain Potts, can you tell me where a washerwoman is to be found for General Longstreet?" relieved the Irishman and tickled his humor.

During the war the men were without many books and eagerly clung to a novel when one came their way. Many old volumes were sent from home, but they did not go far among such numbers. Victor Hugo's "Les Miserables," and Muhlbach's novels, translated from the German, and reprinted at Mobile, had begun to appear and were devoured by readers. Later on, after Gettysburg, Freemantle's "Three Months in the Southern States" was reprinted at Mobile and widely read. These old volumes are now a curiosity and not to be had except at great price. The dirty old type, blurred and worn, the rough paper with florid designs, all attested the stress of the Confederacy in everything entering into life. Among the soldiers in camp there was the usual gambling going on; they played some odd sorts of games, but the greasiest packs of cards were their stand-by.

One day Longstreet received a note from General Lee, after a ride through our camps. This informed the corps commander that he regretted to see so much gambling among the men; they nearly all seemed absorbed in a game called "Chuck-a-luck." "Could anything be done to better the matter?" Longstreet had served much with soldiers, and knew they would, many of them, gamble in camp in spite of all orders and watching; never yet had he found anything that would completely cure the evil. He would, however, see what could be done—but nothing came of it.

CHAPTER X

Second Battle of Manassas, August 29 and 30, 1862.

Major-General Pope in command of Union troops in Northern Virginia—Religious observances in our army—Homesickness—Furloughs—Rations—March against Pope—Artillery duel at Rappahannock—Spy captured and hung—Jackson's marches—Thoroughfare Gap—Longstreet's attack—Enemy routed—General Wilcox and Union general—Wilcox's and Couch's baptismals—Brig-Gen. A. G. Evans—General Toombs and the picket—His arrest—Released and joins brigade in the fight.

McClellan still lay at Westover, recruiting and reorganizing. It was apparent that his army would not be long in that position. Confidence in him had been lost, and there was a new paladin in the field, the doughty John Pope, major-general, with "Headquarters in the saddle." He was a man of some ability, but did not have a reputation for high character in the old Army; and now with elevated rank and command thrust upon him, he turned into abuse of his enemy, explained how he meant to whip him, and filled the air with bombast and threatening. He was in command in northern Virginia, and Lee had marked him for his own.

We were rather a devout army. The men came from their homes deeply tinged with religion. Methodists were in large numbers and next to them Baptists and Presbyterians. There were many meetings and addresses conducted by worthy chaplains. These devoted ministers could always be counted on to follow beside their men, in camp or on the firing line. The men were fond of hearing in camp any kind of address, and were an easy prey to sharpers. I recall that some years later, on the Petersburg line, a crank came along with what he called an artis-avis (a bird of art) with him, and some fifty thousand like it; he was to drop a shell into Grant's army and fleet and destroy them! He wanted permission to address my men and solicit cash for building his wonderful birds. He was sent out of camp. The soldiers were fond of chanting hymns and quaint old plantation airs, and at times they were touching with the recollections of home. Homesickness was often very prevalent, and the awful nostalgia came near crippling us. There is a general order from Longstreet on that matter somewhere and I may be able to find it to attach to these leaves.

At this date, July and August, 1862, food was plentiful and good. No variety, but fresh beef or bacon, flour, coffee and sugar were issued in full rations. There was an abundance of whiskey, but comparatively little drunkenness. Encouragement and incentives to good conduct came from the General-in-Chief down through the officers. Previous to the Chickahominy Campaign a balloon had been constructed for reconnoitering. The enemy had several and we also wanted one, so the women—Heaven bless them!—came to the front with, it may be, tearful eyes but willing hearts and chipped in all their pretty silk frocks and gowns. It was a wonderfully picturesque balloon and at first did some little service, captive to a locomotive pushed far to the front. Then it was packed on a little steamboat in an adventurous cruise down the James. She ran aground, was gobbled up, with the bright ball-dress balloon, by the delighted Yankees, and that was the last of the pretty things of our sisters, sweethearts, and wives.

But the march against Pope is now beginning and must have a little space. The movement was masked as much as possible, a few troops only being at first concentrated at Gordonsville by rail. Lee collected then his outlying commands with great skill and started in earnest against his braggart opponent. Pope seems to have quite underestimated or disbelieved what was awaiting him, and his dispositions were all in favor of Lee. His first rude awakening was the shock Jackson gave him at Cedar Mountain, very costly to him; but we lost Charles Winder, one of the finest and most promising of the brigadiers. The march of the army was in tactical language "left in front," Jackson's position throwing him on the left; and this formation was necessarily observed by all the commands of the army. In these operations Stuart and his cavalry were exceedingly active and performed most valuable service. Our command, the full division, and two smaller ones under D. R. Jones and N. G. Evans, came to a halt hunting a ford on the Rappahannock and found a strong force of the enemy, with good artillery, at the railroad bridge. The gunners (ours the Washington Artillery) on both sides took up an artillery duel for nearly all day, but nothing decisive was achieved. We forded the river in another place without opposition.

It was in these operations that a spy was taken. He had murdered one of our cavalry couriers, and was caught almost red-handed, and with papers on him compromising enough to hang a dozen spies. Nevertheless, we gave him a trial. I convened a drum-head court martial of three brigadiers and they sentenced him to be hanged immediately. The wretch was mounted, arms tied, on a horse, with the noose and limb of a tree connected. He finally admitted he was a spy from Loudoun County, Virginia, but to the last stuck out he had not shot the cavalry courier. A smart blow with the flat of a saber started the horse on the jump and left the spy breathless, and there he hung until the army, continuing its march, passed almost under the tree and perhaps took the lesson to heart.

Jackson's marches, in swiftness, daring, and originality of execution, were almost extraordinary. At one time there was great fear for his safety, widely separated as he was from the right wing under Longstreet. General Lee's route was near Longstreet's and night and day he was always close to us. Longstreet was delayed by the enemy at Thoroughfare Gap. This is a mountain gorge, not long, but narrow, rocky, and precipitous. It was capable of stubborn defense. Its echoes were wonderful—a gun fired in its depths gave forth roars fit to bring down the skies. Here Longstreet had to stop impatiently until he could work his way through. He knew Jackson was hard pressed on the other side and praying for a sight of him. It took a little time, but we sent a flanking force over the mountains by a rocky path and the enemy gave way speedily and left the gap early. Pushing through we saw the dust of Jackson's masses miles away and heard his guns. Forward we pressed almost at a run, and in time. The attack on Stonewall ceased as soon as Longstreet came on the scene.

This was early enough in the day to permit us in turn to make a combined attack. The enemy was disheartened, and Jackson's column, although fatigued and losing heavily, was triumphant and still capable of great efforts. Our own force was large, comparatively fresh, and eager to crush John Pope, but for some reason the attack was not made, although I think General Lee preferred it to waiting.

The great battle that followed, and all these operations covering several days, were called the Second Manassas. Some of the ground was identical with the first. Most of it lay beautifully for good tactical operations, and as the country was quite open much could be observed at considerable distances. When the enemy's masses began again pressing Stonewall on the 30th of August, Longstreet moved quickly up to support. Their dense columns had been left exposed to artillery fire from our position and Longstreet instantly saw it. Planting a battery in the road, the first shots, together with Jackson's incessant fire, began to tell.

We were near enough to see some wavering in the blue masses, then halt, and then a flight back to cover. But it was all up with John Pope. No rest was given his army. Longstreet started every man of us to his division to push them into attack, and soon everything was hotly engaged. The easy, rounded ridges ran at right angles to the turnpike, and over these infantry and artillery poured in pursuit. The artillery would gallop furiously to the nearest ridge, limber to the front, deliver a few rounds until the enemy were out of range, and then a gallop again to the next ridge. And thus it went on until black darkness stopped operations—the enemy defeated at all points and hastening back to the Potomac. Many prisoners, guns, colors, small arms, and large quantities of stores and equipments fell into our hands.

J. E. B. Stuart was highly tickled at his capture of Pope's wagon and personal effects, including a very fine uniform.

Losses on both sides were heavy. Alas! the butcher's bill is always to be paid after these grand operations, and at Manassas especially there were some splendid young lives laid down for our cause and our homes.

Longstreet was seen at his best during the battle. His consummate ability in managing troops was well displayed that day and his large bodies of men were moved with great skill and without the least confusion.

As General C. M. Wilcox was moving forward at the head of his brigade in the open field, he was attracted by the waving of a handkerchief at some little distance. He found time to go to the spot and there mortally wounded was a Federal general, Wilcox's old army friend, who had recognized the Confederate as he passed and wanted to say farewell. His soul soon took flight and his body was cared for by his old-time comrade—the name is forgotten.

Wilcox told me that he once officiated at a christening with D. N. Couch, afterwards a Federal major-general. Wilcox's baptismals were Cadmus Marcellus, and Couch's Darius Narcissus. It is said that when these sonorous designations reached the parson's ear he almost dropped the baby in round-eyed astonishment!

N. G. Evans ("Shanks" Evans) had two brigades with Longstreet and was a rather marked character. A regular soldier, he had served well in Mexico, and at Manassas, on July 21, had done exceedingly well with a small command, a good eye, and quick decision. It was he, too, that commanded at Ball's Bluff on the upper Potomac when Baker attempted to take it with his fine regiment and lost some 800 men. Baker was Senator from Oregon and only a few days before had addressed the United States Senate in full uniform in farewell. It was forever, for he died with hundreds of his men in the waters of the Potomac. Evans was difficult to manage and we found him so. He had a Prussian orderly, with a wooden vessel holding a gallon of whiskey always strapped on his back, and there was the trouble. At the little artillery fight he had on the Rappahannock, G. T. Anderson (Tige), commanding one of the Georgia brigades, was ordered by Evans to attack a powerful battery and silence it. In vain did Anderson explain that it was on the far side of a deep river and that without a bridge his infantry could not get to it. Evans would not listen to reason and Anderson came to me. Of course he was told to make no such attempt, and I proceeded to hunt up Evans, finding him under a tree, too near his "Barrelita," as he called his whiskey holder. But he had to listen and comply. In the progress of the campaign after the Manassas battle he became so unruly as to arrest without reason Hood, one of his brigadiers, and Longstreet had to get him out of the way in some manner. He disappeared afterwards from field work and I don't know his end. He had been a very brave, experienced cavalry officer. Anderson's indignation at the impossibility of the order to take the battery was highly amusing.

In the early part of the march against Pope we made a bivouac near where some Federal cavalry were reported to have been prowling. The enemy had no troops near by to disturb us except this body of horse. It was therefore thought prudent to post a regiment at the cross-road which would warn our camps. General Toombs was ordered to detail one and I saw that it was posted.

During the night a cavalry picket reported that the regiment had been withdrawn. I awoke Longstreet to ascertain if by his orders. "No, but place immediately in arrest the officer who has done so." It proved to be Toombs. He was a great lawyer and a good politician, but in the wrong place when posing as a soldier. He had taken a notion that his regiment was not really needed at the cross-road and the men would be more comfortable with the others in bivouac.

Toombs was therefore put in arrest and the march continued. The next evening on halting it was reported to me that he had followed, as was proper, in rear of his brigade, but had worn his sword, and upon his men going into camp had made them a violent speech. I felt called on to make this known to General Longstreet, whereupon he directed me to order General Toombs back to Gordonsville and confine himself there; also to prefer charges against him on two grounds—withdrawing the regiment from picket duty and breaking his arrest. This was done and Toombs went back to Gordonsville, not many miles away, whence he wrote a short note asking to be released of the charge of breaking arrest, saying he had worn his sword only for convenience and there was nothing improper in his speech to the men. Longstreet always had a decided liking for Toombs, and upon seeing this note he not only withdrew that charge, but the other also and sent him back to duty. Knowing that we should soon be engaged he advised me to be quick about it if I wanted the Georgian to see something of hot work.

An intelligent courier was sent to Toombs with the latest orders, and meantime we were marching forward. He returned; General Toombs was not at Gordonsville. I might well have left the matter there, but it seemed to me that one of our foremost Georgians should have a chance with the army and I sent a second man after him; this time he was found. The situation was explained to him and he was advised to lose no time in joining his men if he desired to be with them in the smoke of battle. And so Toombs came; late, but just in time to be with his brigade in its last victorious charge when everything, as already described, was turned loose.

Toombs stuck to the army through Sharpsburg, where he did good service, and then returned to more congenial fields—politics and oratory. In after years he always showed me much kindness and appreciation for the trouble I had taken to get him back to his brigade for fighting at the Second Manassas.

CHAPTER XI

Battles of South Mountain (Boonsboro Gap) and Sharpsburg (Antietam), Sept. 14th and 17th, 1862.

Accident to General Lee—To Longstreet also—Fight at Chantilly—General Kearny killed—Cross the Potomac—Lee's confidential order found by McClellan—Straggling.

When we got back to Virginia and Toombs's resignation had gone in, Longstreet sent for me to say he had, some time before, about August, 1862, recommended me for promotion to brigadier-general. That Toombs's retirement now left a Georgia brigade open and he wanted me to have it and that I must put out for Richmond forthwith and try to work it through by help of my Congressman and other strong friends. I lost no time about this and was soon on the ground. Hartridge, our M. C., did all he could in my behalf; but there was no possible chance while the brigade had four good colonels, well known representative Georgia men, ready each for the command. It was given to Colonel, formerly Judge, Benning, and his record in command of it was excellent.

The day after great Manassas, General Lee suffered a painful accident. It had rained and he was wearing a rubber poncho and over-alls, his body and legs being thus well protected. With a number of his officers he was dismounted in a thick piece of woods, making some disposition for following the enemy. His horse, a gentle, intelligent animal, was at the General's shoulder, reins on neck; he made some slight movement as if to start away, and Lee taking a step ahead for the bridle tripped in his over-alls and fell forward, not prone, but catching on his hands.

He was instantly on his feet, erect, but his hands were badly damaged; one had a small bone broken and the other was nearly as bad with the twist and strain. Both were put into splints, but were painful and most uncomfortable. For some time the saddle had to be given up and the ambulance called into use. General Lee made the campaign on wheels. At Sharpsburg he was far enough cured to allow him to ride a little. This accident caused widespread report of the General having been wounded, and of course the enemy's papers gave facts in detail of the serious character of the wound and how it was received.

Some little time afterwards Longstreet also got himself damaged. A boot chafed his heel, which took on an ugly look and refused to heal. "Peter" (this was his West Point sobriquet, much used for him by his army friends and to this day not forgotten) therefore was obliged to don a slipper, and at Sharpsburg he was in no good humor at such footwear and the need of occasionally walking in it. In fact, a wobbly carpet slipper was not a good-looking thing for a commander on the field.

General Lee took his army forward to the Potomac. Only a detachment of the enemy was encountered by Jackson, and this was at Chantilly, where toward dark, and in a furious storm, there was a short combat in which Major-General Kearny was killed and left in our hands.

Kearny had been a conspicuous young officer in the Mexican War, where he lost an arm, and coming of a wealthy New Jersey family had resigned from the army and retired to private life. I saw his body next morning. It was given up to the enemy at their request, and his horse also, I think. He was a small, dashing-looking man, possessed, it was thought, of considerable military ability.

After such successes there was a fair prospect of driving the enemy out of Washington or bringing him to terms. General Lee moved his army into Maryland, passing most of the troops across the river at White Ford. The soldiers crossed with joyful excitement, singing "My Maryland," and the whole round of their musical stock, with bands playing and all cheering as well-known officers came in sight. Indeed there was some reason for elation and hope. The enemy had suffered a serious defeat and was driven into his capital, his numbers again very great, but of demoralized and raw-recruited men. On the other hand, Lee also had a strong army (for Confederate numbers—we had been accustomed to be outnumbered). The men were triumphantly rejoicing and confident, and as they believed were moving into the friendly fields of a sister State, whose men would surely rise and join us; and more than all, they were commanded by the first General of the day.

It was early September and delightful marching over Maryland's good roads and through her fields of plenty. We had not yet been pushed for food, the transport so far having kept us supplied. General Lee made a short halt at Frederick City, where we took a rest and got loose ends of the army together; and from here began the movement that after two bloody battles was to send us disappointed back to the Virginia side of the Potomac.

General Lee there issued his famous confidential general order on which the army moved. It provided in detail for the march of his troops and his objective points. It was so full that when a copy came in my possession I wondered what could be done with it in event of my falling into the enemy's hands.

By it Jackson was to move to Harper's Ferry and capture its large garrison—it was a menace to Lee's rear. McLaws was to occupy Maryland Heights, and J. G. Walker, Loudoun Heights, in co-operation with Jackson. Troops were also sent to Crampton's Gap.

D. H. Hill was to occupy South Mountain, or Boonsboro Gap, as it was variously called. Longstreet's strong column was to be in the vicinity of Hagerstown, twelve miles from D. H. Hill's position. Proper directions were provided for Stuart's large cavalry force.

The army moved from Frederick under the confidential order. All should have gone well. The programme would have been carried out, the severed army reunited, with Harper's Ferry captured as it was, and once in front of the already half-beaten McClellan (who had succeeded Pope in command of the Army of the Potomac), what great victory would surely have awaited us! But fate or an unlucky chance decided otherwise. A copy of General Lee's confidential order was handed to McClellan when he reached Frederick. He says in his official report that it was picked up by one of his men on our late camping ground.

Had Lee whispered into the Federal General's ear his inmost plans the latter could have asked for nothing more than the information brought him on that fatal paper.

The effect on McClellan was immediate. His march, up to then, had been cautious and timid, not more than eight or nine miles a day. When the order came to him he knew all about us. He knew that D. H. Hill's five brigades at Boonsboro would be nearly all that lay in his path to cross the mountain, and he began footing it with great speed. His march was rapid, and for McClellan confident. He actually struck D. H. Hill on September 14, on the mountain, with an overwhelming force. Hill defended himself valiantly, Drayton's and Anderson's brigades reinforcing him.

Hearing his guns near Hagerstown, Longstreet's quick military instinct told him what was happening. We instantly broke camp and raced out for Hill's relief. The distance was covered in extraordinary time and we happily got to Hill just as he was being driven from the crest of the mountain, and in time to save him. Darkness coming on, he was able to assemble his shattered battalions below, where with our force a front was shown that McClellan hesitated on immediately attacking. At sun up we prepared to move and were soon on the march to Antietam

Creek, behind which part of the army took position on the 15th and 16th.

But I must go back to Frederick City, asking how a document so vitally important as General Lee's order could have suffered loss. It has often been discussed in special papers, in magazine articles, and in letters. McClellan says it was addressed to Major-General D. H. Hill. There is no disputing this because the document is on file for evidence. General Hill and his adjutant-general, Col. Archer Anderson, both declare it impossible to have been Hill's copy. They are to be implicitly believed. In addition, Colonel Anderson is able to produce a copy addressed to his chief. Thus we find ourselves in a dilemma.

The explanation suggested is that perhaps two copies were sent Hill. Although now an independent division, Jackson considered Hill under his command and sent him a copy of the order. One copy certainly reached him direct from General Lee. Jackson and Hill, although connected by marriage, had it is said no great personal liking for each other, and I can imagine the cross and dyspeptic Hill, with the order from Lee in his pocket, receiving another copy from Jackson with careless irritation. If this theory does not work out, we seem to be quite baffled in finding a solution.

We had a bad night on the mountain, extracting D. H. Hill. He had made a magnificent defense, but was terribly mauled and broken up.

Drayton's brigade had been dispersed. There was great straggling to the rear by some of the men and our staff had to make sharp play with the flats of our swords on the backs of these fellows. It tired and disgusted me. The mountain roads were filled with broken regiments and companies and it was very late before they got to the foot of the mountain and in some sort of order. The material of our army was such that it did not take long for the men to shape up after disaster. It was near daylight before I got to Longstreet's bivouac, made a brief report of things, and threw myself on some fence rails in the bad weather for a chance of sleep. Not for long, however. All hands were soon afoot preparing for the march. During the day I came up with my old friend and schoolmate "Sandy" Duncan, of the Hussars. He was a comical object, but doing good service mounted on a little beast, almost skin and bones, with scarcely any hair. The animal looked badly scalded. He bore Duncan and his arms however, the trooper bearded and with as odd an appearance as his mount. He was gathering stragglers and pushing them forward with hard words and sometimes blows. We had never a campaign when there was so much straggling. Duncan was an excellent cavalry soldier and devoted to his troop. In full health to-day at Savannah, he is considered justly good authority on all things Confederate.

CHAPTER XII

BATTLE OF SHARPSBURG, CONTINUED

Marching through Frederick—Barbara Fritchie and Stonewall Jackson—Commissariat broken down—Green corn for rations—Stampede of horses of a cavalry regiment—D. H. Hill's horse shot—Longstreet's staff served guns of Washington Artillery—Cannoneers killed—Colonel John R. Cooke's gallant fight—Am wounded and carried off the field.

When the army marched through Frederick City it was fine weather, and the poet Whittier has told of Barbara Fritchie and Stonewall Jackson—a stirring poem in winning lines, but quite without fact at bottom. But that matters not in the least. The lines are good and we can well afford to throw in with all the hard words and abuse of those days, the poet's ideas about our Stonewall.

The country through which we marched was beautiful, rich, and fertile, but we were constantly hungry. There were two lines of Whittier's unquestionably true:

> "Fair as a garden of the Lord,
> To the eyes of the famished rebel horde."

In all parts of the army straggling was principally caused by want of food. The commissariat had about broken down and the troops had recourse to anything.

The fields were full of ripened corn, of which too much was eaten. Parched and salted it would help a little, but eaten as it was, bad attacks of diarrhea followed and such sickness became serious.

On the night before the battle we were getting some sleep under thick trees when a stampede of horses nearly trampled us. It was a very surprising thing that happened to the Jeff Davis Legion. The regiment was well lined and picketed in front, part of the officers and men asleep, guards and pickets on good watch, and everything deadly quiet and still, the night well on.

Suddenly something seemed to pass through the animals like a quiver of motion, a faint sound as of a sign, and then the wildest scene ensued. The horses for no reason that could be found had become stampeded, in the greatest panic and excitement. They broke away from their picket ropes, and droves of different sizes, some few, some many, were thundering along over the country and about the army in wild confusion. Fortunately, they drew to our rear, and the troopers were all night and part of the next day recovering them. Duncan has well described to me this extraordinary stampede, the like of which did not occur during the four years' war.

The morning of September 17 opened with battle before us, presaged by the booming of cannon already beginning their noisy work.

Longstreet held the right center, the other wing being trusted to Jackson, Hood, Richard H. Anderson, McLaws, and other divisions. The fall of Harper's Ferry had released the attacking forces and enabled Jackson and part of his command to join Lee, but only after great exhaustion and fatal straggling. The enemy called this battle Antietam, from the little stream that traverses the field. We gave it the name of Sharpsburg, the village that nestled in the hills by the turnpike some little distance back of Antietam. It was a dreadful day of fighting. Beginning early, we were at it until nightfall. Outnumbered three to one, it seemed that at almost any time a strong effort by McClellan would drive us back, but that effort was not made. A third of his fine army did not fire a rifle.

In the early afternoon, Lee, Longstreet, and D. H. Hill ascended a little acclivity near the turnpike to make some observations. All others—staff and orderlies—were kept back under the brow of the hill to avoid drawing fire on the three generals. In truth, they did look conspicuous on the crest, silhouetted against the bright skies, and the shot of course came, a little wide, but the second was from a good gunner. This shot struck the front legs of Hill's horse, cutting them sharp off at the knees. The poor beast did not fall immediately, and made no sound, but put his nose into the grass, nibbling at it seemingly.

The small general in a high-cantled saddle could not get his leg over in the position of the horse until Longstreet helped him down. There is occasional talk of groans and shrieks of horses when wounded. I have seen many badly hurt, but cannot recall an instance in which the animal made any noise. This "gunning" has recently been associated with another incident on the field with which it has really no connection. It was rather later in the day that we came on two of Miller's Washington Artillery guns that had been doing splendid work, but were now silent.

The gunners had fallen by their places, which were temporarily without cannoneers. Longstreet was with us. Fairfax, Goree-Manning, Walton, myself, and perhaps some others took our horses' bridles as we leaped from them to the guns. The position was most important and it would never do for those "barkers" to be dumb, even for a minute; so at it we went, the improvised gunners, and were afterwards cheered by being told we did it well and could always get a gunner's berth when we might want it. I had the rammer, No. 1, I think it is in the drill. Our fire was really strong and effective, until some reliefs from the Washington Artillery came up "ventre à terre," and with hearty shouts took their guns in hand. The enemy opened a severe fire on us, but fortunately none of our party was hurt. We mounted again with cheerful grins at our sudden adventure, and Longstreet, much pleased, turned his attention to other imperiled points.

Now, some fellow writing recently says it was McClellan's own hands that fired at Hill's horse in the morning; and that, in revenge, Longstreet seeing his position in the afternoon, guessed it must be McClellan and his staff and dispersed them with his own hands on the guns. An awful lot of lies circulate nowadays about the Civil War, and it is so long ago there is hardly anybody to contradict them.

Longstreet, whose eyes were everywhere, had noticed a regiment well advanced that had been fighting steadily for hours. It had gathered a few rails and stones for a chance protection to its brave fellows, all the time keeping up a good steady fire on the force in front of them, whose ranks looked so thick as to make one wonder they did not walk over our poor little regiment. Longstreet never failed to encourage good work; he praised freely and liberally where he thought it due, constantly recommending meritorious young officers for promotion. There was no illiberality about him, and the officers knew it and tried for his notice. "Major Sorrel," he said, "go down to that regiment with my compliments to the colonel. Say he has fought splendidly and must keep it up. We are hard pressed and if he loses his position there is nothing left behind him; his men have made noble sacrifices, but are to do still more."

It was Col. John R. Cooke, commanding a North Carolina regiment, that received this message. There were many dead along his lines and some severely wounded who could not be got away. My horse was wounded on the way to him, and the enemy's rifle firing was incessant, while from the saddle Longstreet's praises and encouragement were given this brave officer.

Profanity is justly considered objectionable. I do not approve of it, but there are times when it may be overlooked, and never did such words sound so sweet as when I looked into Cooke's eyes and heard him: "Major, thank General Longstreet for his good words, but say, by —— almighty, he needn't doubt me! We will stay here, by J. C., if we must all go to hell together! That —— thick line of the enemy has been fighting all day, but my regiment is still ready to lick this whole —— outfit. Start away, Major, quick, or you'll be getting hurt too, exposed as you are on that horse!" This is only a faint reproduction of the Colonel's gift of language, but it left with me no doubt that the position would stand until that gallant heart gave the word to leave it. He stuck there until ordered off at night. It was some time before I was able to send a report to Longstreet, the hour being about 5 p. m., but he had Cooke promoted immediately. I had scarcely drawn my hand from Cooke's when a shell burst over us and a fragment struck me senseless from my horse.

CHAPTER XIII

Battle of Sharpsburg, Concluded

Toombs's Georgia Brigade—Longstreet on the field—Lee's war horse—McClellan superseded by Burnside—A horse trade—Richard H. Anderson's division—A lost opportunity—Walton and myself find quarters at Shepherdstown among wounded—Driven away by enemy's shells.

Toombs's brigade of Georgians had fought well at the bridge on the right. It was contested all day and was the scene of some bloody encounters. Some fresher men under A. P. Hill at last came up late, almost dark, and a general advance on the enemy's lines persuaded the timorous McClellan that we were not done fighting, and he ceased his operations. Lee was left, after the long day's work, with thin ranks holding the ground he stood on in the morning, and nothing lost by us in guns, colors, or prisoners. The casualties, however, were very heavy, our list of wounded and killed being awful. Here fell my dear personal friends of school days, McIntosh and Parkman. I had lost several in the battles preceding and my heart was heavy.

Longstreet's conduct on this great day of battle was magnificent. He seemed everywhere along his extended lines, and his tenacity and deep-set resolution, his inmost courage, which appeared to swell with the growing peril to the army, undoubtedly stimulated the troops to greater action, and held them in place despite all weakness. My staff comrades described to me later his appearance and reception by Lee when they met at night after firing ceased. Longstreet, big, heavy, and red, grimly stern after this long day's work, that called for all we could stomach, rolled in on his clumsy carpet slippers. Lee immediately welcomed him with unconcealed joy. "Here comes my war horse just from the field he has done so much to save!" his arm affectionately around "Peter's" shoulder. The latter should surely have been proud and well satisfied. Lee held his ground that night and all the next day (the 18th), caring for his wounded and burying his dead. On the night of the 18th he quietly moved out and successfully passed the Potomac to Viriginia ground without loss. That McClellan with his great army, a third of which had taken no part in the two battles, permitted this escape is unaccountable. In olden times generals lost their heads for such stupidities. "Little Mac" lost his place instead, being soon superseded by Burnside.

I was never good at a horse trade, and here is a story of one. I had a nice little mare of good paces, but she was undersized for my long legs. Walton, my staff comrade, had a big, fine bay, well gaited and apparently all that I could wish. Walton, being a small man, liked the mare, and was ready to trade; but just before getting to Boonsboro, the big bay, "Mott" (he had been brought from Mississippi by that Colonel Mott who was killed at Williamsburg, and we named him "Mott"), had broken loose and was astray somewhere, Walton being unable to find him. Having some mounted men I could use and knowing the cavalry officers near by, I believed he could be found, so taking the chances I made the trade by paying Walton $275 to boot, and this too in '62, when Confederate money was not so very *bad*. That much cash could then buy considerable stuff. Longstreet was an excellent judge of horse-flesh and to him I gave the details of my trade. In answer I got a little stare and smile as he said, "Why, Major, I would not give $275 for the horse tied to a corn crib; no quartermaster in this army can furnish forage enough for that beast!" This was soothing and encouraging to be sure, and in the mean time bay "Mott" refused to be found. Boonsboro and Sharpsburg were fought, the army back in Virginia, and I on my way back, when at last came my cavalrymen, bay "Mott" in hand, and in a fortnight or so I was on him, a powerful, well-paced animal; but Longstreet was right, he could never get enough to eat, and after some time his ribs and bones were disagreeably in evidence, and the beast was turned over to a quartermaster to do with as he would. He had pickings in the corral and was probably hitched to a hay wagon.

When struck down by that bursting shell, Colonel Cooke had me immediately carried off on a stretcher to a less exposed place, and on regaining consciousness good old Fairfax was pouring whiskey down my throat. We had been severed by one of those unnecessary camp differences and were not on good terms. Needless to say all that was now forgotten and we were comrades once more. He managed to get an ambulance and sent me off to the army field-infirmary. There was another officer stretched by me in the ambulance, very bloody and very terribly wounded. I did not think I was hurt badly, but seemed to have no motion or feeling about the legs. We were soon at the surgeon's camp, Dr. Guild medical director in charge. I knew him well, a cheerful soul. "What, you too!" he cried. "Now, turn over." And he began pinching my legs unmercifully. I kicked and cried out loudly, and he laughed and said: "O, you are quite right, I feared for your back. Now away to the rear across the river; you will be on duty again in a fortnight." The hurt was a violent contusion below the right shoulder and made the whole side of the body black and blue with extravasated blood. Off we started and came up with my staff comrade, Walton, slowly trotting to the rear with a bullet in his shoulder. He took charge of things energetically, managed by threats and bullying to get a boat, and had us ferried across the river at Shepherdstown. There Walton got some men to carry me, hunting a resting place; he tried everywhere, his wound paining him all the time. The little town was full of wounded and it looked as if we should have to lie out in the street, but some gentle hearts were melted. At the house of the Hamtrammocks, already crowded with wounded, the ladies gave up their last room and put us in it, fed and cheered us, providing that sweet sympathy and goodness that was ever present among the noble women of battle-torn Virginia.

The Hamtrammock family was unknown to me, but stood very well in the village and all through the Valley. It was said that their father, long dead, had commanded a Virginia regiment in the Mexican

War. The only members of the family we saw were the two pleasant girls, Elsie and Florence, and an aunt, Miss Sheperd. That evening the doctor relieved Walton of acute suffering by cutting out the bullet, which had buried itself in the muscles of the shoulder, and dressed my battered back. So we awoke next morning refreshed and easier, charmed with our luck in such good quarters. We were soon quite ready to be entertained by the young ladies, and they were nothing loth after the nurses had made us presentable. There was a Georgian in the house, Captain D'Antignac, badly wounded in the head, and in charge of Miss Sheperd. She would sometimes rush into our room, laughing immoderately; the poor fellow was out of his head and talking all sorts of nonsense. Our hostesses were very gracious, gay, happy, well educated girls; they played and sang prettily, and were such Confederates! We had much curiosity to know how they had fared during the night, since they had been robbed of their rooms; it finally came out that they had shared the bathroom between them. But this elysium could not last long, for next day the enemy planted some guns on the river bank and began shelling everything. The wounded were in great peril and the surgeons hurried them to the rear. An ambulance was sent at once for us, and with grateful farewells to our friends, we were taken away to a little old farmhouse fifteen miles distant, behind Lee's army.

CHAPTER XIV

Our Personnel—Visitors

On duty again, recovered—Army refreshed and in good condition—Reorganization—First and Second Army Corps, Longstreet and Stonewall commanding—Divisions composing them—Cavalry under Stuart—Visitors to our camp in Valley—Three Englishmen, Wolseley, Lawley, and Vizitelly.

Within the fortnight I was returned to duty, rather stiff but quite fit, and pleased with the hearty welcome of my brother officers. Walton's wound proved severe and he was sent to a hospital at Richmond. The army had picked up wonderfully, stragglers were back in ranks, the lightly wounded were again ready with their rifles, rations were abundant; some clothing and shoes had come, for a small part of it, and we were just eager for Burnside or any other fellow. Our General, like his army, was high in spirit and controlling absolutely its destiny. Its devotion for Lee and unfaltering confidence in him had never been surpassed. It was now that he found it necessary to reorganize his various commands. They were all comfortably camped in the Valley, except a small detachment sent to the vicinity of Fredericksburg, and covered a good deal of ground. The enemy was silent and showed no sign of movement, but we could guess where he was likely to strike next. Somewhere about Spottsylvania or Fredericksburg, Lee divided his army into two great infantry corps—the First Army Corps under Lieut.-Gen. James Longstreet; the Second Army Corps under Lieut.-Gen. T. J. Jackson. The First had five divisions under Pickett, McLaws, Hood, Richard Anderson, and J. G. Walker; all had from four to five brigades, except Walker's, only two, but it was known that his command was to be but temporarily with the Virginia army. Jackson's Second Army Corps had also four divisions under A. P. Hill, R. S. Ewell, D. H. Hill, and Jackson's old division under Taliaferro.

The strength of the two great bodies was thus about equal. To each division there was a battalion of artillery of four batteries, and to each corps a reserve battalion of six batteries. Longstreet had two of them, the Washingtons, and Alexander's battalion.

There was also a strong body of reserve artillery to the army under command (and indeed he claimed some authority over the rest) of Brig.-Gen. W. N. Pendleton. This officer had graduated from West Point, had changed his uniform to the cassock and was rector of an Episcopal church in Western Virginia. He was an especial friend of General Lee, and leaving his pulpit brought a good battery to Jackson's command. A well-meaning man, without qualities for the high post he claimed—Chief of Artillery of the Army.

The cavalry under Stuart completed the good organization of that wonderful army. An excellent body of horse it was, in fit hands, and its commander, true body and soul to Lee, was already a great cavalry leader. It was not, however, until next year that he rose with it to its high-water mark of strength, efficiency, and renown.

While camped there in the Valley we had all at once three interesting visitors, Col. Garnet Wolseley, of the British Army; Hon. Francis Lawley, correspondent at the South for *The London Times,* and Frank Vizitelly, Southern correspondent and artist for *The London Illustrated News.* Wolseley was on duty in Canada and had just slipped across the border and the army lines to have a look at the Confederate forces. He was a small, spare man, modest and soldierly. It was from Lawley that we learned more about him, and that he had distinguished himself while a subaltern in the Crimea and was considered a rising officer. It fell to me to make better acquaintance with Wolseley and we have kept up some communication since. It has, therefore, been good to follow his "steps" and note the more than fulfillment of the favorable expectations of him. Commander of the Red River Expedition; general in charge of the Ashantee War; severe, successful service in India; command in Egypt and defeat of Arabi at Tel-el-Kebir; operations in the Soudan—these have been some of his various services up to five years ago, when he was made commander-in-chief of the forces, his tour of duty having just ended. We had a review of one of our divisions, gave him a good mount, and he rode well with Longstreet, admiring with an experienced eye the hardy material of our soldiers. In a day or two he returned to Canada. He has attained the rank of Field Marshal, and is Viscount Wolseley in the Peerage of England, with many high orders of merit.

This distinguished officer has written well and often of his Confederate observations. He places

Lee in the first rank of generals of the English-speaking race, with Marlborough and Wellington; and his admiration for our leader is constant—of the very highest. A letter pointing to his interest in Confederate autographs will be found in the Appendix.

Frank Lawley, tall, handsome, and of distinguished appearance, had started in English political life with everything in his favor. A fine University education, natural aptitude, and a polished pen aided him in becoming secretary to Mr. Gladstone when Chancellor of the Exchequer. Soon, however, a shadow fell on Lawley. He gave up his post and political life, taking to writing, for which he was well fitted. *The Times* had sent him South, and he was about Lee's army nearly two years, making many friends. He is now one of the principal editors of the *London Telegram,* with a great salary, which, as of old, does not go far with him.

Frank Vizitelly (Italian family, for centuries settled in England) was a burly-looking, reckless "Bohemian," of many accomplishments. He could write, could sing, could draw and paint, could dance and ride, could tell good stories (good only in the telling, not in the matter) by the hour, and, finally, could drink like a fish, and did so. He made spirited drawings of battles, persons, and all sorts of scenes during the two years he was with us in the South, and managed to get them through the blockade to his paper.

When Vizitelly left us he served his paper all over the world, whenever there was war; and finally joining Hicks Pasha's Expedition for subduing the

Soudan, perished in the complete massacre of that ill-fated column.

His name, with six other war correspondents who fell at their several posts elsewhere, is carved in a tablet set in the walls of St. Paul's Cathedral, London. I never thought Vizitelly could possibly come to such respectable distinction.

CHAPTER XV

The Staff

Staff of First Corps—Kirkwood Rangers escort—A camp dinner party in state—Lee's aggressiveness—Ropes's description of Lee—Duties of the staff.

The organization of the army having been described, it is time to show the staff of the First Army Corps; thus, October, 1862:

Major G. M. Sorrel, A. A. G. and Chief of Staff.
Major John W. Fairfax, A. A. G. and Inspector.
Major Osmun Latrobe, A. A. G. and Inspector.
Lieut.-Col. P. T. Manning, Chief of Ordnance.
Captain F. W. Dawson, Assistant to Chief of Ordnance.
Major Thomas Walton, A. D. C.
Captain Thomas Goree, A. D. C.
Lieutenant Blackwell, A. D. C.
Major R. J. Moses, Chief Commissary of Subsistence.
Major Mitchell, Chief Quartermaster.
Captain J. H. Manning, Signal Officer.
Surgeon J. S. D. Cullen, Medical Director.
Surgeon R. Barksdale, Medical Inspector.
Surgeon Kellum, Medical Inspector.

Assistant Surgeon Thomas Maury, Assistant to Medical Director.

Major Chichester, Commissary of Subsistence.

Major I. G. Clarke, Engineer Corps.

Of the names of those starting out with Longstreet at the beginning only a few have already been given. The others were added as the command grew in strength and wants. Some of those here named may not have joined until a little later than this time, which I fix at about November 15, 1862. Latrobe, a Marylander, had been serving with D. R. Jones's small division. Upon its being broken up he came to us and proved most acceptable to the Lieutenant-General, and a valuable staff officer. He was eventually to succeed me when I was in 1864 promoted to command in another corps. Moses, the chief commissary, had been a leading lawyer in Georgia, and was now a most intelligent, efficient officer. He was much older than most of us, but "bon comrade," and had an exhaustless fund of incident and anecdote, which he told inimitably.

Latrobe, whom I often see, is my dear friend as I write; in fine health and good condition; big in body and frame as he is in heart. To corps headquarters at this time was attached a good troop of cavalry for courier and escort service. It was the Kirkwood Rangers, from South Carolina, first commanded by Captain Shannon, then by Captain Tobey. Captain Shannon was that excellent man, somewhat advanced in years, and retired, who was forced into a duel in South Carolina, and killed. The staff well understood their General and he knew them; they worked together with good results and never did one of them fail him.

An officer who might also be numbered on the staff was Colonel E. P. Alexander, although he commanded the reserve artillery; but Longstreet thought so well of his engineering and reconnoitering abilities that he kept him very near headquarters.

While the three Englishmen were visiting us it was decided to give them a dinner. Two hospital tents were thrown together and made a fine mess hall, embellished with trophies of arms and flags. Flowers and ferns did the rest for decoration. For the table there were planks on trestles, and the same for seats. The countryside was generous in lending, as well as giving provisions, and our fête did not lack a good white covering over its bare boards. Provisions were plentiful outside the army rations, and I aver that on this occasion they were paid for honestly. Young pig well fattened, turkeys, fowls, fresh beef, and vegetables topped off the commissary's pork and hardtack. There were good cooks at our call, and the negro servants of the officers fairly grinned with delight at such a feast. We had many officers of note to meet our guests, and the function went off most agreeably. The absence of wine was conspicuous, but no one lacked for good whiskey, and perhaps before parting it had been tasted too often by some. After dinner came cards—poker. The Englishmen, except Wolseley, knew the game and enjoyed it. I know that I was a considerable loser, then a turn of chance brought me even, and soon we quit for bed, my last real game of poker to this date.

The army had now been long enough under Lee to satisfy all that he meant fighting, always fighting. That was the business of the army, and only by fighting could Virginia be cleared of the enemy and Richmond made secure. When he first took command there were a few unthinking speeches made. He had fortified Richmond, and like a skilful general knew the value of field-works and temporary entrenchments. Some in the army were given to speak of him as the "King of Spades" who would never allow us to show fighting. The past fourteen months had indeed opened the eyes of these sneerers.

Ropes, the distinguished Northern military historian, writing always, even in the most heated controversy, fairly and dispassionately, has this to say for our hero, en passant, in one of his books, having already once declared him "The most accomplished soldier of the day":

At the time of his appointment to the command of the Army of Northern Virginia, General Lee was 55 years of age, in perfect health, vigorous, robust, of a commanding presence. His character, public and private, was of the highest. In intellect it may be doubted whether he was superior to the able soldier whom he succeeded; indeed, Joseph E. Johnston possessed as good a military mind as any general on either side; but in that fortunate combination of qualities, physical, mental, and moral, which go to make up a great commander, General Lee was unquestionably more favored than any of the leaders of the Civil War. He possessed at once the entire confidence of his Government and the unquestioning and enthusiastic devotion of the army. He had no rival, either in the councils of the Richmond War Department or in the colloquies around campfires. Lee's position was unique. No army commander on either side was so universally believed in, so absolutely trusted. Nor was there ever a commander who better deserved the support of his Government and the affection and confidence of his soldiers.

With the growth of Longstreet's command my duties had become doubly important, and with weighty responsibilities. The General left much to me, both in camp and on the field. As chief of his staff it was my part to respond to calls for instruction and to anticipate them. The General was kept fully advised after the event, if he was not near by at the time; but action had to be swift and sure, without waiting to hunt him up on a different part of the field.

The change of movement of a brigade or division in battle certainly carried a grave responsibility, but it has often to be faced by the chief staff officer if the general happened to be out of reach. Nearly two years of war on a grand scale had given me experience and confidence, and Longstreet was always generous with good support when things were done apparently for the best. This gave me good prestige in our large corps, and I found hosts of friends among officers and men.

The reorganization had made the First Corps 40,000 strong, effective, by the time it got to Fredericksburg in December. Jackson's Second Corps was fully 38,000 strong.

CHAPTER XVI

Events Preceding Fredericksburg

Burnside in command of Army of the Potomac—Sketch—Lee's plans—At Fredericksburg—General Patrick, U. S. A.—Flag of truce—Arrival of army in position—Poor defensive works—Bad-weather march—Some expedients by Longstreet—The stone wall—Major-General McLaws, Major-General Hood, Major-General Anderson, Major-General Walker—Sketches.

The new commander of the Army of the Potomac was one of the most highly respected officers of the United States Army, but he was not equal to the command, and so stated to the officers who brought him Mr. Lincoln's commission and orders.

McClellan was of decided ability in many respects; timorous, but safe; and there was no better organizer. He seemed to hate battle, and it is surprising that with such a record he should have secured and retained the devotion and confidence of his men to the very end. There was no lack of physical courage; it was a mental doubt with him.

Burnside had no prominent reputation, but made a success of an unimportant expedition into North Carolina. He conspicuously failed at Sharpsburg, where all day the bridge on the right was the scene of combat, without his movement to seize it. His great corps, held idly in hand, was equal to it ten times over. But he may have been waiting on McClellan, with whom he was in the closest intimacy of friendship.

At all events, Burnside could and would fight, even if he did not know how, and after "Little Mac" this was what Mr. Lincoln was trying for. He was a handsome man, from Rhode Island, of fine, courteous bearing.

Franklin should have been, I think, the man for Lincoln; but who knows? There was a powerful clique always about McClellan, most unwisely at difference, sometimes, with the Administration.

A pause in the operations ensued while we lay about Bunker Hill and Winchester. But Lee had, in the first half of November, decided where he should make Burnside fight. It was Fredericksburg. Longstreet had previously sent McLaws's division east of the mountains to the vicinity of Culpeper, and about November 16 started him for the old town on the Rappahannock, following a day or two later from his Valley camps with the remainder of the corps.

The gaps of the Blue Ridge were well occupied and defended by Jackson and Stuart's cavalry during Lee's transfer of his army in this delicate strategical operation.

I parted from Longstreet for a day or two, and arrived near Fredericksburg with some of the leading troops, before him.

My ride was in the worst weather, roads deep in mud, with rain in torrents. Fredericksburg is one of the oldest and most aristocratic of the Virginia towns. A dwindling trade had thinned the population and quieted its ambitions. At this time the place was the home of families of historical importance and present interest, with a thorough knowledge of good living, and still respectable cellars of old Madeira that had been imported by them many years before.

The enemy had a small garrison there and a provost marshal, an elderly United States officer, kind and gentle in his authority, and much liked by the citizens.

From this officer I received a request to meet him under flag of truce, and we made acquaintance in a little block-house just outside the town. The good old General Patrick was quite in ignorance apparently of the great operation that was then culminating. Expecting to hold the city with his little garrison he wished to avert any shelling of the town by our guns.

His friends had not yet made their appearance on the Falmouth Hills, commanding the town on the left bank of the river. We had outstripped their march.

General Patrick was informed that he must at once withdraw from Fredericksburg, that we should occupy it in force. He smiled, thinking it a bluff, and wanted to know where the soldiers were. On this point he got no information, of course, and we parted. However, he was soon to see our men pouring forward, and McLaws's division seizing the city and posting his gallant Mississippians on the river front, under the intrepid Barksdale.

Patrick's little gang had, of course, immediately slipped away when they saw what was coming.

This I think was about November 21. The entire army soon after arrived and took position behind the Rappahannock, a wide, undulating plain for the most part stretching between our lines and the river itself. Longstreet took the left and Jackson the right; the former's most important point being the stone wall and sunken road at the foot of Marye's Hill.

Looking back at the situation, it seems surprising that we did so little in the way of defensive field-works. The enemy in great masses were crowding the Falmouth Hills, and we knew intended to cross and strike us. But yet we contented ourselves with the little stone wall (which proved helpful), and two or three tiers of light trenchwork extended on the slope of the hill behind and on our left.

The like observation applies to Jackson, whose lines were about the same as ours in strength, except the stone wall.

Later in the war such a fault could not have been found. Experience had taught us that to win, we must fight; and that fighting under cover was the thing to keep up the army and beat the enemy. He knew it, too, and practised it, so later on veterans no sooner got to facing each other than they began to dig, if ever so little; a little trench, a tiny hillock is often a very helpful defense and protection.

The march to Fredericksburg in bad weather and over almost bottomless roads had caused great suffering to the men and some losses among the animals. It was then that Longstreet told his men of an expedient that as an old soldier he had often resorted to. "Rake," he sent word to the men, "the coals and ashes from your cooking fires and sleep on that ground; it will be dry and warm." And so it proved. Also, there being many barefooted men, "Take the rawhides of the beef cattle, killed for food; cut roughly for a moccasin-like covering for the feet, and there you are with something to walk in." But this did not go. This foot-wear had nothing like soles of stiffening, and in the mud and icy slush of the Virginia roads the moist, fresh skins slipped about as if on ice. The wearers, constantly up or down, finally kicked them aside and took the road as best they could, barefooted or wrapped with rags or straw. Richmond did its best to supply, but there was always trouble for want of shoes. Great quantities were run in from England by blockade, but they were worthless, shoddy things that might be done for in a day's use. I once wore a pair of them, and in a single day of wet and mud the cheats came to pieces and developed bits of paper and odds of leather things, where should be good, strong, well tanned cow skin.

It is said that our friends, the enemy, across the lines fared badly as well in shoddy, and that too from their own neighbors and countrymen.

It was awfully nasty work getting down to that stone wall for giving orders or receiving information, the way swept by the enemy's volume of fire over every foot. Once at the wall it was fairly snug, but the coming back was still worse, and one drew a long breath on emerging safely from that deadly fusilade.

We could only manage it on foot by making short rushes from point to point, affording perhaps some little cover. It was on such a duty that my friend Lord King was killed. He was A. D. C. to McLaws, of the family of Kings of southern Georgia.

The ranking major-general of our corps was L. McLaws, his division made up of Georgians, Mississippians, and South Carolinians. He was an officer of much experience and most careful. Fond of detail, his command was in excellent condition, and his ground and position well examined and reconnoitered; not brilliant in the field or quick in movement there or elsewhere, he could always be counted on and had secured the entire confidence of his officers and men.

Maj.-Gen. John B. Hood's appearance was very striking; in age only 34, he had a personality that would attract attention anywhere. Very tall and somewhat loose-jointed; a long, oval face shaded by yellowish beard, plentiful hair of same color, and voice of great power and compass.

With very winning manners, he is said to have used these advantages actively for his own advancement. But apart from that, his services in the field were of the best. Resigning from the United States Army he was made colonel of one of the three Texas regiments that were sent to Virginia. There he quickly showed his soldierly qualities and was made brigadier-general over the brigade formed of the three Texas regiments and the Third Arkansas. It was conspicuous in all of the many combats in which it was engaged, and Hood soon came on for promotion to one of the divisions of Longstreet's corps. As major-general he continued to display high qualities and he might be considered an ideal officer of that rank and command. At Gettysburg he received a wound in the arm. It is said that at Richmond, while convalescing, he suffered himself to criticize very freely our operations in Pennsylvania. As soon as recovered he resumed his division, which he took to Chickamauga, where his conduct was magnificent. There he lost a leg. Longstreet immediately recommended him to promotion to lieutenant-general, which was done, and on recovery Hood was assigned to the Western army under J. E. Johnston. There I must leave him. His biographers will relate his promotion to the rank of full general; his superseding Johnston; his march to the enemy's rear; the sanguinary battles of Franklin and Nashville, and the crushing defeat of his expedition by Thomas, making possible the great decisive strategic operation of Sherman's "March to the sea."

Maj.-Gen. G. E. Pickett we already know. He had a very fine division of five Virginia brigades, all well commanded by brigadiers who greatly helped the Major-General to the high reputation gained by this gallant body of men.

Maj.-Gen. Richard H. Anderson, of South Carolina, had been a captain of cavalry in the United States Army, and was rather an interesting character. His courage was of the highest order, but he was indolent. His capacity and intelligence excellent, but it was hard to get him to use them. Withal, of a nature so true and lovable that it goes against me to criticize him. He had served well as a brigadier-general, and now with Longstreet, commanding a division, had more to do. Longstreet knew him well and could get a good deal out of him, more than any one else. His division was of Georgians, South Carolinians, Alabamians and Mississippians.

Maj.-Gen. J. B. Walker was commanding two brigades of North Carolinians. I had no intimate knowledge of this officer, who it was known would be with the Virginia army but for a short time. He bore a high reputation among those of his acquaintance.

CHAPTER XVII

Battle of Fredericksburg, December 13, 1862

Enemy massed on Stafford Heights—Heavy artillery fire—The pontoon bridge—Splendid defense of Mississippians—Enemy crosses—Preparing for his assault—Sumner's attack on Marye's Hill—The deadly stone wall—General Cobb killed—General Lee's position—Jackson in uniform—His answer to Longstreet—Franklin's attack on Jackson—Enemy escapes across the river—Strength and losses—Bursting of a gun—Old Madeiras in Fredericksburg—An incident, "one touch of nature"—Enemy not pursued.

But now it is time to sketch something of the remarkable battle that the quiet waters of the Rappahannock were to see fiercely fought in torrents of blood across the plain that bordered the stream. I attempt no description, limiting myself to some stray observations.

The enemy had finally massed his great force (122,500 men) on Stafford Heights and was to force the passage of the river. Franklin had wisely advised Burnside to do the work with half the army against our right, and Burnside, at first assenting, then resumed his original intention to attack our center with Sumner's grand division. Well for us that he did so!

On December 11 his movement began by attempting to set his pontoon bridge opposite the city for the crossing.

It was opposed by General Barksdale's Mississippi Brigade of McLaw's division, and stands as one of the finest acts of heroism and stubborn resistance in our military annals.

Burnside first poured an artillery fire in the devoted town and defending brigade—that was literally an "enfer."

There had been nothing like it before in this war. Every shot, all kinds of missiles, were thrown at the Mississippians to dislodge them. The brave fellows were there, however, to stay. They hid themselves in cellars, wells, holes of any kind where they could get a little cover, while their rifles picked off the pontooners pluckily trying to throw their boats across the stream. The latter fell in great numbers and this went on nearly all day. The Confederates would not budge, although so stubborn a defense had been no part of our expectation. We knew the town would be seized.

Quite late the bridge effort was abandoned by the Federal engineers. Calling for volunteers to fill the boats and cross in mass, it was gallantly answered. A number of them were quickly crowded, and notwithstanding our fire their landing was soon made and the town occupied, but not before Barksdale had safely withdrawn his hard-fighting fellows.

They had the cheers of the army for their day's brave work.

Then began that night and all next day and night the movement of Burnside's great army across the river. More brigades were added and there were several in Franklin's possession. He had no trouble in laying what he wanted in his front.

Thus stood Burnside, his army facing us with nothing between, on December 13, and bitter cold, Franklin operating on his left against Jackson. Sumner in the center and center-right against Longstreet, who also guarded the lines extended considerably to our left. Hooker's grand division was held on Stafford Heights during the night of the 12th.

But Marye's Hill was our strong point. Burnside wanted it and there he threw his men in blind and impotent fury. It was held by T. R. R. Cobb's brigade of Georgians behind a stone wall at first and another brigade in support. The front here was quite narrow. Ranson's and Cook's North Carolina brigades were in light trenches higher up the hill, but in position to deliver deadly fire, and did so. The defense at the stone wall was also kept carefully reinforced as needed. There was some artillery in pits near the crest of the hill that did effective service.

General Lee's position with his staff during the day was on a small hill with a good plateau, from which he had a fair view of Sumner's attack on Longstreet, as well as Franklin's on Jackson. Longstreet was much of the time with him. Before the hot work began, "Stonewall" rode up to have a word with Lee. As he dismounted we broke into astonished smiles. He was in a spick and span new overcoat, new uniform with rank marks, fine black felt hat, and a handsome sword. We had never seen the like before, and gave him our congratulations on his really fine appearance. He said he "believed it was some of his friend Stuart's doings."

Franklin was in great masses before Jackson, and before mounting, Longstreet called out, "Jackson, what are you going to do with all those people over there?" "Sir," said Stonewall, with great fire and spirit, "we will give them the bayonet."

There is really now but little more to be said in detail of the battle. In front of us it was hammer and tongs all day from 11 a. m. until finally Burnside had to desist in sheer weariness of slaughter. His troops advanced to their assaults with the finest intrepidity, but it was impossible for them to stand before our fire. I afterwards saw that perhaps not more than half a dozen of their men had got within sixty yards of our wall and dropped there. Not once was there any sign of faltering or weakness among our troops; the solid bodies of troops attacking might easily have made it otherwise with unseasoned soldiers.

On our right Franklin had been more successful. He managed to pierce a salient that should have been corrected and worsted a considerable number of Jackson's men. The line was retaken and restored, but with some loss, among whom was Captain Edward Lawton, a young brother of General Lawton, of Georgia. We also lost at Marye's Hill General Cobb (T. R. R.), of Georgia, deeply mourned as one of the most promising officers and whole-souled patriots of the South.

When darkness fell on this great tragedy, hostile movements ceased and the two armies were caring for the "butcher's bill." Ours was small comparatively, but the enemy had lost very heavily.

A thick fog or mist also arose and enveloped the enemy's movements in strangeness and uncertainty. They were actually started on hastily recrossing the river, but we don't appear to have known it. Most of the day of the 14th it was thick and misty, veiling successfully the enemy's movements, but all the time he was preparing for his retreat.

He was not attacked while in this exposed position. Why not? It is generally thought it would have been fatal to the Federals and it is indisputable that they were in hourly dread of it. Some say Jackson proposed a night attack, but I doubt it, and am glad it was not made.

It is impossible to describe the confusion of such an attempt or to anticipate what might happen. I was in one later on with three picked brigades of the highest order and efficiency.

The roar of battle between Lookout Mountain and Brown's Ferry on the Tennessee River words cannot express, and in the black darkness the three brigades achieved worse than nothing.

But why did we not attack on the 14th in daylight? Not my part to attempt this explanation, but it looks much as if we were "building a bridge of gold for the flying enemy."

On the night of the 17th Burnside withdrew his army to his old camp in the Falmouth Hills.

We lost in killed and wounded—Longstreet, 1,519; Jackson, 2,682; total, 4,201. Jackson was also reported as having lost in missing 526. These figures are also adopted by Ropes, and he gives Burnside's army as 122,500, ours as 78,500. I do not think that more than half of our forces were engaged on the 13th. The Federal losses, attacks on

Marye's Hill, 8,000; loss of whole army, Federal, 12,650 killed and wounded. (Ropes's figures.)

The hill referred to as affording General Lee at Fredericksburg a point of view, had a light trench in which was mounted a 30-pounder Parrott gun, made in Richmond. The 10-pounder guns of that make had done well, but those of heavy caliber were treacherous. The one on "Lee's Hill," as it came to be called, burst after a few discharges. Happily it did not send fragments flying about, and no one was hurt. The immense breech just appeared to have split into a dozen pieces of various sizes and then fallen heavily to the ground. We were rather glad to have done with such a piece of metal.

The old wines of the good people of Fredericksburg have been referred to. They suffered in the fortunes of war. A few nights before the opening of the battle, which was then imminent, considerable quantities of fine old Madeira and other varieties were taken out of cellars and bins, and sent by the citizens to our fellows in camp, equally ready for drink or for battle. It was known that the town would be shelled and occupied by the Federals, probably looted and plundered; therefore it was thought safest to see priceless old vintages passed around campfires and quaffed in gulps from tincups. Of course the men would have better liked whiskey, but they did not refuse the wine.

An incident on the river may bear telling. It was after the battle, when the pickets had resumed their posts and had become friendly; more given to trading than shooting each other at less than one hundred yards. The authorities had to set their faces sternly against this trading. It led to desertion. A fine Federal band came down to the river bank one afternoon and began playing pretty airs, among them the Northern patriotic chants and war songs. "Now give us some of ours!" shouted our pickets, and at once the music swelled into Dixie, My Maryland, and the Bonnie Blue Flag. Then, after a mighty cheer, a slight pause, the band again began, all listening; this time it was the tender, melting bars of Home, Sweet Home, and on both sides of the river there were joyous shouts, and many wet eyes could be found among those hardy warriors under the flags. "One touch of nature makes the whole world kin."

Of course the enemy's powerful artillery on Stafford Heights would have been an efficient aid in resisting an attack on his infantry before, and while recrossing the river. But they were badly demoralized and would probably not have stood long with that threatening river in their rear and the triumphant Confederates in the front. There was much private discussion then, and after, among the intelligent of the Federals as to why they were not struck after their sanguinary defeat. A general belief existed among them that we were deficient in ammunition, the only explanation many of them were able to arrive at. We had no want of it.

CHAPTER XVIII

After Fredericksburg—Reminiscences

Fredericksburg after the battle—Flag of truce—Burying dead—General Wadsworth, U. S. A.—Again on enemy's side with flag of truce—At their picket fire—Colonel Brown, of Rhode Island—Bitter cold—All night in their camp— Luxuries for the wounded—First Georgia Regulars—They are ordered home—Want of shoes—Captain Cuthbert, of South Carolina.

The battle was indeed fought and finished, and although the triumph of victory rested with us, and the enemy was back in his lines, beaten and dispirited, yet it cannot be said that there had been achieved a result so decisive as to bring us near the end of the war.

We were caring for our dead. The enemy was to do so for his. They lay in great numbers on the plain. General Lee wrote Burnside and I carried the letter under a flag of truce through the town to the ferry, where was found a pontoon, and my men took me across. It was pitiful riding through the town, considerably damaged as it was by the artillery fire from Stafford Heights, but more still from the plundering and looting that had gone on while in possession of the United States troops. Furniture, bedding, mattresses, carpets, china, domestic utensils, indeed all that went to make up those comfortable old homes, were strewn helter skelter, broken and ruined about the streets. The streets were filled with distressed women and children, both black and white. But we passed on—"C'est à la guerre comme à la guerre!" My pontoon landed me at the foot of a steep road that ascended the hill and I was immediately met by a number of officers in brilliant uniforms. For myself I must have been awfully shabby; never at any time given to military finery, while campaigning, I think I was worse off than usual here at Fredericksburg. The weather had been atrocious, and mud and I were closely acquainted day and night. There was, too, so much to do that one had no time for repairing damages.

But my reception by the Federal officers was extremely courteous while awaiting an answer to General Lee's missive, now on its way to Burnside, whose headquarters were near by.

There were Major-General Park, chief of staff to the army; Major-General Wadsworth (whom I was to see in eighteen months at the "Wilderness" under different circumstances); Brig.-Gen. Jim Hardie, and many others, all having some inquiries to make for friends on our side. General Wadsworth asked me how many dead I thought lay on our front. "I ask, Major," he said, "so as to make my burying parties strong enough."

I said: "I cannot possibly guess with any approach to accuracy. I have only ridden through the slain in front of Marye's Hill, and it seemed that there must be at least 800 there awaiting burial." "My God, my God!" groaned the old officer, deeply depressed by such mortality. Instead of 800, they buried nearly 1,200 men in that small front, besides some 300 in front of Jackson's position. General Burnside's answer soon came, and saluting my Federal acquaintances I was quickly on our own side of the river and the Federal commander's letter in Lee's possession.

Strong burial parties immediately came across for their ghastly duty. General Wadsworth was a wealthy, middle-aged man from the lovely Genessee Valley, New York, owning great tracts of land; but considered it his patriotic duty to raise some battalions for the army and did so, placing himself at their head. The Government showed him all honor, conferring at once high rank.

A day or two later it became necessary to see the Northerners again. Their burying parties were making hideous work with the dead soldiers; throwing them in heaps in shallow trenches, barely covered; filling the country ice houses and wells with them; indeed, doing this work most brutally for themselves, and intolerably for our citizens. General Lee called Burnside's attention to the revolting conduct of the latter's men and I went across the river, with also some verbal details.

The pontoon had been drawn in by the owners and was in the Union rear with the bridge train. There was naught to cross in except a broken, leaky little batteau that was found in a cellar. The river was smooth and one of my men managed to paddle the crazy thing safely across. There I was met by Colonel Brown, commanding a Rhode Island regiment on picket duty, who civilly invited me to the comfort of his camp fire while awaiting the communication from his army headquarters, now quite a distance off. I was detained some time, and the Colonel (a lawyer of high reputation from Providence, Rhode Island,) had time for much general talk. At last, making my thanks and farewell, I started back, only to find my man at the river's edge almost frozen and the batteau sunk out of sight with darkness on us! A pretty kettle of fish, indeed! The water rough, wind strong, and already freezing. There was nothing for it but to take my man back with me to the picket and get a message to headquarters of my plight, with request of assistance to cross. After another considerable wait there came an officer and several mounted orderlies leading a good horse; this was for me. The officer brought a civil message from the adjutant-general regretting that they had nothing at hand to float (their pontoons being in the rear), and hoping I could be made comfortable for the night. Leaving my soldier to the good care of the friendly pickets, I mounted and was led to the large house on the hill, at that time in use as a hospital. There my escort left me and I found myself for the night in the great kitchen of the establishment, filled with bright warmth and savory smells of good food.

A blanket or two had to do me for bedding, but I was soon asleep, after the soldier cooks had given me food, always with full respect to rank and authority.

To see what they had, its quality, its abundance, filled one's heart with envy when contrasted with the doled-out, bare necessities of life the lot of our own uncomplaining fellows.

Here in this great kitchen were huge swinging vessels of odorous real coffee; immense chunks of fat, fresh beef of all parts of the animal; great slabs of dessicated vegetables, which, when thrown with knuckles of meat and good flesh into the boiling cauldron, puffed out, swelling each vegetable into something like freshness, and then with free dashes of salt and pepper, behold, a soup of strength and tastiness fit for Faint Heart himself to fight on. They gave me of it all and I tasted all, sleeping well and early up. My man, who had fared well too, was soon at hand, and the boat raised, bailed out, landed us safely on our own bank. The soldier with me was Jesse Beall, private from Milledgeville in a Georgia regiment. I was disposed at first to be vexed by such rough lodgings (a parlimentaire being entitled to the best), but Colonel Kip explained that there was really nothing else to be done at that hour of night. Of course they could not carry me through the lines to their own comfortable staff quarters in the rear.

Many years after, hearing that there was in Savannah, passing through, a Colonel Brown, of Rhode Island, with his wife, I called on him. It proved to be my friend of the picket fire, and his wife, with much enthusiasm, declared he had spoken of the incident fifty times. Colonel Brown had some more talk this time, quite free, and like very many Union officers marveled why they were not attacked after a repulse so bloody and disastrous. He said that want of ammunition could only explain it to him. Brown was a middle aged, delicate man, a member of the well-known Brown family of Rhode Island.

He said he had raised his regiment from patriotic convictions and carried it through the battle of

Fredericksburg; then he gave way to younger, stronger men and resigned. He was a broad, fair-minded man, with no deep prejudices against the South. Next year he died, his townsmen showing in every way the honor and respect in which he was held.

The First Georgia Regulars were posted at Hamilton's Crossing, near Fredericksburg, and had its ranks much thinned by the casualties of several campaigns. It could not be recruited like other regiments, being enlisted from all parts, and the Department therefore ordered it home to fill its ranks.

I rode myself, orders in hand, to its camp. I had many friends among the officers and knew how delighted they would be; and so it was, a wild shout of happiness at seeing old Georgia again, and the skeleton battalion began packing almost immediately for the route. After doing some enlistment it took an honorable part in the battle of Olustee, fought in Florida. Lieutenant Sorrel was with them until a captain's commission in the Adjutant-General's Department sent him to report in Virginia to Gen. John Bratton's South Carolina Brigade.

I was in Europe in the summer of 1860, and traveled on the continent a few weeks with George Cuthbert, of Beaufort, South Carolina. He was a pleasant fellow, and handsome, of good height and figure, and the fairest blonde, with beautiful blue eyes. Even in fair-haired Saxony, people turned to look at him.

The war broke out and I did not know where Cuthbert would be serving. One day, however, in the winter of 1862-63, riding by the lines of one of our South Carolina regiments, up rose Cuthbert, and I was immediately on my feet beside him. He was a line captain, had been wounded, and was at the moment as shabby a Confederate soldier as could be found anywhere. Razors had been discarded, and the German girls who liked to look at the handsome Southerner would not have deigned him a glance. I resolved to do something for his advancement, but the channels were such that I could not get him out of them. Soon after, however, an order came from Richmond to detail 160 shoemakers for the use of the Quartermaster-General—such was the stress we were in for shoes. Half the detail was ordered from Jackson's corps and half from Longstreet's. I sent out orders for our eighty crispins, and when they were picked out of the whole corps, word was given to Captain Cuthbert to report at corps headquarters and a brief colloquy opened.

"I say, Cuthbert, would you like to go to Richmond?" "Wouldn't I!—clean clothes, soap, a bath and a shave!" "Eighty shoemakers are to be taken there by rail and then turned over to the Quartermaster-General, and an officer must take the detail. Will you have it?" "My dear Sorrel, give it to me; for God's sake, give it to me—such a change after my long trench service. I'd land them safely with the Q. M. G. if they were eighty raving demons instead of the happy fellows they doubtless are in getting such a detail." "All right, old chap, take your fellows off by train to-morrow; here are the orders. And I say, Cuthbert, while you are in Richmond don't hurry too much; you can make the duty last you a week or ten days."

He was very grateful for being thought of, performed his work satisfactorily, and then enjoyed himself hugely.

I was glad to think of this later, since he was one of many personal friends who gave up his life in battle. The incident also illustrated the great straits the Confederate supply department was in to keep the troops equipped for the field. This was especially the case with shoes.

CHAPTER XIX

To South Virginia for Supplies

Burnside's "mud march"—His removal—Hooker superseding him—Our great want of supplies—Longstreet ordered to south Virginia—Hood's and Pickett's divisions with him—I precede them—Inspecting fort at Washington, N. C.—Rejoin the command at Suffolk—Gathering supplies—Operations against Suffolk not successful—Ordered back to Lee—All haste—No time lost, but too late for Chancellorsville—Pickett's courtship—Harrison, the scout—Death of Stonewall Jackson—Lieutenant Habersham.

Here then for some weeks did the two armies lay in the peace of camp life after the fever of battle. Burnside attempted a movement, known as the mud march, quickly made abortive by the condition of roads, and then Mr. Lincoln reluctantly removed him, placing Hooker—"Fighting Joe Hooker"—in command of the Army of the Potomac. It was in May before he attempted his disastrous move against Lee and Jackson.

Meantime, our army was in want of all supplies. The subsistence department lacked fresh meat. In southern Virginia and eastern North Carolina there were said to be large quantities of small cattle which, fattened on the good Virginia pasture lands, would greatly help the subsistence officers. There were also there large stores of bacon and corn. It was decided to send part of Lee's army to operate in that region, and, at the same time, by covering large wagon trains, we should be enabled to use that part of the country for the Virginia army.

It had sometimes been occupied by the enemy, at all times exposed to their sudden incursions. But these, it is thought, formed the least of the reasons governing Lee when sending Longstreet and two of his strong divisions to Nansemond and Suffolk. It was daring to make such a large draft on his army, but Lee was given to daring efforts, with a great objective in view. The Northern army was becoming dangerously strong for him to view calmly, and another strong body was preparing to threaten Richmond from a different quarter. Lee may have reasoned, as he did in some of his Valley operations, that by detaching Longstreet, Hooker would be quickly induced to follow him, by sending from his army a still larger force for the safety of the threatened districts. But it proved they had enough troops for such reinforcements without impairing Hooker's great strength.

Our two divisions, Hood's and Pickett's, and a battalion of artillery broke camp and halted at Petersburg, whence the force found camps on the Nansemond River, in a manner besieging the town of Suffolk, strongly held by the Federals.

By Longstreet's order I set out alone for a short visit of inspection to the eastern boundary of North Carolina. It was the little town of Washington, on the head of a tidal river, that, I think, I first visited. There was nothing there but a well-built, strong earthwork fort, and a fine, full regiment, doing nothing and eager for action. It was not likely to come to them at that dull place, and on my recommendation the regiment was sent to Lee.

The lieutenant-colonel (Lamb) gave me a warm fur collar, which was always a comfort, and he was delighted with the pair of spurs I made him accept from me (they were made from the brass trunnion beds of the monitor *Keokuk,* sunk by our forces at Charlestown). Poor Lamb was killed in the first engagement of his regiment. My instructions were to lose no time, but, after a glance around, hasten back to the command. When I returned it was seen that nothing had been achieved. Some little bluffing had been made at the town of Suffolk, in which we lost two pieces of artillery and gained nothing. Time was passing, the Virginia roads improving, and some restlessness apparent among us. We knew, of course, that Hooker must soon fight, and that we should be there. At last General Lee sent for us in haste, not a moment was to be lost. Not a moment was lost; we threw everything into movement, realizing how keenly our beloved commander and comrades on the Rappahannock would be wanting their Lieutenant-General and his two splendid divisions. But it was humanly impossible. We were late, Hooker had attacked rather earlier than expected, and on May 3 the battle was given, and our great Jackson fell in glorious victory while we were miles distant by railroad from the memorable field of Chancellorsville.

General Pickett was a widower, but had recently suffered himself to fall in love with all the ardor of youth. The object of these fiery, if mature, affections dwelt not far from Suffolk. Pickett's visits were frequent, a long night ride and return for duty early next day. Perhaps he had wearied Longstreet by frequent applications to be absent, but once he came to me for the authority. My answer was, "No, you must go to the Lieutenant-General." "But he is tired of it, and will refuse; and I must go, I must see her. I swear, Sorrel, I'll be back before anything can happen in the morning." I could not permit myself to be moved. If anything did happen, such as a movement of his division or any demonstration against it, my responsibility for the absence of the Major-General could not be explained. But Pickett went all the same, nothing could hold him back from that pursuit. He married some time after. I don't think his division benefited by such carpet-knight doings in the field.

While Longstreet was holding this brief independent command, a scout, more properly a spy, was placed at his service by the War Department. He was a man of about thirty years, calling himself a Mississippian, and was altogether an extraordinary character. He was paid in United States greenbacks. I approved requisition on the quartermaster every month for $150 for him. His time seemed to be passed about equally within our lines and the enemy's. Harrison (such was his name) always brought us true information. There was invariable confirmation of his reports afterwards.

While always suspicious that such secret instruments give away as much as they bring and may be in the pay of both sides, it was difficult to be sure of this in Harrison's case. He went everywhere, even through Stanton's War Office at Washington itself, and brought in much. We could never discover that he sold anything against us; besides, we had means, and did verify his account of himself as coming from Mississippi. When Longstreet gave him up in September, he was sorry afterwards and missed the man. He made me try to get him back for our command, but I failed.

There will be more to say of Harrison before losing him. On the whole he appears to have been a daring Southerner, hating Yankees most bitterly, but loving their greenbacks, and fond of secret, perilous adventure. Latrobe recently heard from him in Baltimore, in want, and asking some small assistance.

Upon rejoining our army after Chancellorsville we were, of course, eager questioners and listeners for everything about the battle.

Gratifying it was to hear on all sides of the conduct of our two divisions, which bore so large a part of the attacks on Lee. Anderson and McLaws had never fought better; while Lee, to hold his position and beat off Hooker, had to have the very best every man could give him. It was a battle most extraordinary in its execution and development. The powerful movement on Lee's rear by Sedgwick's force from Fredericksburg was enough to disconcert any ordinary commander. Lee, calm and undismayed, met it by thinning out his lines to almost a frazzle, and throwing a good division before John Sedgwick, while he and Jackson were preparing the blow that made "Fighting Joe Hooker's" head split with surprise and agony and sent him flying back across the Rappahannock.

The great flank movement of Stonewall had been carefully planned by Lee and most brilliantly executed by the Lieutenant. But the army had suffered the irreparable loss of that hero. Struck down in the gloaming and thick foliage of the forest, by his own men, his dauntless spirit clung to his army for a week, among ever-hopeful soldiers, and then took its warrior's flight to its Supreme Maker. There was none left in his place; there was but one Jackson.

When Marye's Hill was attacked by Sedgwick in Lee's rear, the battery in action there had to make a hurried escape. One of its officers, a dear friend of mine, Lieut. Frederick Habersham, had been killed at his section. His comrades determined to have his body, and lashed it to the trail of a gun, and there it hung, firmly bound, a sight not often witnessed, while the battery, already late in retiring, was at a gallop in escape from the pursuing enemy. It was accomplished handsomely, and the brave fellow received his interment by the hands of loving wife and friends at his home in Savannah. It was my brother, Doctor Sorrel, in Richmond, who, with many difficulties, arranged for the care and transportation home of the slain artillerist.

CHAPTER XX

Preparing for Gettysburg

Preparations for summer campaign—Army reorganized—Three Army Corps—A. P. Hill made lieutenant-general, commanding Third Corps—Lieutenant-General Ewell commanding Second Corps—Stuart's cavalry reviewed—Its fine condition—Longstreet and his scout Harrison—Lee's intricate operations—Stuart's cavalry movements—He crosses below—The loss to Lee—The march through Maryland and Pennsylvania—No depredations—Halt at Chambersburg—Scout Harrison reports Meade in command, superceding Hooker—Ewell ordered to leave—March resumed, A. P. Hill leading, gaining decided success.

General Lee began now to prepare for his summer campaign. It was secretly settled that it should be an invasion of Pennsylvania. There were many things that assisted in arriving at this decision in the conferences with the president and chiefs of the Government at Richmond. Virginia had been fiercely fought over, and ravaged by the tramp of hostile armies. Now, it looked as if the enemy should feel something of such sacrifices. If we could live on the supplies we hoped to find north of the Potomac, the already serious question of food and forage for our men and animals would lighten up temporarily, at least; and finally, the men of arms were eager for the movement and most enthusiastic at the start.

First of all, Lee had to reorganize his army. Jackson's death made this necessary; besides, the two corps had grown, individually, rather large for effective handling. He created a third corps and placed A. P. Hill in command of it, perhaps the best arrangement possible at the time. One division was taken from Longstreet—Anderson's; one from Jackson—Heth's, and the third, under Pender, was made up of unassigned commands, of which there were quite a number between Richmond and the General's camps.

The second (Ewell's) was of Early's, Rodes's, and E. Johnson's divisions.

The first (Longstreet's) was of Hood's, McLaws's and Pickett's divisions.

Suitable artillery details were made to meet these changes, which went in effect smoothly and effectively.

On the cavalry, special care was bestowed. It had been heavily strengthened and much improved by selections of men and horses. For some time, during inaction, they had been getting good forage and pasturage. Now, when the time was near for the use of this formidable arm under Stuart, its able and famous leader, it was ready for the Commander-in-Chief.

What irony of fate that the great approaching campaign should be fought and lost without that bold leader and his riders being at Lee's touch, when indeed he wanted them, bitterly missing having Stuart and his great body of unsurpassed horse near by him.

The activity of preparation went through all departments—Quartermaster's, Subsistence, Ordnance, and Medical. It could be guessed that the military operations would be of great severity and exaction and it behooved all officers of supply to be ready; to fail would be fatal.

The cavalry were assembled under Stuart in Northern Virginia, on lands growing richer and richer in grass with the advancing weeks. It was a magnificent day, befitting the superb body of cavalry that, under Stuart, marched rapidly in review before the Commander-in-Chief. A sight it was not soon to be forgotten. The utmost order prevailed. There could be no doubt that the cavalry was as ready for the work before us as was our matchless infantry.

Longstreet sent for his favorite scout, Harrison. His instructions were to proceed into the enemy's lines, where he was to stay until the last part of June. Then he was to report to General Longstreet, it was hoped, with the amplest and most accurate information. "Where shall I find you, General, to make this report?" asked Harrison. "With the army," was Longstreet's grim answer; "I shall be sure to be with it." He was very far from giving even to his trusted scout information as to his movements. But Harrison knew all the same; he knew pretty much everything that was going on.

The operation now performed by General Lee was intricate, of much delicacy and hazard. It was to move from his position in front of Hooker without exposing any part of his forces, or Richmond, to be attacked in detail, and this important part of the grand maneuver was left to Longstreet and his corps, with the cavalry in communication.

The corps of Ewell (formerly Jackson's) and A. P. Hill were sent ahead by easy marches, keeping a certain distant touch with Longstreet. The mountain gaps were filled with Stuart's cavalry and the enemy held in close observation. All went well. Hooker made no attempt to follow. Lee moved toward Washington leisurely, as if to meet him there later.

Stuart's part with his cavalry was now most important. It is contended by some that Lee left it finally optional for him to decide upon his movements. Whether to follow the army by crossing the river in the west of the ridge or by one of the lower fords. In the latter event it was, as it proved, to lose Lee and leave him without his strong arm in an enemy's country. It has been attempted to show also that the order by which Stuart moved came from Longstreet. But this must be dismissed; positive information to the contrary being at hand. Surprising to say, it now appears that Stuart left the army with his fine command and started on his too fascinating raid, not only by his own preference, but actually in violation of Lee's orders, which failed to reach him. All doubt had passed from Lee's mind and he had ordered Stuart to keep with him. The latter was raiding, and Lee's campaign was lost.

Major McClellan, Stuart's A. A. G. and chief of staff, in his history of that cavalry (an excellent work) declares that in his opinion the absence of Stuart was the cause of Lee's trouble; and for myself I have never doubted it. It is not to be supposed that no cavalry whatever was left with the army. Stuart's defenders have taken pains to point that out. There was a squadron or two, here and there, a regiment at one place, and a brigade under an efficient commander left in the rear. But these separate little commands amounted to nothing. It was the great body of that splendid horse under their leader Stuart that Lee wanted. He was the eyes and ears and strong right arm of the commander, and well may he have missed him. All through the marches he showed it.

Stuart was on a useless, showy parade almost under the guns of the Washington forts, and his horse, laurel-wreathed, bore the gay rider on amid songs and stories. He met some opposition, of course, and had a share of fighting in Ashby's Gap and the plain on the east.

When he rejoined Lee it was with exhausted horses and half worn-out men in the closing hours of Gettysburg.

Had he been with Lee where would our commander have made his battle? Possibly, not on that unfavorable ground of Gettysburg. Lee with his personally weak opponent, and Stuart by him, could almost have chosen the spot where he would be sure to defeat the Union Army.

This, however, somewhat anticipates; going back we find our three corps with their military pushed across the river with energy. The Second (Ewell's), the Third (A. P. Hill's), and Longstreet last. All infantry and artillery across, leaving only about a brigade of cavalry on the south side. The enemy for some days had quite disappeared from our observations. The march proceeded through Maryland and Pennsylvania in good form, General Lee's orders against depredations being most peremptory. At Chambersburg a halt was made over Sunday and our corps had the place well guarded and protected from plunder by loose bodies of men. Our chief commissary, Moses, made a forced requisition and got some supplies and necessaries, not very much.

At night I was roused by a detail of the provost guard bringing up a suspicious prisoner. I knew him instantly; it was Harrison, the scout, filthy and ragged, showing some rough work and exposure. He had come to "Report to the General, who was sure to be with the army," and truly his report was long and valuable. I should here say that in every respect it was afterwards fully confirmed by events and facts. Harrison gave us the first complete account of the operations of the enemy since Hooker left our front. He brought his report down to a day or two, and described how they were even then marching in great numbers in the direction of Gettysburg, with intention apparently of concentrating there. He also informed us of the removal of Hooker and the appointment of George Meade to command of the Army of the Potomac. How many commanders had Lee made for that army! Harris son's report was so exceedingly important that I took him at once with me, and woke Longstreet. He was immediately on fire at such news and sent the scout by a staff officer to General Lee's camp near by. The General heard him with great composure and minuteness. It was on this, the report of a single scout, in the absence of cavalry, that the army moved. Important as was the change, the commanding General was not long in deciding. He sent orders to bring Ewell immediately back from the North about Harrisburg, and join his left. Then he started A.

P. Hill off at sunrise for Gettysburg, followed by Longstreet. The enemy was there, and there our General would strike him.

The march was much impeded by too many troops and trains on one road and Ewell's men breaking in on the route next day to get to their position.

The army thus moved forward, and A. P. Hill leading, struck the enemy near, and in, the town of Gettysburg sharply on the afternoon of July 1. We were following some little distance in rear, and heard the lively fire of cannon and rifles, and soon after got the news of Hill's and Ewell's decided success in an important preliminary engagement. Many prisoners and much material remained with the Confederates. This stimulated every one forward, and Ewell taking position on our left, we were all snugly in bivouac at a good hour, with Longstreet's two divisions, McLaws and Hood, about four miles in rear, but ready for movement next day. Pickett had been doing guard duty at Chambersburg and was not yet up, but would be in the morning. The serious mishap of the day was Ewell's failure to seize the heights on the left. General Lee expected it of him, and we know of no impediment.

CHAPTER XXI

Battle of Gettysburg, July 1, 2, 3, 1863.

Expectation of revelations—Longstreet and Lee—Attacks not in good combination between the three corps—July 2, situation unfavorable—Our heavy attack on the right—Ground and guns taken—Round Top reinforced checks us—Longstreet leads—Hood and Longstreet—Am slightly wounded—Lieutenant-Colonel Freemantle, Coldstream Guards—Captain Ross, Austrian Army—July 3, necessity of a stroke—Pickett's charge—His repulse—Lee's noble encouragements—July 4, not attacked—Holding ground—Withdrawal at night—The retreat, and passage of the river.

On the tremendous and decisive battle of Gettysburg, now about to engage the two armies, more has probably been written than on any battle since Waterloo. There seems to be a feeling abroad that great secrets explaining why we were beaten are yet to be told and that they are locked up in the breasts of a few men, one of them the present writer, Longstreet's chief of staff. There is absolutely nothing in that expectation; no living man knows more about the battle than has already been written.

Lee has made his report. Longstreet has written a book and said his say. The staff has little or nothing to add. Communications were in the main between Lee and Longstreet, verbally, or occasionally by note direct.

The story has been in part told by Longstreet. We can discover that he did not want to fight on the ground or on the plan adopted by the General-in-Chief. As Longstreet was not to be made willing and Lee refused to change or could not change, the former failed to conceal some anger. There was apparent apathy in his movements. They lacked the fire and point of his usual bearing on the battle-field. His plans may have been better than Lee's, but it was too late to alter them with the troops ready to open fire on each other. Ewell on the left, A. P. Hill and Longstreet on the right, seemed never able to work together, and I can well imagine the great soul of our Commander deeply furrowed with the difficulties about him and what was going on to the disadvantage of the army. This is all I shall permit myself to express on this well-worn but ever interesting subject. One can build many theories, but theories only will they be; besides, my opinion is already given that the loss of the campaign was due to the absence of Stuart's cavalry.

I proceed to jot down idly some "choses vues" of the military events and incidents of the three great days of this remarkable historic battle and the days immediately about it.

The situation on the morning of the 2nd was far from favorable to us. First of all, our position, compared with the enemy's, was not good. It may be said to have been decidedly inferior. We were the outer line, he held the inner. We were the cord to the arc on which his heavy columns were massed. True, there were some positions on the left that were in Ewell's possession and could be well used. Round Top and his high shoulders were on our right, and held by us would be everything. This Lee quickly saw and tried for. They made the key for the position, and with it dangling at our girdle the lock would have yielded and the door opened. But we were too late on our right. An attack, powerful indeed, at 4 p. m. was quite different from the commanding General's expectation of one in the forenoon.

Late on the first, and early on the second, Hill and Ewell were heavily engaged with apparently no satisfactory results.

On the second, quite late, 4 p. m., Longstreet made his long-deferred attack on the enemy's left. It was done in smashing style by McLaws's and Hood's divisions and a few of Hill's troops, Longstreet personally leading the attack with splendid effect.

His fine horsemanship as he rode, hat in hand, and martial figure, were most inspiring.

We gained ground rapidly and almost carried Round Top, but the morning delay was fatal. It had been heavily reinforced while we were pottering around in sullen inactivity. Undoubtedly Lee's intention was to make the attack in the forenoon and suport it with strong movements by Hill and Ewell. I think it would have won, notwithstanding the difficulties of position. The attempt was made to move the troops to the right into position without discovery by the enemy, but it was abortive.

We were seen from the start and signaled constantly. Much valuable time was lost by this trial, which with better knowledge of the ground by General Lee's engineers would not have been attempted.

At nightfall the combat was over and we were dragging off our captured cannon and standards, and caring for our dead and wounded.

The loss in storming the position on the right was heavy. When Hood's division was across the turnpike, under orders to attack, he begged me to look at it, report its extreme difficulty, and implore Longstreet to make the attack another way. This was done, but the answer I took to Hood was that the attack must instantly be made, that General Lee had so directed; and forward and upward the gallant Hood charged, almost gaining the plateau of Round Top, the key of the enemy's left.

The staff had been hard at work day and night, and my exhausted frame found rest that night in the snuggest fence corner in sight. The ground to weary bones felt as good as a feather bed. In addition, I had been suffering from a painful but not serious wound. Riding with Dearing's artillery late in the afternoon, while exchanging some shots, a shrapnel burst directly over us, one of the large projectiles striking me on the right arm near the shoulder. It was not broken or pierced, but paralyzed for use for at least ten days, and quite black down to the wrist. Painful, of course, it was, but a small matter where there was so much death and mangling.

On the march through Virginia we had received a delightful acquisition to our headquarters party, in Lieutenant-Colonel Freemantle, of the Coldstream Guards.

He had entered the Confederacy on a visit of observation, well fortified with credentials from his own government, and, traveling through all the Confederate States, had arrived in Richmond just in time to join Lee's army in its invasion of Pennsylvania.

With good letters of introduction he had been sent to us and there could not be a finer fellow. He roughed it with the hardest, and took everything as it came. A quick, observant eye and indefatigable sightseer, apparently nothing escaped him. When the campaign was ended and the Confederates making their way back to Virginia, Freemantle said his farewells and made the best of his way to New York, whence he immediately took steamer for England. There he published an entertaining little book, "Three Months in the Southern States," which was later reproduced by a worn-out, decrepit old press at Mobile, a copy of the issue being now a great rarity. Freemantle had met Southern men of all kinds, and his book has many pen pictures by this fine officer and friend of ours. His regiment, a corps d'élite, soon sent him to the staff, where he distinguished himself, and successively obtained rank as major-general, lieutenant-general, and general, with several military orders of coveted distinction. He is now Sir Arthur Lyon-Freemantle, K. C. M. G.,* and of other good-service orders. He commanded the brigade of guards in Egypt, and has just finished (about retiring) his four years' tour of duty as Governor of Malta, one of the greatest of the British military posts. He is delightful to every Confederate he can put his hands upon.

There was another foreign officer with us at this time, and for some months later, Captain Fitzgerald Ross, very Scotch as to name, but Austrian to the

* Sir Lyon-Freemantle has since died.

core. He came of one of those military Scotch or north of Ireland families that centuries ago settled in many parts of Europe and generally rose to distinction.

On the morning of July 3, it was apparent that a great blow must be delivered to Meade's army. He could not be persuaded to leave his formidable positions and instruments and attack us, and Lee could not retreat without another effort, indecisive as had been those of the 2d. Our General, as has been said, did not mind blood when it had to be shed. It is the soldier's calling. Here was a case in point: His army and trains could only be saved by a tremendous strike straight at the enemy. The time for maneuvering had passed and he prepared for what was before him. He believed his troops could do what he asked of them; never yet had they failed him.

The attack was to be made as soon as possible, under direction of Lee's "War Horse," that stout warrior James Longstreet, with three brigades of Pickett's division (right), Heth's division of Hill's corps (left), with supports of several brigades of other divisions thrown into position.

An artillery "feu d'enfer" was to precede the attack, directed by E. P. Alexander, who was to give the signal when in his judgment the artillery had made the greatest impression, and then the troops were to move instantly across the wide, lead-swept plain, against the heavy masses of blue on the crest of the heights. All this was done at about 2 o'clock, Longstreet accepting Alexander's signal message with dejection, it seemed. Indeed, the delay in attacking which undoubtedly hurt us was apparently caused by his objections made known to the Commander-in-Chief, but of course all this is set out from that standpoint in Longstreet's own book.

It was soon over. Pickett's men got far up the acclivity and many were soon among the enemy. There was, however, some wavering on our left, which weakened us, and we broke, tearing back pell-mell, torn by shot and shell across the width of that bloody plain, a sight never before witnessed—part of the Army of Northern Virginia in full, breathless flight.

But there was no pursuit and the run soon stopped. The soldiers got together, picked up arms, and in a short time were ready for another combat.

If there was repulse and its usual result, a quick flight for cover, there was also something else. A charge that, considering the difficulties of position, comparison of numbers, was so steady to the objective point, and so near success as to make it one of the greatest feats of arms in all the annals of war. Every brigade commander and colonel and lieutenant-colonel of Pickett's division was shot down. The brave Armistead and Garnett at the head of their brigades fell inside the enemy's parapet, and the gallant Kemper, hard hit and left for dead, lay with the men of his leading line. To-day, the detail of the great charge, not as barely hinted at here, but as described in full with ample particulars, mounts one's blood, stirs all hearts with deep tragedy and pride. Well do we know that amid all things to happen, the memory of Pickett's charge will forever live in song and story of that fair land for which the Southern soldier poured out his blood like water.

While Longstreet by no means approved the movement, his soldierly eye watched every feature of it. He neglected nothing that could help it and his anxiety for Pickett and the men was very apparent.

Fearing some flank attacks if we succeeded, he had sent Latrobe to the left to warn the officer against its possibility. I went sharply off in search of Pickett to watch his right and if necessary move some troops in for meeting such an attempt. I did not meet with General Pickett and was soon up with Garnett and Armistead. The former was ill that morning, but was at the head of his men where he was to fall. Just here a shell burst under my horse (my best), a splendid chestnut mare, and down she came, both hind legs off. I luckily got another from a mounted man near by, who rather ruefully gave up his horse and saved my saddle for me. Latrobe also had his horse killed over on the left; other staff officers were also sent forward with the troops and shared in the charge.

General Lee's extreme agitation when he witnessed the repulse and race of our men for cover from that murderous fire has not been exaggerated in the prints. The noble soul was stirred to its inmost depths at the sight of the awful and fruitless sacrifices his men had made at his command. His generous heart could only say, "It is my fault, I take it all—get together, men, we shall yet beat them." I saw no man fail him.

It was on July 3 that a mail from the Department at Richmond brought my commission as lieutenant-colonel, A. A. G. Latrobe's and Fairfax's, as inspectors, came along a few days later.

Notwithstanding our great losses of the second and third, we were permitted to hold the field on the fourth by Meade's inactivity. His army was very strong, had not suffered as had ours, and an enterprising general might seemingly have had us on the run in short order.

But no! he had taken a taste of our mettle the day before and wanted no more of it. A bridge of gold for his enemy was the card for Meade's hands. It is said on good authority that at a council called by Meade he was in favor of retiring, and it was only by strenuous, bold opposition of two or three of his generals that he was prevented and induced to keep his ground.

Thus during all the fourth we were in preparation for the rear movement that must begin that night. Lee's position had become serious, but undismayed were the Confederate Chief and his three corps commanders. He knew he could count on their tried courage and experience.

The night of July 4, 1863, was of awful weather—rain in torrents, howling winds, and roads almost impassable; all trains had been sent back during the day, as well as the reserve artillery. At night artillery in position and pickets were withdrawn and the army moved back by its left—Ewell, Hill, and Longstreet. It marched all night and part of next day, and then Lee with characteristic audacity selected a line of defense, entrenched and fortified it, and offered Meade battle for several days, while his immense trains were safely crossing the Potomac. Meade declined the challenge, and Lee resuming the retreat, crossed on the bridge of boats that had been thrown over the river at Falling Waters by the engineers—and a crazy affair it was, too.

Our corps was all night crossing, and at dawn I was able to approach General Lee on the south bank, "tête de pont," with a report to that effect, adding that now everything was clear for General Hill's infantry. The General's anxiety was intense. He expected to be attacked at the passage of the river. There was good reason to fear; why Meade failed to do so is yet to be explained. General Lee, like every one, had been up the whole night, and his staff officers were stretched in sleep on the ground. He desired me to recross the bridge for him, see General Hill in person, and urge him to the utmost haste in getting his men over, stopping only when imperatively necessary.

I immediately pushed back, finding the road deep in mud but clear of any impediment to the men. Broken wagons or a dismounted gun or two had been cleared away and thrown one side. General Lee's message was given and Hill asked me to assure the Commander that he should safely get across, notwithstanding a slight attack that was even then developing itself on his rear brigade—Pettigrew's. Some men were captured, but we suffered most loss in the death of that promising officer.

Returning, I reported to the General that "all was clear. Hill was about three-quarters of a mile from the bridge and marching rapidly to it." "What was his leading division?" I was asked. "General Anderson, sir." "I am sorry, Colonel; my friend Dick is quick enough pursuing, but in retreat I fear he will not be as sharp as I should like." Just then a heavy gun was fired lower down, filling the gorge of the river with most threatening echoes. "There," said the General, "I was expecting it, the beginning of the attack." But he was wrong. The enemy made no further demonstration and Hill came safely across. Our corps had found camp some ten miles south of the river and there I soon threw myself down for rest and food. After a week of the most exhausting physical and mental trial it was indeed time for some repose.

CHAPTER XXII

Gettysburg Aftermath

Retrospective—Invasion of Pennsylvania—Some characteristics — Pickett and perfumery — An acquisition — The inhabitants, Pennsylvania Dutch—Their cookery—Colonel Freemantle's activity—Figures as to strength and losses—Lieutenant Dawson—A curious meeting—The sweating soldier—Death of Captain Fraser.

The invasion of Pennsylvania had many features of interest to our army. The country itself contrasted greatly with our own. It was rolling in plenty, high cultivation was apparent on all sides, and the ripening wheat stood tall and golden. General Lee's orders caused it to be well protected, and there was not much looting. The people seemed a queer lot. Hostile looks and imprecations were constantly leveled at the good-natured Southerners footing it amid such new scenes. The cherries were ripe and the trees bending with delicious fruit. I recall one especial tree near Chambersburg that seemed beyond all others to tempt me. Sitting quietly in saddle, branch after branch was gently drawn down to the rider's thirsty lips almost to repletion, and good is the recollection even to this present day. The roads were magnificent in our eyes—metaled macadams, bearing the heaviest loads, and well drained and graded. The animals were nearly all for farm use, great lumbering, powerful horses, capable of enormous draughts on those hard roads, but quite impossible to do anything out of a heavy walk,

We thought to renew some of our quartermaster's and cavalry mounts from this source and a few horses were got across the river. They proved useless and were soon abandoned. As we marched, the people were drawn to the roadside arrayed in their Sunday best, gazing viciously at the invaders. All work in town and country had stopped. Chambersburg being quite a town, was subject to requisition, which did not, I think, yield much.

We "persuaded," however, the principal shopkeepers to keep open, and they displayed some of their wares, doubtless old or unsalable stuff that they could not hide. Everything was strictly paid for in our national currency—Confederate bills!

I did get something, however. Our good commissary, Major Moses, managed to secure (by payment, of course) a bolt of excellent velveteen, wearing quite as well as corduroy. Indeed, he got some of the latter also, and sent the plunder to our headquarters, where the stuff went around sufficiently to give me a coat and trousers, which did good service, I think, till the end of things. He also managed to get a few felt hats, and deserved more, for he was grumbling furiously at the ill success of his important requisition for cash, stores, and army supplies; also for the sound rating and liberal abuse he had taken from the irate females in furious rage at his work.

Lee and Longstreet were bivouacked near by in a beautiful grove of large trees not far from town. They both had many visits from citizens, generally with some trumped-up complaint as a means of seeing the two celebrated soldiers.

The women of the country were a hard-featured lot. The population, principally Pennsylvania Dutch, are an ignorant offshoot of a certain class of Germans long settled there.

Many can speak no English. A hard-working, thrifty class, with, it seems, no thought but for their big horses and barns, huge road-wagons like ships at sea, and the weekly baking, and apple-butter. This last appeared to be their staple food. On the morning of the 3d, already mentioned, waking in my fence-corner, I took thought of breakfast and sent my man to an abandoned farm-house near by. The terrible shell and musketry fire of the previous day had driven off the owners hurriedly, for safety. But here was food galore. My soldier came back loaded with loaves of well-baked bread and jars of apple-butter—a week's baking of the bread, and the abominable butter once a year, I suppose. It did for once or so when very hungry, but I don't call it a nice breakfast anywhere.

The drain of war had not here shown itself—none of the men out of this populous region seemed to have gone to the front. There was no need. The Government, the State, counties, towns, and villages were all paying great bounties for the substitutes. The drafted man was serving at home, and there was joy at so much money among the foreign mercenaries brought over by the rich Northern and Eastern States, and among the ever-present and agile bounty-jumpers, who were indeed making their golden harvest.

Our British friend, Colonel Freemantle, was bound to see everything. During one of the hottest hours of fire he climbed a tree with great agility, and notwithstanding I bawled to him to come down, there he stuck with his binoculars. He was a very small, slight man, wiry, and much enduring. I don't believe he changed his clothing or boots while with us, and I never saw him use a note-book or any scrap of paper as an aid to memory, and yet his book puts down things with much accuracy.

In this great campaign and battle the numbers and casualties and lists may be fairly accepted as follows: Col. W. H. Taylor's figures as to strength—Army of the Potomac, of all arms, 105,000; Army of Northern Virginia, of all arms, 63,000, or say 50,000 infantry, 8,000 cavalry, 5,000 artillery.

His figures are about right as to the Army of Northern Virginia. They would be verified by those of our own corps.

Confederate losses, 2,292 killed; 12,709 wounded: 5,150 missing.

It was about this time that Lieut. F. W. Dawson, C. S. Artillery, reported to our corps for duty. A few words of the career of this young man may not be without interest. He was an Englishman of university education, able and capable. He had come to see hard service. Colonel Manning, chief of ordnance, wanting some assistance at that time, I assigned Dawson to do duty with the ordnance train. He was thoroughly competent, and made himself indispensable to Manning, whose taste took him more to adventures in the field. Dawson was made captain and also acquitted himself well under fire. With return of peace I lost sight of him until a year or two later he turned up as the able and aggressive editor and part proprietor of a leading newspaper of Charleston, South Carolina, and had reason to call for my help in a dangerous crisis. He was strongly on the respectable white side in the dark days of reconstruction, was bold and unflinching, showed extraordinary abilities, made many friends, married, and was assassinated at the very height of an adventurous career.

This is curious in the way of happenings. It has been mentioned that the soldier who passed the night at Fredericksburg with me inside the enemy's lines was Private Jesse Beall. It has not been said, though, that my staff comrade and friend, Manning, had been desperately assailed, stabbed almost to death, by a fellow-student at the Georgia Military Institute. Manning recovered after long care, spoke only once, even to me, of what had happened, and then with a curious tension of feature. Another time we were riding together across fallow fields near camp, when a soldier came out, saluting us, and asked to speak with Colonel Manning. On rejoining me, Manning's face was set and deathly pale. "Sorrel," he said, "that was the man who came so near murdering me. I had sworn to kill him on sight, and it was all I could do to stop myself while he stood by my horse. But he had a tale, and I believed him. It was remorse and horror of his deed. He humbly begged my forgiveness. Nothing else would content him, and I yielded to the man's suffering and evident sincerity. I gave him my hand in parting, but never do I wish to see him again." It was Jesse Beall, Manning's assailant, and my man of the batteau. He was afterwards killed in battle.

On a hot day's march across the river, General Lee, Longstreet, and their people had made a short midday halt in a little rising grove by the roadside, where we found a spring to wash down our soldier's fare. It was the hottest of July days, and the troops were moving by in long column, listlessly, and suffering from the heat. Soon I saw one of the men leave the ranks and approach General Lee. Some one tried to stop him, but the General kindly encouraged his coming forward. He was a stout, well-built soldier, equal to any work, but sweating awfully. "What is it you want?" said Lee. "Please, General, I don't want much, but it's powerful wet marching this weather. I can't see for the water in my eyes. I came aside to this old hill to get a rag or *something* to wipe the sweat out of my eyes." "Will this do?" said the General, handkerchief in hand. "Yes, *my Lordy,* that indeed!" broke out the soldier. "Well, then take it with you, and back quick to ranks; no straggling this march, you know, my man."

Lee's talk and manner with the soldier were inimitable in their encouraging kindness. It is only a single little example of what he was with them.

At Gettysburg, on the 3d, I lost another dear personal friend, Captain John C. Fraser, of Georgia, commanding a battery of artillery. He was working it most effectively in action when struck down. Only a few days before he made me a visit, and noticing his very bad hat, I sent him off rejoicing in one of the felts Major Moses had given us. Then it pillowed his shattered head.

CHAPTER XXIII

In Virginia Again

Lee moves across the ridge into the Piedmont country—Camps taken near Rapidan—Our Headquarters at Taylor's—Festivities and gaieties—Buying remounts—Scout Harrison again—Longstreet and two divisions start for Chickamauga—In Richmond—Harrison as Cassius—His dismissal—The First Army Corps—Dissensions in Hood's Division—Jenkins and Law.

The army being after some days refreshed and strengthened by rest and food and the return of wounded and stragglers, General Lee began preparing to move to a good position east of the mountains. It lay now in the Valley, and General Meade with great consideration molested us not nor gave us any uneasiness. As usual the cavalry filled the gaps of the Ridge and covered efficiently every approach, while the army slowly poured through its defiles to well-known camping grounds on the sunny slopes of the Piedmont glades and meadows. Gradually without incident we found good camps for several weeks in a rolling country bordered by the Rapidan. Our headquarters were in the grounds of Mr. Erasmus Taylor, a well-known gentleman, farming largely in that county, and everything was done by him for our comfort and amusement. The house was spacious, well fitted for dances and entertainments, and being crowded with joyous, happy Virginia girls there was no lack of fun and gaiety. We got out our best, cleaned up, kept the barber busy, became very particular as to the shine of our boots, and put forth all of our long disused bravery in honor of the lovely eyes and true Virginia hearts that were joyfully giving us welcome. There were for those young officers who had time to give, dances by day and evening at Taylor's or elsewhere in the well-settled neighborhood, horses in plenty for riding parties, picnics, excursions—everything indeed for the happiness of the young warriors and their captivating maidens. Hard, brave work had earned the guerdon and it was no niggard hand that gave it.

It was here I had to provide my remounts. My best had been lost in Pickett's charge and the other had broken down and was left. I was consequently up to buying two horses, and after many trials and tests selected from a certain commissary given to horse dealing, two beasts that I thought would do my work. They both broke down under the demands of our Georgia and Tennessee expedition, and later I shall have something to say about the sharp officer who was so ready to put these animals on me. I have already said that I cannot call myself successful in horse selection. These two cost about $2,500.

Ah! those were lovely days; that short rest amid such delightful environments. We were soon to change it, plunge into the forests of Georgia and Tennessee, and fight in the former one of the fiercest, bloodiest battles on record. But meanwhile time went merrily and there was enjoyment throughout the army. The soldiers were in high spirits and ready any day for the enemy.

Supplies of clothing and shoes had come down from Richmond and the ranks looked decidedly better.

Harrison, our scout, had been with us since Gettysburg. His report, all important as to the results of that campaign, was not forgotten. With no immediate duties assigned him, he trotted along from day to day, but he was sure of something to come, and it came. He asked permission to go to Richmond for a few days. As there was nothing to keep him, leave was given.

"Colonel," said this dark character, "if by any chance you should be in Richmond next week, I hope you will take in the theater one evening. (There was then not the slightest expectation of my being in Richmond at that time.) "What is the attraction?" I asked. "Myself," said Harrison. "I have made a bet of $50 greenbacks that I play Cassius and play him successfully." "Are you an actor?" I asked. "No, but I can play." The matter was dismissed as so much nonsense, but he was not a man for nonsense. It so happened that I was in Richmond the next week with Longstreet and the staff on the way to Georgia to strike our great strategic coup, and *did* happen into a friend's box at the theater. "Othello" was on the boards with all the splendor the times could muster, and my Harrison and "Cassius," one and the same, were before me. He had lied in part. His acting was as if he had regularly strutted the boards for a stock company. But the play was rather lively at times. "Othello" was in drink, "Cassius" was really quite far gone, and even "Desdemona" was under more than one suspicion that evening.

The occurrence induced me next day to set on foot some minute inquiries about Harrison's life. I learned that he was drinking and gambling. On reporting it to General Longstreet he thought it better to let him go and so directed me; accordingly I had him paid off, with an order to report to the Secretary of War, from whom he had originally come.

This is the last I saw of the mysterious fellow. Longstreet missed him afterwards while we were in East Tennessee, and I made a careful effort to find him and bring him out to us.

While writing I hear from Latrobe that the man is alive and in Baltimore, seeking some small assistance from the Confederate veterans. I should like to see his last days made comfortable.

The organization of our First Army Corps had suffered no material damage. The ranks were kept fairly well filled by constant recruiting, and the feeling of confidence and pride of this splendid force of infantry and artillery could not be surpassed, from the Lieutenant-General down to the teamster. It was a very remarkable body, inspired by great sacrifices and victories in its history, and with a cohesive strength and belief in itself that spoke nobly for the future. This is said on the eve of a separation of many months, by which the larger part of the corps was sent to strange fields and new sacrifices and laurels.

There was, however, an ugly flaw in one of the divisions, that long uncured was eventually to lead to disaster. When Hood was borne wounded from the Gettysburg field his division of five brigades—

Alabama, Texas, Georgia, and South Carolina—fell under the command of the senior brigadier, Mr. Jenkins, of South Carolina. Between this officer and General E. M. Law, of Alabama, there was the most intense rivalry. They were both from South Carolina, and it was but a continuation, it was said, of what stirred them at school together, at college, at military exercises, and finally in Longstreet's corps. They had been made colonels about the same time—Law of an Alabama regiment—and had advanced almost contemporaneously to be brigadier-generals. Longstreet had recommended them both for promotion to major-general, and they were both unquestionably officers of high attainments and the greatest promise. Here we had a situation that made it useless to think of one of these men serving under the other in the same division. A major-general must be assigned to command, or else one of the aspiring brigadiers transferred to another place. Neither was immediately done and Longstreet had considerable trouble. Both officers were highly valued by him and he wanted full justice done to each, but the situation grew no better with time and service, and Longstreet's efforts at the Department commanded apparently no attention.

CHAPTER XXIV

Longstreet to Reinforce Bragg

The movement to reinforce Bragg—Good work of the Quartermaster-General—General A. R. Lawton, of Georgia—The journey through the States—Ovations to the troops.

The important movement now impending was the subject of deep and secret discussion by the President, Generals Lee and Longstreet, and General Lawton, Quartermaster-General, whose part in it would be of the first consideration. Its gravity can scarcely be overstated.

Rosecrans, commanding the Federal forces in Tennessee and Georgia, had suffered himself to be in position inviting attack by a competent force. It was believed that Bragg, his opponent, if reinforced, could strike a swift, crushing blow, relieve the wide region in which he was operating from the presence of the enemy, and enable masterly reinforcements to return rapidly to Virginia without endangering the safety of the Confederate capital or that of Lee's army, thus temporarily weakened.

Indeed it was the military calculation that so large a detachment from the Southern army would be instantly followed by a still greater withdrawal of troops from Lee's front, and that too by the outer line of the segment, while our own contingent was hurrying by the short, straight cord of the circle.

This expectation proved correct. Meade was silent and inactive, and our own army was stiffening in material and numbers. Meade was apparently without a plan. His predecessors had suffered so cruelly at Fredericksburg and Chancellorsville that his well-known prudence and lack of initiative might be trusted to keep him quiet during our great strategic coup. The movement was, therefore, determined on, and in the first half of September the details were settled. Longstreet was to take on the expedition his two splendid divisions, McLaws and Hood, the latter by this time quite cured of his wound, and Alexander's battalion of artillery—six batteries. Supply trains were to be furnished at destination.

The movement was to be wholly by train, and to any one familiar with the railroad service at the South in the last part of 1863 little need be said of the difficulties facing the Quartermaster-General.

He was to pick up their camps near Gordonsville and the Rapidan, nine strong divisions of infantry and six batteries of artillery, and land them without serious accident and no delay with their ambulances and light vehicles near Chattanooga or Lookout Mountain. This feat was accomplished without stint of honor or praise, be it said, to the Quartermaster-General's department. Never before were so many troops moved over such worn-out railways, none first-class from the beginning. Never before were such crazy cars—passenger, baggage, mail, coal, box, platform, all and every sort wabbling on the jumping strap-iron—used for hauling good soldiers. But we got there nevertheless. The trains started day after day from Virginia and worked through North Carolina, South Carolina, and Georgia by different routes, all converging at a point not far east of Chattanooga—Catoosa Station, I think, was the name.

The Quartermaster-General, Brig.-Gen. A. R. Lawton, was my fellow-townsman. He had graduated from West Point in the class of '39 and entered the artillery. Soon resigning, he took up the study and practise of law, married, and resided in Savannah, where he achieved success. An admirable, well-rounded character, with many friends, Lawton was a leading man in municipal and State affairs for years.

When the clash came in 1861 there was no doubt as to where he would stand. It was for his State, and he was immediately commissioned a brigadier-general, stationed on the coast assembling and organizing troops.

Called by General Lee to Virginia in 1862, he took a brigade of nearly 6,000 strong to Jackson in the Valley operations, and served with distinction in the Chickahominy battles, the campaign against Pope, and at Sharpsburg.

At the latter he was severely wounded and retired from field service. He was, however, not long left in quiet ease. Lawton's abilities suggested him for administrative work, and he was made Quartermaster-General. It was by him and his department that our reinforcements were moved to the help of Bragg and the victory of Chickamauga—an admirable piece of railroad military transportation under adverse conditions. General Lawton was Minister to Austria during Cleveland's Administration.

The journey through the States from Virginia was a continuous ovation to the troops. They were fed at every stopping place and must have hated the sight of food. Kisses and tokens of love and admiration for these war-worn heroes were ungrudgingly passed around, and as the two divisions were from States all south of Virginia, it was good for the men to show up in this fashion even for a few minutes with their home people.

Many of the companies were carried through their own towns and villages and surrounded by the eager faces of kinsfolk and neighbors. But there were no desertions or stops. The brave fellows pressed stoutly on with comrades to meet the foe.

The first arrivals plunged into the battle of September 19th, and on the 20th, when the final stroke was delivered, five of our brigades were up and hotly engaged in that bloody, all-day battle. The glory and renown of the Army of Northern Virginia were fully upheld by Longstreet's men. Some general outlines of the day's events will be attempted in the next chapter, to be filled out at close, as hitherto tried, with brief reflections and observations on the occurrences of the great struggle and the days before and after it.

CHAPTER XXV

Battle of Chickamauga, September 20, 1863.

Arrival at Catoosa—Riding to General Bragg—The meeting —Order of battle—Polk the right wing, Longstreet the left—Attack to begin on right—Delayed some hours—Left wing takes it up victoriously—Attack on right checked —Thomas reinforces his right against Longstreet's assaults —Cannot stand and retreats toward Chattanooga—A great victory for the Confederates—Pursuit next day expected—Bragg says no—Army marches to positions in front of Chattanooga—A barren result—Lieutenant-General Polk —Sketch.

It was about three o'clock in the afternoon of September 19 that our rickety train pulled up, with jerks and bangs, at the little railway landing, called Catoosa Platform. Longstreet and some of his personal staff, Colonels Sorrel and Manning, were in this train and immediately took horse. The remainder of the staff, with most of the horses, were on a train two or three hours later. The Lieutenant-General and part of his staff at once started to find General Bragg.

That General should surely have had guides to meet and conduct us to the conference on which so much depended. A sharp action had taken place during the day and it would appear that if Bragg wanted to see anybody, Longstreet was the man. But we were left to shift for ourselves, and wandered by various roads and across small streams through the growing darkness of the Georgia forest in the direction of the Confederate General's bivouac. At one point in our hunt for him we narrowly escaped capture, being almost in the very center of a strong picket of the enemy before our danger was discovered. A sharp right-about gallop, unhurt by the pickets' hasty and surprised fire, soon put us in safety, and another road was taken for Bragg, about whom by this time some hard words were passing.

But all things have an end, even a friendly hunt for an army commander, and between 10 and 11 o'clock that night we rode into the camp of Gen. Braxton Bragg. He was asleep in his ambulance, and when aroused immediately entered into private conference with Longstreet. It lasted about an hour, and in that time the plan of battle for next day was definitely settled, and then we all took to the leafy ground under the tall oaks and hickories for some sleep against the work before us.

An hour was quite enough to settle the plan and details, since nothing could be simpler than the operation proposed for Rosecrans's destruction.

Bragg's army was already occupying favorable ground and but little preliminary movement was positively necessary. The enemy's force was not far off in our immediate front, seemingly easy to attack. Bragg's army was, however, strange to say, rather deficient in artillery, and its want was felt the next day. Our own batteries, under Alexander, had not yet detrained. Bragg made a good disposition of his separate divisions and commands, dividing his army into two wings, the right under

Lieutenant-General Polk and the left under Lieutenant-General Longstreet. There was consequently thrown under the latter three of Hood's brigades and two of McLaws's (under Hood), and Stuart's and Preston's divisions (under Buckner), and a division of B. R. Johnson's, and Hindman's with artillery. The order for the day was simple in the extreme.

There was no question about all the troops being in position by daylight, and at that hour the attack was to be opened by General Polk on the extreme right and followed up vigorously by the lines to the left, until the entire front of Bragg's fine army should be engaged and charging the enemy, exposed to an attack so furious it was not believed he could sustain it, and he could not. It will be shown how he was partially saved after the roughest handling he had had since Bull Run. The right wing was formed of Breckinridge's and Cleburne's divisions under D. H. Hill, Walker's and Biddell's divisions under Walker, and Cheatham's division, besides artillery.

Longstreet's front had Wheeler's cavalry on his extreme left, then Hindman, Hood's corps, Stuart, and Preston in the order named, and they were ready for their work at daylight on the 20th, the other commands in close support. Unhappily, a most serious delay occurred on the right, by which Polk's attack was retarded until near 10 o'clock, a loss of at least four previous hours. Lieutenant-General Hill's command was on Polk's extreme right and should have begun the attack. Orders sent during the night by General Polk failed to reach him. On our part we waited with the utmost impatience for the guns, but no sound came until 10 o'clock. Then Polk's attack was made, but does not appear to have achieved a decided success. The enemy were able to hold their ground against most of the right wing commands.

When it came, as it quickly did, to the left wing to put in its work there was another tale. The ground was in parts difficult in front of us, but never was a more determined, dashing attack made, never a more stubborn resistance. But our men would not be denied. The fighting lasted nearly all day. Finally everything broke before us, and the enemy's right was in full flight. It was a panic-stricken host that fled. Our Virginia contingent was always to the front and seemed to fire their western comrades with emulation of the grand example of the Army of Northern Virginia.

Unhappily, amid shouts of victory, General Hood was shot down at the head of his seasoned veterans. His leg was taken off on the field, the operation being well borne. But we were forced into a temporary halt.

Reinforcements were pouring fresh and ready against our front. The attack of the right wing having partly broken down, the enemy in front of Polk was not held to their own, but were in large numbers free for a masterly movement by that fine soldier, Gen. George Thomas. He was a Virginian, and it is said started to join his Southern friends at the beginning, but was finally won over to the Northern side.

He was one of the ablest of their soldiers, perhaps none equaled him, and I heartily wish he had been anywhere but at Chickamauga. Thomas pressed rapid columns to relieve his overwhelmed right and was in time to make a good stand, but it was unavailing, although costing more blood and time. His defenses were finally broken down, about dark, by our incessant hammering, and it was right-about-face and hasty retreat to Chattanooga.

This was just as darkness spread its mantle over the fields and forests, and simultaneously there sprang up on that bloodstained battle-ground camp fires innumerable, and the wildest Confederate cheers and yells for victory that ever stirred the hearts of warriors—and such warriors as had that day borne the battle-flags forward. It was one of the greatest of the many Confederate successes.

That night was passed in caring for the wounded, burying the dead, and cooking rations, for in all that host there was probably only one who did not believe that "pursuit" would be the word early next day, and that was the commander-in-chief. It is thought by some that General Bragg did not know a victory had been gained. He does not appear to have been closely present on the battlefield, nor for that matter was Rosecrans. A unique instance of a great battle being fought out of the immediate presence of the respective commanders. The next morning Bragg asked Longstreet for suggestions. "Move instantly against Rosecrans's rear to destroy him," was the instant reply. "Should we fail, we can put him in retreat, and then clear East Tennessee of Burnside and the Union forces."

Apparently, Bragg adopted this view, and gave orders to march out at 4 P. M. The right wing marched about eight miles, ours next day at daylight. We were halted at the Chickamauga Red House Ford, I think it was, and then directed to march to Chattanooga. At the close of the battle we could have strolled into that town; now it was vigorously defended. This was the fruit of the great battle; the pitiable end of the glorious victory that was ours. The spoils were 8,000 prisoners, 36 pieces of artillery, 15,000 small arms, and 25 stands of colors.

It was a lasting regret that I had no more than a passing glimpse during these operations of the distinguished soldier, Lieut.-Gen. Leonidas Polk, second in command of Bragg's army.

A pure and lofty character, nothing but the most self-sacrificing, patriotic convictions, and the almost peremptory wishes of the Executive had led him to lay down his great Episcopal station and duties and take to arms. His training at West Point had well prepared him for the stern efforts in the field awaiting Southern men. Throughout his army career he was never without a desire to put by his sword and take up again his dearly loved people, his Bishop's staff, for prayer and strength and consolation in their many trials and sufferings. But the President, holding him in the highest esteem and confidence, insisted on retaining him in the armies of the Confederacy. He could not but yield. Of commanding presence and most winning address, he served with distinction and renown. While suffering at the hands of Bragg treatment unjust and harsh, he on the other hand had won to himself the abiding affection and confidence of all officers and men whom he commanded.

On June 1, 1864, near Marietta, Georgia, that noble life ended. In the distance lay the hills of the Etowah; on the right, Kenesaw reared its lofty heights. The Generals—Johnston, Hardee, and Polk—had together walked off to observe a portion of the enemy's lines, some distance away. Soon after they slowly separated.

Dr. W. M. Polk, the General's son, eminent in his profession, and author of his interesting biography, simply relates what then happened (Vol. II, p. 349):

General Polk walked to the crest of the hill, and, entirely exposed, turned himself around as if to take a farewell view. Folding his arms across his breast, he stood intently gazing on the scene below. While thus he stood, a cannon shot crashed his breast, and opening a wide door, let free that indomitable spirit. He fell upon his back with his feet to the foe. Amid the shot and shell now poured upon the hill, his faithful escort gathered up the body and bore it to the foot of the hill. There in a sheltered ravine his sorrow-stricken comrades, silent and in tears, gathered around his mangled corpse.

CHAPTER XXVI

CHATTANOOGA—INCIDENTS

The Western army—Its general appearance—Feeling toward Bragg—President Davis's visit—An incident in battle—General W. W. Mackall, chief of Bragg's staff—Losses—A captured saber—General Forrest—General Benning and Longstreet—Vizitelly's battle-picture—Quartermaster Mitchell dead—Manning wounded—President Davis's escort—The Austrian captain's brilliant uniform.

We were therefore marched back to what was called the siege of Chattanooga, finding the enemy there in fine spirits after the indulgent reprieve granted him; strengthening his works, perfecting his communications with the rear, and pouring in men from the East, who, following our own movements, were necessarily late in arriving by the outer line. Bragg put his army in position across Missionary Creek (subject to perilous overflow) and occupied Lookout Mountain with his left and Missionary Ridge with his right, and here I shall leave the army while jotting down some observations and incidents since we left Virginia.

The personal appearance of Bragg's army was, of course, matter of interest to us of Virginia. The men were a fine-looking lot, strong, lean, long-limbed fighters. The Western tunic was much worn by both officers and men. It is an excellent garment, and its use could be extended with much advantage.

The army gave one the feeling of a very loose organization. There were indeed corps, so called, but not that compact, shoulder-to-shoulder make-up of Lee's army. There a First Corps man would so speak of himself, just as a Third Georgia Regiment man would speak of the regiment to which he belonged. The artillery, which seemed to me not as strong as should be, looked a bit primitive. The battalion unit was not often met with; but, on the contrary, many single independent batteries, nominally attached to infantry commands, but on the day of the battle wandering loose, hunting for their supports. The subsistence and quartermaster's departments were well supplied with food and forage, but weak in transportation.

The tone of the army among its higher officers toward the commander was the worst conceivable. Bragg was the subject of hatred and contempt, and it was almost openly so expressed. His great officers gave him no confidence as a general-in-chief. The army was thus left a helpless machine, and its great disaster in November at Missionary Ridge and Lookout Mountain could easily be foreseen with Bragg retained in command.

Mr. Davis made his celebrated visit to the camp to see and hear for himself. It is difficult, even now, to recall and realize that unprecedented scene. The President, with the commander-in-chief, and the great officers of the army, assembled to hear the opinion of the General's fitness for command. In the presence of Bragg and his corps commander he asked of each his opinion, and his reasons if adverse. This was eye to eye with the President, the commander-in-chief, and the generals. There was no lack of candor in answer to such challenge with men like Longstreet, Cheatham, Hill, Cleburne, and Stewart. Some very plain language was used in answer, but it seems that one and all were quite agreed as to Bragg's unfitness for command of that army. These opinions were received by the President and his general without comment, and Mr. Davis got more than he came for.

An incident of the day of battle will indicate some differences between the Eastern and Western armies in the reception of orders. While Thomas was heavily reinforcing his right, a column of fours was seen marching across Gen. A. P. Stewart's front. If attacked, its destruction was certain. I pointed out the opportunity to General Stewart, his position being admirable for the purpose. His answer was that he was there by orders and could not move until he got others. I explained that I was chief of staff to Longstreet and felt myself competent to give such an order as coming from my chief, and that this was customary in our Virginia service. General Stewart, however, courteously insisted that he could not accept them unless assured the orders came direct from Longstreet. Valuable time was being lost, but I determined to have a whack at those quick-moving blue masses. Asking General Stewart to get ready, that I hoped soon to find Longstreet, I was off, and luckily did find him after an eager chase. Longstreet's thunderous tones need not be described when, in the first words of explanation, he sent me back with orders to Stewart to fall on the reinforcing column with all his power. Stewart was ready and pushed forward handsomely. In a few minutes, with little or no loss to himself, he had broken up Thomas's men and taken many prisoners. This was quite late in the afternoon, twilight coming on.

My brother-in-law, General W. W. Mackall, was serving with Bragg as chief of staff, although his rank and attainments qualified him for higher duties. But the Executive at Richmond was not favorably disposed toward him, and the best that could be had for service must content him. It seems that he and Bragg had been long friends, having served together in the old Army. I was glad to come up with him, and delighted his soul by a gift of a five-pound bale of Virginia Killikinick smoking tobacco, in place of the vile stuff he was blowing off.

The numbers on both sides, and the casualties, are generally accepted as follows: Rosecrans's strength, 60,867; Bragg's strength, 60,366. Rosecrans's losses, 16,550; Bragg's losses, 17,800.

It was during the battle that I became the possessor of a handsomely mounted saber. In a part of the field near us there was a sudden sharp, deadly scrimmage between some of our mounted men and the enemy, a small force on each side. It was soon over, and Hardy, one of my couriers, a stout, ready Georgian, came to me with a beautiful saber, evidently a presentation to the lieutenant-colonel whose name was engraved on it. My fellow made me a gift of the handsome blade, and I wore it until peace came. What became of the lieutenant-colonel I could never ascertain.

> "His sword it is rust,
> His bones they are dust,
> His soul is with the Saints I trust."

The good sword was treasured until a few years ago, when the ladies of the Confederate Museum at Richmond asked me to put it among their collection, and there it hangs to-day, I hope for many years.

It was on the 20th that I had my look at the celebrated Forrest. Truly a most powerful, impressive figure of a great cavalryman. He was yet to become still greater, as one of the first commanders of the South, and subsequent studies of his life and career only expand this admiration into deeper feelings for the great soldier.

Dr. John Wyeth's interesting biography of Forrest, published only in the past few years, is most fascinating, and has gone far to place him as one of the greatest leaders of the Civil War. During the battle a queer scene between Longstreet and the valiant old brigadier, Benning, commanding one of Hood's brigades, illustrates Longstreet's grim calm in action, and the excitability of "Old Rock," as his men called him. A sudden counter-stroke of the enemy had smashed his brigade and they were badly scattered. Benning thought that they were "all gone." Seizing an artillery horse that was galloping by, harness flying, he threw himself on the terrified animal and found Longstreet. "General," said the brigadier, "I am ruined; my brigade was suddenly attacked and every man killed; not one is to be found. Please give orders where I can do some fighting." Longstreet saw the excitement and quickly cooled it. "Nonsense, General, you are not so badly hurt. Look about you. I know you will find at least one man, and with him on his feet report your brigade to me, and you two shall have a place in the fighting-line."

Benning saw it, took the hint, hunted up his men, who were not so badly mauled after all, and with a respectable body was soon ready for work.

Vizitelly, the English artist, had started from Richmond with us, to sketch and draw for the campaign; something stopped him on the way, drink, probably. At all events, he arrived very sheep-faced, long after the battle. He took me aside with: "Colonel, I am in an awful mess. I must send drawings and a picture of this great battle to my paper somehow. Cannot you help me?" We were at the time not very far from a little field that had a scene during the fighting which struck me, even then, as somewhat picturesque. The open field crowned with thick woods at one side, through which frowned half a dozen Federal guns and a brigade of ours moving up in beautiful order to capture it. I said as much as this to Vizitelly, and sent him to look at the spot. He returned, on fire with his artist's fancies. and shut himself up for several days. Then he emerged with drawings, and much letter-press of what he had *actually* seen; and principally a very large drawing beautifully finished of the so-called "Little scene." But heavens! all resemblance had ceased. Instead of the slight affair, three solid lines of infantry were moving across a great stretch of ground against hundreds of guns that were devastating our troops in fire and smoke. In the central portion there was the wounding and fall of a great officer and the closing in of the soldiers to protect him. "What think you?" said the proud Vizitelly. "Splendid, but nothing like it took place." "No matter, it might have happened, and besides all battle-pictures are drawn with such freedom." "Who is the general just falling?" "That, sir, is General Hood, drawn the instant of being shot." "But, my good Vizitelly, Hood was not within a mile of that little field I gave you." "No matter, he was shot, no one will deny that; and I must have a great interesting center for my picture. You fellows are altogether too particular. This goes by first underground chance, and you will see it in the *London Illustrated News.*" And so I did in the quiet sitting-room of a Northern friend later on.

He is not the only one of artistic imagination for battle-pictures.

At Chicakamauga we lost our quartermaster, Major Mitchell, of Virginia, a valuable officer. A sudden attack of diphtheria carried him off like a stroke of lightning. Major Erasmus Taylor, of Orange Court House, Virginia, was immediately appointed in his place, and served with us efficiently until the close of the war.

Lieutenant-Colonel Manning, of our staff, was slightly wounded in the battle of the 20th. A fragment of shell pierced his scalp, causing much loss of blood, but otherwise no great damage. He was soon about his ordnance duties as good as ever.

When President Davis came to Bragg's army on his visit of conciliation and support to his general, there was a universal turnout to give the Executive our best reception. At all headquarters the least shabby uniforms were looked up and our best belongings for horse and man were brought out. Mr. Davis had a really fine escort to the top of Lookout Mountain and back to quarters. At First Corps headquarters we still had the pleasure of Captain Fitzgerald Ross with us, a companionable and honorable officer and gentleman. On this occasion we thought it time for Ross to show the quality of his Austrian corps, and most reluctantly he consented to ride with us in full uniform. It was a beauty and a wonder! Sky-blue tunic and trousers, fitting skin-tight to the body and legs, loaded down with the richest gold braid and ornaments. Tiny boots, tasseled and varnished, incased the Captain's shapely Hussar legs. And then the pelisse hanging from the left shoulder!—it would be the envy of any woman. The color, still sky-blue, of the finest cloth, lined with buff satin, gold braided and richly furred. A smart, richly plumed Hungarian busby, with handsomely mounted curved saber and gold cords, completed the costume of this brilliant representative of his corps d'élite.

We gave Ross our plaudits and thanks for his fine appearance, and only on returning was there any annoyance. The large cortege about the President parted and some of us found ourselves riding with Ross under Maj.-Gen. John C. Breckinridge. Our route lay through one of his divisions camped in the noble primeval forests. The men were scattered all about attending to their personal matters, cooking, cleaning arms, mending, and, as it seemed, many stripped to the waist examining very closely their shirts and undergarments.

Without going into particulars, all soldiers in the field must be careful in this respect. Long-worn clothing had a way of "gathering" things, and it was what had to be done in all our armies. But when the scattered troops saw the brilliant apparition of Captain Ross riding with their General there was a shout and a rush to him. Such was the rough admiration exhibited that harm might have come to him but for Breckinridge. He motioned the men back, said the Captain was his guest, and, "When you fellows get to his army on a visit you will find him treating you more civilly; so get back to your bivouacs and make yourselves clean."

There was a good-natured cheer for Breckinridge, Ross, the President, and all the rest of us, and we got back to camp with much cheerful chaff for poor Ross and his gay uniform.

CHAPTER XXVII

THE EAST TENNESSEE CAMPAIGN, NOVEMBER 1863, TO APRIL, 1864.

Ordered by Bragg to move against Burnside and Knoxville—Our two divisions—Wheeler's cavalry with artillery—Burnside's strength—At Sweetwater, November 21st—Disappointed in supplies—The railway—Pontoons, but no train—Cross Holston at Loudon—Enemy escapes into Knoxville—Hood's old division—Generals Jenkins and Law—Siege of Knoxville—Bull Winthrop—McLaws ready for an assault—Troops ordered to support—General Leadbetter, of Bragg's staff, orders assault—Brigadiers Wofford, Humphreys, and Bryan attacked—Repulsed at Fort Saunders—General Longstreet assumes the blame—Losses.

After a long wait, General Bragg settled on something. He decided to make a move against Burnside and Knoxville. About November 3, Longstreet received his instructions. They were about in line with what the Lieutenant-General wanted instantly after Chickamauga and what should have been done, but the General-in-Chief could not see it, and, welcoming the orders even at this late day, we prepared for a hearty support and active campaign.

The troops of the expedition were to be the two divisions (nine brigades of infantry) brought from Virginia and Alexander's fine battalion of artillery, six batteries; also Leyden's artillery, and Wheeler's powerful body of cavalry (four brigades) and horse artillery. We were also to take up all the loose bodies of troops to be found in the wide district to be covered. A force of about 3,000 men was promised from southwest Virginia.

It was an ill-disciplined body, not well organized, but accomplished wonders under Wheeler as a screen to the army, and an unceasing menace to the enemy's communications. He had some able officers with him, Generals W. J. Martin, John T. Morgan, G. G. Dibbrell, and Thomas Harrison. When Wheeler left us with instructions for a movement calling for some night work his cheerful words to his fellows were: "Come, boys, mount. The War Child rides to-night." That being, it seems, one of his pet names among the men.

Major-General Wheeler was not long with us, Bragg, to whom his services were invaluable, having sent for him. I saw him I think but once. He had reported to Longstreet for orders and was followed by a rather numerous staff and escort. A small, slight man, very quick and alert in his movements, quite young, only recently from West Point, he had justly earned great distinction as the cavalry leader of our Western army.

Burnside's force south of Knoxville was computed at about 15,000, and if we could get all the troops Bragg held out to our commander, there would be enough of us to crush Burnside. But the Federal general had within reach some five thousand more men than General Bragg estimated.

The expedition, glad to be on the move, set out smartly for Tyner's Station, where it was to be entrained for Sweetwater, but things went decidedly wrong. We had brought no transportation from Virginia and General Bragg's officers supplied us with wagons and teams, but held themselves under Bragg's order. A most inconvenient disposition then, and until we parted company with that commander for good.

With these and other difficulties it was November 12th before the last of our brigades came to Sweetwater. Here there were more disappointments as to rations, supplies, and transportation. We were dependent on Bragg's provisions, which cruelly failed us. Not to dwell too long on these mishaps, I need only add that they beset the entire campaign.

The cars and railway by which we helped the transportation were almost comical in their inefficiency. The railroad was of heavy grades and the engines light-powered. When a hill was reached the long train would be instantly emptied—platforms, roofs, doors, and windows—of our fellows, like ants out of a hill, who would ease things by trudging up the dirt road and catching on again at the top; and so it went on as far as the railroad would serve us.

A bridge train had been prepared by the engineers, and it had been our intention to use it across the Little Tennessee, or Halston, above its confluence and through Marysville. But here again was disappointment; there were pontoons but no train for hauling.

We were thus forced to throw our bridge across at Loudon, where, fortunately, the boats could be floated direct from cars without need of wagons, and there that curious bridge was laid by our worthy engineers. It was a sight to remember. The current was strong, the anchorage insufficient, the boats and indeed entire outfit quite primitive, and when lashed finally to both banks it might be imagined a bridge; but a huge letter "S" in effect it was with its graceful reverse curves. But no man should abuse the bridge by which he safely crosses, and this one took us over, using care and caution. I shall always love the looks of that queer bridge.

The enemy was well advised as to our movements, and evidently conducted his retreat with skill and no serious losses. At Lenoir's Station he was forced to leave nearly a hundred loaded wagons, though the running-gear had been broken up so as to make them of no immediate use to us.

I do not give in detail the various movements of our advance from one point to another, their character generally not being of the highest credit to us in rapidity or co-operation of our several commands.

A fine opportunity of crushing Burnside was lost at Campbell's Station. Burnside's retreat was in time to cover the roads leading into it, and there he had to make a stand. We should have beaten him badly, but he escaped and was soon safe in Knoxville. The roads were deep in mud and caused hard travel and labor, but they were no better for the Union force.

Campbell's Station cannot be termed a serious battle. It was principally an artillery fight, in which the gallant Alexander was tormented by defective ammunition. It should have been a strong and decisive battle, but things went wrong with the infantry divisions and an effective co-operation was not secured. Ah! would that we could have had Hood again at the head of his division.

As it was, the five brigades of this fine command were practically paralyzed by the differences between the senior brigadier in command, Jenkins, and his competitor, General E. M. Law. It was a most unhappy condition of things, but by no fault of Longstreet. When Mr. Davis visited us at Chickamauga the Lieutenant-General laid the situation before him and urged the promotion and appointment of Jenkins, to which Mr. Davis would not listen. He was asked then to appoint Law, but this also met the Executive's "No," that officer being junior; and then Longstreet begged the assignment of any good major-general to be found elsewhere. But none came then; months after one was sent when irretrievable mischief had been done by the unfortunate condition of the division. It lasted during all the subsequent operations in East Tennessee throughout the winter.

Thus it came about that the enemy eluded us at Campbell's Station, and the next day was behind his works at Knoxville, except his cavalry, which lingered to retard our march. Our army followed closely, at once put the enemy's works under fire, and so began what is called the "Siege of Knoxville."

By many it is thought to have been a serious error on the part of the Confederate commander, the resorting to so slow a process. "He should have attacked immediately;" and I am disposed to consider intelligent statements of Union officers and citizens of Knoxville, long after, as indicating that an energetic movement, without the slightest delay, would have carried us into the town and brought Burnside to terms.

On the 18th of November McLaws advanced against some defenses of skirmishers, but part of his line halted before reaching the crest of the hill. Captain Winthrop, an Englishman serving with Alexander, dashed forward, and encouraging the men got through the hill in handsome style. It was well done by "Bull" Winthrop, as we called him, and he picked up a nasty wound in the doing of it.

Burnside's strongest defense was Fort Loudon, later called Fort Saunders, for the gallant officer of that name who fell in its defense. It was a strong earthwork, closely under McLaws's eye, who was expected to capture it. Of course he had done much work toward it—ditches, parallels, and many devices for success. A night attack was proposed and at one time favored.

On the 22d General McLaws thought the time had come and he was ordered to prepare his assaulting column, supported by the division. Longstreet also ordered up other troops for support and following up a success. Later on McLaws reported that his officers preferred daylight for the work before them and the movement was for the time deferred. On the 23d we heard that Bragg had been attacked at Chattanooga. Bushrod Johnson's division of two brigades was at Loudon moving to us, and our strength then would be eleven brigades of infantry, Wheeler's cavalry of four brigades (Wheeler himself had been ordered back by Bragg, leaving the horse under command of Maj.-Gen. Will T. Martin), Alexander's artillery, and Leyden's battalion.

On the 25th, Bragg's chief engineer, General Leadbetter, brought orders from the former to attack immediately. Longstreet was reluctant. Troops from Virginia were on the march, due with us in eight or ten days, and with them the investment could be made complete. The enemy was also said to be on half rations, and an attack now with chances of our repulse would be all in his favor. But Leadbetter felt that Bragg's orders were imperative and the assault must be attempted. Minute orders were then sent to McLaws for the effort. The details are rather lengthy for the scope of these recollections. It was intended for the 28th, but because of bad weather put off until the 29th. At the appointed time the vigorous assault was made in fine form by the brigades of Wofford, Humphreys, and Bryan in the early gray of the morning. At first we seemed to be going right ahead, shoving everything aside, but some stops were made and the wounded men began coming back.

General Longstreet says that when Major Goggin, an old Army man on McLaws's staff, reported to him that it would be useless to persevere, that the fort was so surrounded with net-works of wire that no progress could be made without axes and not an axe was to be found—"Without a second thought, I ordered the recall." He says later that the accounts of General Poe, the engineer in charge of the works, convinced him that the few wires met with were far from being the serious obstacle reported and that we could have gone in without axes. It also seemed sure that the fort was nearly ours by the retirement of part of its garrison, only some two hundred men being kept with the guns.

General Longstreet takes upon himself the failure of the assault. It seems conclusive to him that it was due to the order for recall. He had long known Goggin. Some of our men pushed into the fort. One gallant young officer, Adjutant Cumming, from Augusta, Georgia, leaped through an embrasure and instantly demanded the surrender of fort and garrison. The Union troops cheered the feat while making him a prisoner of war. Almost immediately after the repulse General Longstreet received a telegram from the President to the effect that "Bragg had been forced back by numbers and that we were to co-operate with his army." A euphemism on the part of the President—Bragg had suffered a severe defeat and was in full retreat. He made for Dalton, which put out of the question any co-operation by us. Our own safety was to be considered and how it could be accomplished.

The casualties at Knoxville are thus given: Confederate loss in assault, 822; Union loss in assault, 673; Confederate loss in campaign, 1,296; Union loss in campaign, 1,481.

CHAPTER XXVIII

The East Tennessee Campaign, Continued

In front of Knoxville after repulse—Position serious—Bragg defeated at Missionary Ridge—Reinforcements pressing to Burnside—We withdraw to the eastward—Halt at Rogersville—Foraging good—Supplies in valleys sufficient—We decide to winter there—Occasional operations without importance—Affair at Bean's Station—Much uneasiness at Washington at Longstreet's presence in East Tennessee—General Grant ordered to drive him out—Affair at Dandridge—Great want of shoes—A supply from Quartermaster General—General McLaws relieved from duty—The correspondence — General McLaws's resignation — Intense cold—Roads almost impassable—Inhabitants of the valleys and mountaineers—The fierce old woman—Mountain fastnesses—Deserters from a North Carolina regiment—Their capture and execution—General Schofield in command of Union army—We take position and make camps near Bull's Gap.

Our position was now becoming serious. Some additional troops under Ransom would soon join us, but the enemy was being heavily reinforced. Grant had decided to drive us out of East Tennessee. A letter from him to Burnside by courier was captured, advising him of three columns en route for his relief—one on south side by General Sherman, one by Dechared under General Elliott, and one by Cumberland Gap under General Foster. Longstreet decided to march past Knoxville on the north side of the river and aim for the column reported coming from Cumberland Gap. The enemy did not see fit to molest our flank as we marched past his defenses on the 2d of December.

There was good foraging in the country, and we halted at Rogersville on the 9th to accumulate supplies. Up to this date it had not been our General's intention to stay in the Tennessee Valley. He was looking eastward, but more hopefully toward some combinations and increase of force by which a powerful demonstration could be made into Kentucky through Cumberland Gap. But at Rogersville the foraging officers brought in roseate reports of plenty in the land. It appeared to be overflowing with subsistence for an army; cattle, swine, corn, sorghum, and honey were abundant, and it was decided we should winter in these beautiful valleys, watered by the Holston, the French Broad, the mouth of Chucky and Nolachucky. Truly was it a fertile and smiling land to be still showing all this abundance, ravaged and harried as it had been alternately by Union and Confederate forces, and with such a population! It could well be said that "Only man was vile."

General Longstreet in his book, "Manassas to Appomattox," has written up his movements from the time he left Bragg to that of leaving Tennessee, at great length and with extreme particularity. Its recital had apparently occupied him more than any part of the four years' war. We may therefore well leave these details; they are correctly stated, although without the interest of a successful campaign. We turn therefore to matters more general, but perhaps attractive, of our doings in that country.

There was occasional skirmishing and outpost fighting, but nothing of importance. At the affair of Bean's Station we expected to accomplish something, but little came of it. Gradually a good force had been assembled at scattered points under Longstreet's orders, and he was most confident and eager for an opportunity to deal the enemy a blow. President Davis, on December 10th, gave him discretionary authority over all the troops in the department, and on this he held, for the present, Martin's cavalry by him, that Bragg had called for. It was positively necessary for holding East Tennessee, which seemed the best possible use to make of the troops while Bragg's army was in a state of demoralization and uncertainty.

Indeed, in the published annals there is appearance of intense uneasiness by Halleck and Mr. Lincoln as to Longstreet's presence in Tennessee. The emphatic tone of many letters and orders from the Federal capital was that we should, under any circumstances and apparently at any sacrifices, be driven out. Our presence there took the form of a political peril. As long as we had a good foothold and a good army in reach of Cumberland Gap there was the chance of a successful movement into Kentucky, and once there that State would have been in an unpleasant and dangerous attitude to the Federals. Its Confederate sentiments were in parts still strong and shared by large numbers of the population. Longstreet's correspondence always took a squint at such an eventuality, and nothing would have better pleased him than to lead such a movement. But the winter coming on sharp, we found camps in the great forest about Morristown before Christmas and began collection of food supplies in earnest.

The men were happy and cheerful, but awfully in want of clothing and shoes. Some of the latter were made by themselves, but this supply could not go far. I recall a movement against General Granger at Dandridge when the corps turned out to march. It was bitter winter weather, the ground hard and sharp with ice, and not less than 2,000 of our little army were without shoes. Their bleeding feet left marks at every step.

They were useless for the work and quickly sent back to camp. Not long after, however, all were made happy by a shipment of three thousand pairs of shoes by General Lawton, our Quartermaster-General. He had listened to our earnest, almost desperate appeals.

About the middle of December, Major-General McLaws was relieved from command of his division by Lieutenant-General Longstreet and ordered to Augusta, Georgia. Part of the correspondence concerning this matter will be found in the Appendix, sufficiently explanatory. The commanding General had for some time been dissatisfied with his second in command. Later on, at Greenville, McLaws had the court of inquiry for which he at once applied. The charges were three in number, principally alleging neglect and want of preparation at Knoxville, supported each by one specification. The court absolved McLaws from all fault, but found him guilty on one of the specifications. The proceedings went to the President, who immediately disapproved them, restored McLaws to duty, and assigned him to a command in Georgia.

General E. M. Law handed in his resignation and asked leave of absence on it—this about December 20th. It was cheerfully granted, and then General Law asked the privilege of taking the resignation himself to Richmond. It was unusual, but was allowed. From this afterwards grew serious complications, involving Law's arrest by Longstreet, his support by the Executive, and Longstreet's threat of resignation from the army, in which he was upheld by General Lee. And the Lieutenant-General had his way. Law was not again in Longstreet's command.

The cold was intense, the record showing the lowest temperature for many years. During the last days of 1863 the glass went down to zero and the entire army was quiet in the effort to keep warm.

Fortunately there was fuel in abundance. The primeval forests of oak and hickory were food for some of the grandest campfires ever seen, but we froze in front while scorching in back, and vice versa. And as to sleeping, many a fine fellow woke to find his shoes crisp from the too generous blaze. At this time the roads were so bad as to be almost impassable; artillery and wagons would be drawn hub deep. The artillery horses, Leyden's especially, were in bad condition, very weak, and six or eight pairs would be hitched to a single gun or caisson. It amused the infantry footing it on the side paths, and they would call out, "Here comes the cavalry, but what's that gun tied to the tail for?"

The people of these valleys made an interesting study. They doubtless went through much during the Civil War, and part of their disposition at the period of our occupation may be accounted for. There were, of course, some exceptions to be found in families of wealth, intelligence, and breeding, but the general run of people was hard in the extreme. Apparently they were without pity or compassion—generosity and sympathy were strangers to them; but hatred and revenge made their homes in the breasts of these farmers.

When the Confederates came on the ground, then was the time for acts of brutality against their Union neighbors, the political feeling in the valleys being about equally divided. Burnings, hangings, whippings were common—all acts of private vengeance and retaliation. When the turn came and the Unionists were in authority, Confederate sympathizers were made to suffer in the same way, and so it went on throughout the bloody strife.

Once an old woman came to my quarters with a request. She was a fierce, hard creature, strong, of wrinkled skin, but set, relentless features, clothed in the homespun worn by all, and like all, dipping snuff. Stick in mouth she made her statement. Some men had come to her house that morning—she knew them name by name. They had taken her old man from her and hung him to a tree by his own porch, and there left him—dead. She wanted the murderers caught and punished. Not a word of sorrow or softness, not a tear of regret, but only vengeance, and that instantly. I immediately sent a good troop of cavalry to seize the men, if to be found, but little hoped it. They had, as usual, taken refuge in the mountains, quite inaccessible to ordinary attack, and were safe there with numbers of others.

These mountain fastnesses were filled with evil-doers of both sides, Union and Confederate; murderers, thieves, deserters—all crimes could there be known.

The authorities had found it quite impossible to break up these formidable gangs by any ordinary force. A special expedition for the express purpose would be necessary.

It was to these mountains that a large body of deserters from a North Carolina regiment in Virginia was making a little time back.

A whole company had broken away, but were overtaken at a crossing of the James above Richmond. They showed fight and killed several of the pursuers, but were taken back and the leaders tried by court martial. Ten were convicted and sentenced to be shot. There had been too much leniency, and General Lee had the sentence executed. The unfortunates were tied to small sunken crosses in line about ten feet apart, with a firing party in front of each. Their division, Major-General Edward Johnson's, was drawn up in three sides of a hollow square, the deserters being on the fourth. At the word the firing was accurately executed and the men sank dead or dying at their stakes. The division was then marched by, close to their bodies, and it was hoped the lesson would be salutary.

General Grant made a visit to Knoxville about January 1st, General Foster in command. Before leaving he ordered Foster to expel us from Tennessee, if not altogether, at least beyond Bull's Gap and Red Bridge. Washington was still uneasy and pressing him hard to put us out of the way.

Preparing for it, he ordered the Ninth and the Twenty-third Corps to Mossy Creek, Fourth Corps to Strawberry Plain and the cavalry to Dandridge—a formidable force. That army moved about January 15th. Dandridge is on the French Broad River, about thirty miles from Knoxville, and was the enemy's objective.

General Foster was invalided, and Sheridan for a short time took command until relieved by the corps commander, Gordon Granger. A smart affair ensued, General Martin's cavalry doing our principal work. Granger retired and Longstreet rode into Dandridge and was soon in the house occupied by his old friend Granger. Pursuit was made impracticable by the condition of roads and want of a bridge train. Practically nothing was accomplished on this trial, and our troops as well as the enemy were sent back to camps.

On February 9th General Schofield took command at Knoxville of the Union army in East Tennessee. The pressure on him continued from Halleck, whose uneasiness at one time became almost uncontrollable. Grant at first made strong effort to carry out these wishes, but we were not moved. Later on he found the field too far from his other operations and likely to interrupt plans for the summer. He preferred resting on the apparent apathy at the South and using his East Tennessee strength in Virginia and Georgia where he should have full need for it. This view was to leave us in inactivity in East Tennessee, and no further serious effort was made. Longstreet had to move east when he was refused more troops for extended aggressive operations and received orders for return of Martin's cavalry to Georgia. Our march was begun about February 20, 1864, and was not disturbed. A fair position was found at Bull's Gap, and then we distributed our commands in good camps from the Holston to the Nolachucky.

CHAPTER XXIX

At Home in Savannah—Sketches

Leave of absence—Visiting home with Doctor Sorrell—Traveling by rail—Old Savannah—Few changes—Many friends—Happiness in meeting them—Return to the army—Longstreet's correspondence with Schofield—Attempt in same line near Richmond with General Ord—General Grant declines negotiations for peace—Andrew Johnson's Masonic paraphernalia saved by Captain Goree—Sketch—Longstreet at Richmond—In conference with President and General Lee—Without result—First corps ordered back to Lee—Began moving late in April—Arrived at Mechanicsville last of month—Major-General Field assigned to command of Hood's division—Sketch—Congress votes thanks to First Corps (see Appendix)—Charlottesville—Sketch—Prices of various articles.

I had now opportunity for yielding to my father's pressing urgency to take leave of absence and see him once more in life. I arranged for thirty days absence. The railroad was not yet fully repaired and my nearest station was about fifteen miles to ride. An agreeable medical officer gave me his company so far, but was constantly weeping that he was not on his way "to see his dear, beautiful little wife." I tried to comfort him by the reminder that no such attraction was waiting for me, but without success. He was, however, braced up by a horse trade we managed to get off, which as usual I incline to think I got the worst of. I think so by reason of a memorandum about horses in which the animal then acquired is named "Deceit." The train soon reached Bristol, whence a change of cars brought me through Lynchburg to Richmond. There Doctor Sorrel met me, like myself on leave, and light-hearted we started for home to see our dear kith and kin.

It was my first absence from duty since July 21, 1861. Slow railway traveling in those days was the rule without exception—gauges not uniform, routes deviating, and engines of low power. The time was, I think, quite three days between Richmond and Savannah, traveling day and night, and of course such luxuries as sleeping-cars were then unknown.

It was a great delight to see home again; to be welcomed and made much of, after the stern scenes of more than two years. Our friends were not backward or ungenerous. Hospitalities were showered upon us, but better than all was the loving home circle of aging father and happy young sisters. The latter, gladdened to have their brothers once more with them, sang, played, and danced to heart's delight.

There were many changes. Only six companies had gone to the Eastern army. The remainder of the very large forces sent by the city was distributed through the Western armies and the coast defenses; consequently I had seen but few of my old comrades and associates in Virginia. The happiness of meeting many awaited me in Savannah, and it will easily be imagined what our talk was about—the camp, the battle, the march, the enemy, and our own commands.

There was no great change in the appearance of the town, then of about 30,000 population. Eighteen miles from the sea, and beautifully situated on a high bluff, it enjoyed a large commerce and much lucrative business. Shady walks, numerous small wooded parks, and thousands of branching, leafy trees made it a very attractive and beautiful little city. The rigors of war had not yet touched it. The forts at the entrance to the river were the enemy's, but he had not yet penetrated to the city. That was preserved for Sherman in December, from the West.

The days slipped by. Our time was nearly up, and with cheerful farewells we were soon on our way back to Virginia. Dropping my brother, the Doctor, at Richmond, I went directly back to my familiar duties with our army in its winter camp in East Tennessee.

Affairs had been very quiet within that thirty days, and I was well satisfied to be again with the colors. My leave and my home became, as it were, but a pleasant bit of dreaming.

Not long after Schofield took command of the Union forces our Lieutenant-General succeeded in getting into a short correspondence with him. The Federal commander was an able soldier, of liberal views, from which Longstreet had hopes. The latter's intentions were commendable. Like most of us, he wanted peace and the honorable termination of the war and cessation of bloodshed. He felt that it was not to be accomplished by the politicians. They had plunged the country into civil war, he reasoned. They would be the last to bring it to an end. The hope was that the generals on both sides might give the movement such an impetus that statecraft must necessarily take it up with probably good results. It was with this view that some letters passed between Longstreet and Schofield. The former pressed that view, and, assuming the Union General, like himself, wanted peace, he urged a joint initiative from which much could be hoped. It was illusory. Schofield's letter was calm and noncommittal. Finally he had to say what was sure to be said, that it was not his part to deal with such matters, which were properly to be discussed by the Executive in Washington. It was necessarily so. The military were not clothed with authority for the purpose. Even the convention between Sherman and Johnston at the close of hostilities was disapproved and annulled by the Federal civil authorities.

The idea, however, did not vanish from Longstreet's thoughts. It took fresh shape later in front of Richmond through General Ord, the officer immediately in command, as intermediary by which it was hoped a meeting between Grant and Lee could be achieved. General Grant declined a meeting for discussion on such a subject. The correspondence relating to these two incidents is probably to be found in the records published by Congress, and should be interesting. I refer to them entirely from memory.

While quartered near Greenville some straggling soldiers found their way into the house once occupied by Andrew Johnson, then Vice-President. He was a Mason of high degree, and the emblems and paraphernalia of the order were very numerous in the dwelling. Our fellows thought they had made a find of value and were about starting off with it when halted by Captain Goree, A. D. C. of our staff.

He had everything carefully repacked and put in a safe place for the rightful owner. I have never known whether he finally recovered them uninjured.

Goree was a Texan and had been with Longstreet from the beginning. The General was fortunate in having an officer so careful, observing, and intelligent. His conduct on all occasions was excellent and his intrepidity during exposure in battle could always be counted on. He was with the corps until Appomattox, and then returned to Texas, where he occupied responsible public office by vote of the people for many years. He enjoys good health and good Confederate memories now at his home in Galveston.

About this time Generals Lee, Johnston, and Longstreet were called on by the Richmond authorities for suggestions as to further operations on a comprehensive scale. General Bragg was in office as adviser to the President. Having failed in all field operations, he had now the President's ear and the President's support for experimental strategy. Longstreet submitted an elaborate proposition, having for its objective a powerful demonstration in Kentucky by combination with General Johnston's army and the eventual command of the State under Confederate auspices. It is said that plan had General Lee's approval when submitted to the President in counsel with the Secretary of War, General Bragg, and General Lee. The proposition was not accepted and nothing apparently was settled. General Lee returned immediately to his army on the Rapidan and the Lieutenant-General set out for his headquarters at Greenville. Feeling himself entitled to the privilege, he stopped two days at Petersburg to see his wife, and to have his infant son christened "Robert Lee." It appears this short stop subjected him to rebuke by the President for loitering.

The country was now in wintry weather and there was much snow. Everything went into quarters that could and all military operations were suspended. The second division of General Johnston's cavalry was ordered to him through the mountains—a hard march. It should be stated that Johnston was now for some time in command of the Army of Tennessee in Bragg's place. In the first half of April our command started back to join General Lee on the Rapidan. It was made on cars collected as fast as possible. The troop detrained at Charlottesville. After a short stop in that country, we began, about the 22d, the march to Mechanicsville, not far from Gordonsville, and on the last of the month had the happiness to be reviewed by our beloved commander, General Lee. The troubles in Hood's old division would, it was hoped, be ended. Maj.-Gen. Charles W. Fields had been some time back assigned to command and was to prove an active and capable commander. He was an old Army man of much experience and unquestioned valor. In the Appendix may be read the vote of thanks given by Congress to Lieutenant-General Longstreet and his command.

When we detrained at Charlottesville I had the good fortune to meet some most hospitable friends. Judge William J. Robertson, eminent on the bench, and his charming wife insisted on having me in their handsome residence and agreeable family circle. It was a welcome contrast to the asperities of a winter campaign in East Tennessee. The town itself was interesting and full of Virginia historic lore. Its chief pride is the Alma Mater of many Southern men, the University of Virginia, beloved of Jefferson. Near by, on steep Monticello, stands his own house, where youth and age, in admiration of the sage, the statesman, the philosopher, sought him for a word, a touch of the hand. The property is still well maintained by its present owner, proud of its history as part of Thomas Jefferson. The county of Albemarle (its deep red-clay soil remembered by many a sore-footed soldier), is of ancient settlement, abounding in wood and meadow and shining streams. Its tasty, luscious pippins are widely known to lovers of the apple. Some stately old residences, the "great houses" of large estates of the early Virginia families, are still to be seen; but alas! the ravages of war and its bitter results have left such properties but as so many reminders of an opulent past. It was this delightful resting place of a few days that we were now to leave for the great campaign of the Wilderness and its subsequent battles.

In April, 1864, the Confederacy had reached a point of great financial embarrassment, as shown by the depreciation of its paper currency. The pay of the officers was in reality a pittance, and those without other resources were often in straits. Many boxes and hampers, however, came to the camps from home and were of some help to all.

A petition from officers in the field had gone to the War Department, asking that rations might be issued to them as to the private soldiers. It had attached a scale of prices charged the officers by the army commissaries, presumably the average cost price, and not the price of retail market. The officers paid for bacon, $2.20 per pound; beef, 75 cents; lard, $2.20 per pound; molasses, $6 per gallon; sugar, $1.50 per pound. A coat cost $350; boots, $250; trousers, $125; hat, $80 to $125; shirt, $50; socks, $10 per pair. General Johnston in approving and verifying the petition said that at existing prices the pay of company officers was worth less than that of a private soldier.

The shrinkage of the value of our paper currency continued with the progress of the war until, near the close, it almost ceased to have any purchasing power whatever.

CHAPTER XXX

Battle of the Wilderness, May 6, 1864.

General Grant in command of all the Union forces—Takes station with Army of the Potomac—His career—His successes—Later kind feelings of Southern people toward him—His dinner party at Savannah—His plan of campaign—The policy of attrition—Grant moves his army—The Wilderness—Disparity of numbers—Courier service an example of our economy in men—Kershaw promoted major-general, commanding McLaws's division—Sketch—Lee decides to strike—Grant on the march—They meet on May 5th—An indecisive partial contest—Early on May 6 Longstreet comes up—Finds situation serious—Hancock's successful attack on Third Corps—It is checked—Our flank attack on Hancock's left—He is rolled up and sent back—General Lee wants to lead troops—Longstreet wounded and Jenkins killed by fire of our own men—Major-General Wadsworth, U. S. A., killed—Attack resumed later—Not successful—Night ends long day's fighting.

The Army of Northern Virginia was now to deal with a new force—a general with the great prestige of repeated victories in the West, and of undeniable ability. Lieutenant-General U. S. Grant had been made Commander-in-Chief of all the Federal armies in the field, and realizing the extraordinary achievements of Lee's army, left the scene of his operations, and retaining Meade in command of the Army of the Potomac, took his station by that army for the supreme direction of military affairs. Grant's career was wonderful; were it not a fact, it would be thought a fairy tale. A West Point graduate of mediocrity, serving well in Mexico, but so given over to drink that his retirement from the Army may be said to have been compulsory. This was followed by hard-working attempts to make a living for his family, in humble occupations, until the stirring events of 1861 brought him forward, as they did every one who had enjoyed the opportunity of a soldier's education. Obtaining command of an Illinois regiment, his field service began, and was followed up with much success; until, placed in command of important armies in Tennessee and Kentucky, he was able to break up the Confederate plans, and finally, by his crushing defeat of Bragg at Missionary Ridge, prepared the way for Hood's destruction at Franklin and Nashville, and Sherman's "march to the sea."

Now came his work in Virginia, which is to be touched on, and then his Presidency for two terms. During much of this time he was said to be intemperate, but if true it made no difference in the results accomplished. Mr. Lincoln was thought to be looking up Grant's brand of whiskey for some of his other generals. This General's character made him very dear to his friends. He was always true and helpful to them, and possessed a certain directness and simplicity of action that was in itself most attractive.

General Grant's conduct toward our leader in the closing scenes at Appomattox and his vigorous defense of Lee when threatened by unprincipled and powerful Northern politicians are not likely to be forgotten by the Southern people. With the passing of time his fame as a great commander appears to be growing, and will probably still grow after careful study of his campaigns. Only once did I have the opportunity of meeting this remarkable man. It was during the "third term" plans of the Republican party that his friends were carrying him on visits to various parts of the country. He was in Savannah with Sheridan and others for a few days and was entertained at a handsome dinner-party, of some dozen or more leading gentlemen of the city, by General Henry R. Jackson, a wealthy and prominent Democratic citizen. He was himself a marked personality—a lawyer of eminence; had been Minister to Austria under Buchanan; was to be Minister to Mexico under Cleveland; was a poet and an orator, besides of the highest character, attainments, and social attractions. The dinner was a great success, served lavishly in the old Southern fashion, with various courses of wine, which the rough Sheridan brusquely put aside. "He wanted champagne, must have it at once." And he *did* have it from start to finish.

Grant was in excellent form, looked well and talked well; his glass was not touched. Fresh from his tour around the world he had much to say. He had been deeply interested in Japan and talked incisively of that wonderful country, really a monologue of a full hour, the table intent and absorbed in the fresh observations that fell from him. Then it became time for his departure to meet a public appointment, and we rose to bow him out. Resuming our seats and attention to the old Madeiras, we agreed that for a silent man Grant was about the most interesting one we had recently found. His talk was clean-cut, simple, direct, and clear.

The General-in-Chief made his headquarters near Culpeper. The Army of the Potomac was about 130,000 strong in aggregate, and consisted of Hancocks' Second Corps, Warren's Fifth, and Sedgwick's Sixth; besides Burnside's Ninth, held apart near Rappahannock railroad bridge. Lee's army lay west of the Rapidan, R. H. Anderson's division facing Madison Court House; the Second and Third Corps (Ewell's and Hill's), two divisions of the First, and Alexander's artillery were at Mechanicsville; Pickett's division of the First was south of the James. Our strength is stated by Colonel Taylor to have been 63,998.

We were at no loss to understand Grant's intention. The Northern papers, as well as himself, had boldly and brutally announced the purpose of "attrition"—that is, the Federals could stand the loss of four or five men to the Confederates' one, and threw nice strategy into the background. It was known that we were almost past recruiting our thin ranks, and the small figures of the army as it now stood; while the double numbers of the Federals could be reproduced from the immense resources in population, not to speak of their foreign field of supplies under inducement of liberal bounties.

Grant started his march the night of May 3d, via Germanna and Elys Fords, Wilson's and Gregg's cavalry leading. Burnside was also ordered to him.

The Wilderness was a wild, tangled forest of stunted trees, with in places impassable undergrowth, lying between Fredericksburg and Orange Court House, probably sixteen or seventeen miles square. Some farm clearings and a shanty or two for a few poor inhabitants might occasionally be seen. Two principal roads penetrated this repulsive district, the Orange Plank Road and the turnpike. The ground generally lay flat and level.

And now was to begin the last and greatest of the campaigns of the Army of Northern Virginia. The campaign of *attrition* on one side met and foiled by the fine flower of the ablest strategy on the other. It was Grant's stubborn perseverance, indifferent to the loss of life, against Lee's clear insight and incessant watchfulness. Our army always ready, ever fighting, was to hold the Federal forces from the Wilderness to the final break at Petersburg, from May to March, ten months of supreme effort, most exhaustive to a commander. Marshall Marmont says, "The attacking general has, to a large extent, command of the mind of his defensive opponents." It is doubtless true, but Lee often gave his mind necessary relief and chanced success by a sudden initiative against Grant. The latter would unexpectedly find part of his army attacked with swift energy and would get something for his mind to work on besides the control of Lee's.

Referring to the disparity of numbers, we did in truth want men. A little detail will show how we had to economize them. Until recently there had been small cavalry details at general headquarters and with corps and division chiefs. These, however, were all sent back to serve with the regimental colors, and the courier service they had been doing taken up by assignments of men from the infantry ranks who could keep themselves mounted.

Six were allowed for corps headquarters, four for divisions, and two for brigades. Being picked men, the service was well performed; but the time was not far off when these able men had again to take up their muskets by their colors. Disabled fellows who could ride but did no marching were put at the important courier duties and did well! The enemy said we were robbing the cradle and the grave, and it was more or less true.

Maj.-Gen. J. B. Kershaw, a lawyer from South Carolina, was one of the most distinguished and efficient officers of the Virginia army. His service had been long and uninterrupted. Coming out with a fine South Carolina regiment among the first to be sent to Virginia, his abilities soon made him its colonel. He served long in that rank, his steady courage and military aptitude invariably showing handsomely in the arduous service of his regiment.

It was one of those forming the South Carolina Brigade of McLaws's division. Longstreet was quick to perceive Kershaw's merit and recommended him for promotion. It was sometime coming. But when he was brigadier-general and placed in command of the brigade he maintained his high reputation fully. In 1864 he was promoted to be major-general, and continuing his service with Longstreet's corps, his conduct and abilities were conspicuous until the very end of hostilities. General Kershaw was of most attractive appearance, soldierly and handsome, of medium size, well set up, light hair and moustache, with clean-cut, high-bred features.

Grant's movement was soon made known to Lee, and the latter prepared to strike. It was his way, he waited not for the blow; better give it, was a large part of his strategy. It was thought Grant could best be met by a stroke as he marched. The Second and Third Corps were ordered forward by the Plank Road. Our own two divisions, Field's and Kershaw's, the latter commanding in McLaws's place, and Alexander's batteries were near Gordonsville and ordered to move by the Plank Road to Parker's Store. The route was changed at General Longstreet's request, and he found a good guide in James Robinson, well known to our Quartermaster Taylor, who lived at Orange Court House. We were at Richard's shop at 5 p. m. on May 5th, Rosser's cavalry then being engaged at that point with part of Sheridan's; the latter moving off when we came up. The march had been twenty-eight miles, and there orders from the Commanding General were received for changing direction so as to unite with other troops on the Plank Road. Directions conforming were issued to resume march at midnight.

Both armies being now in quick motion, the collision was soon to come; indeed, had already come with Heth's and Wilcox's divisions, ending late that night after fierce battle. I make no attempt at detail of all Confederate and Union movements, but the great battle of the Wilderness is now to be fought and the important part in it taken by the First Army Corps briefly sketched.

Strange to say, the two divisions of our Third Corps, Heth's and Wilcox's, after their severe battle made no attempt at defensive field work or trenching when firing ceased that night. In explanation, it is said they expected to be withdrawn and consequently did no work nor replenished their ammunition. But Hancock, accomplished general that he was, suffered himself to fall into no such pit. He had his men at work all night strengthening his position, and was thus enjoying the soldier's high feeling of confidence; and then with the sun he let fly at the troops in front of him, apparently inviting attack with no ground defenses whatever. It was distressing to realize such failure in the field work, and the result came near a great disaster.

Longstreet had moved at 1 a. m., the march being difficult and slow in the dense forest by side tracks and deep furrowed roadways. At daylight he was on the Plank Road and in close touch with Lee when Hancock struck the two unprepared divisions. The situation when we came on the scene, that of May 6th, was appalling. Fugitives from the broken lines of the Third Corps were pouring back in disorder and it looked as if things were past mending. But not so to James Longstreet; never did his great qualities as a tenacious, fighting soldier shine forth in better light. He instantly took charge of the battle, and threw his two divisions across the Plank Road, Kershaw on the right, Field on the left. None but seasoned soldiers like the First Corps could have done even that much. I have always thought that in its entire splendid history the simple act of forming line in that dense undergrowth, under heavy fire and with the Third Corps men pushing to the rear through the ranks, was perhaps its greatest performance for steadiness and inflexible courage and discipline. Hill's men were prompt to collect and reform in our rear and soon were ready for better work. General Lee was under great excitement immediately on the left. He wanted to lead some of our troops into action, but the Texas brigade was about him and swore they would do nothing unless he retired. A confident message from Longstreet through Colonel Venable that his line would be restored within an hour also helped him to regain his calm; and then at it we went in earnest, on both sides of the road. Hancock's success had loosened his ranks somewhat, which helped us when we fell on him. It was a hard shock of battle by six of our brigades, three on each side of the road. No artillery came into play, the ground not being fit for it. The enemy's advance was checked, then wavered, and finally relinquished; our troops pushing forward into the recovered lines. Longstreet had redeemed his promise to his commander. Meantime sharp work had also been going on at the left by Lieutenant-General Ewell—the never sleeping Ewell—and the prospects were bright.

R. H. Anderson, with Hill's corps, had come up and reported to Longstreet, who posted part of it on the right. Latrobe, of our staff, had received painful wounds in the thigh and hand, in this fight, while pushing the men forward. It had taken several hours to achieve this and a slight pause in the activities of the armies occurred. Gen. M. L. Smith, an engineer from General Headquarters, had reported to Longstreet and examined the situation on our right, where he discovered the enemy's left somwhat exposed and inviting attack; and now came our turn. General Longstreet, calling me, said: "Colonel, there is a fine chance of a great attack by our right. If you will quickly get into those woods, some brigades will be found much scattered from the fight. Collect them and take charge. Form a good line and then move, your right pushed forward and turning as much as possible to the left. Hit hard when you start, but don't start until you have everything ready. I shall be waiting for your gun fire, and be on hand with fresh troops for further advance."

No greater opportunity could be given to an aspiring young staff officer, and I was quickly at work. The brigades of Anderson, Mahone, and Wofford were lined up in fair order and in touch with each other. It was difficult to assemble them in that horrid Wilderness, but in an hour we were ready. The word was given, and then with heavy firing and ringing yells we were upon Hancock's exposed left, the brigades being ably commanded by their respective officers. It was rolled back line after line. I was well mounted, and despite the tangled growth could keep with our troops in conspicuous sight of them, riding most of the charge with Mahone's men and the Eighteenth Virginia. Some correspondence will be found in the Appendix about it. A stand was attempted by a reserve line of Hancock's, but it was swept off its feet in the tumultuous rush of our troops, and finally we struck the Plank Road lower down. On the other side of it was Wadsworth's corps in disorder. (I had last seen him under flag of truce at Fredericksburg.) Though the old General was doing all possible to fight it, his men would not stay. A volley from our pursuing troops brought down the gallant New Yorker, killing both rider and horse.

There was still some life left in the General, and every care was given him by our surgeon. Before they could get to him, however, some of his valuables—watch, sword, glasses, etc.—had disappeared among the troops. One of the men came up with, "Here, Colonel, here's his map." It was a good general map of Virginia, and of use afterwards. We were then so disorganized by the chase through the woods that a halt was necessary to reform, and I hastened back to General Longstreet to press for fresh troops. There was no need with him. He had heard our guns, knew what was up, and was already marching, happy at the success, to finish it with the eager men at his heels.

There was quite a party of mounted officers and men riding with him—Generals Kersaw and Jenkins, the staff, and orderlies. Jenkins, always enthusiastic, had thrown his arm about my shoulder, with, "Sorrel, it was splendid; we shall smash them now." And turning back I was riding by Longstreet's side, my horse's head at his crupper, when firing broke out from our own men on the roadside in the dense tangle.

The Lieutenant-General was struck. He was a heavy man, with a very firm seat in the saddle, but he was actually lifted straight up and came down hard. Then the lead-torn coat, the orifice close to the right shoulder pointed to the passage of the heavy bullet of those days. His staff immediately dismounted him, at foot of a branching tree, bleeding profusely.

The shot had entered near the throat and he was almost choked with blood. Doctor Cullen, his medical director, was quickly on the spot. Even then the battle was in the leader's mind, and he sent word to Major-General Field to go straight on. He directed me to hasten to General Lee, report what had been accomplished, and urge him to continue the movement he was engaged on; the troops being all ready, success would surely follow, and Grant, he firmly believed, be driven back across the Rapidan. I rode immediately to General Lee, and did not again see my chief until his return to duty in October. The fatal firing that brought him down also killed General Jenkins, Captain Foley and several orderlies. Jenkins was a loss to the army—brave, ardent, experienced and highly trained, there was much to expect of him.

The firing began among some of the Virginia troops that had rushed the attack. Our detour was such that it was quite possible to expect the capture of prisoners, and when Longstreet's party was seen, followed by Jenkins's brigade and part of Kershaw's command, in the shaded light of the dense tangle, a shot or two went off, then more, and finally a strong fusilade. The officers of our party acted splendidly in the effort to avert confusion and stop the deadly firing. General Kershaw was conspicuous about it, and our signal officer, Captain J. H. Manning, deliberately, calmly rode through the fire up to the Virginians, holding up his hands and making signs that we were friends. This happened between twelve and one o'clock. My report to General Lee was, as instructed, immediate. I found him greatly concerned by the wounding of Longstreet and his loss to the army. He was most minute in his inquiries and was pleased to praise the handling of the flank attack. Longstreet's message was given, but the General was not in sufficient touch with the actual position of the troops to proceed with it as our fallen chief would have been able to do; at least, I received that impression, because activity came to a stop for the moment. A new attack with stronger forces was settled on. It was to be made direct on the enemy's works, lower down the Plank Road, in the hope of dislodging him.

But meantime the foe was not idle. He had used the intervening hours in strengthening his position and making really formidable works across the road. When the Confederate troops assaulted them late in the afternoon they met with a costly repulse, and with this the principal operations on our part of the field ceased for the day; it was coming on dark.

CHAPTER XXXI

Coincidences—Longstreet's Successor

Longstreet borne from the field—His letter to Lee from Lynchburg—Return of General Wadsworth's map to his son—Coincidence in the wounding of Jackson and Longstreet—General Lee summons me—Talks of assignment to command of First Corps—He decides on General Richard H. Anderson.

General Longstreet was first taken to the house of his quartermaster, Major Taylor, near by, and thence, when he could be moved, to Lynchburg. From there he wrote to General Lee of this attack on Hancock's left as conducted by myself, and I trust it may not be considered out of place to insert that letter here.

"General Longstreet's book has caused to be brought forth quite a number of incidents of the late war which that distinguished Confederate necessarily passed over briefly in his narrative. In the battle of the Wilderness, May 6, 1864, Longstreet's corps moved to the support of A. P. Hill's corps early in the morning and checked the onward movement of the enemy. In this attack General G. M. Sorrel (then lieutenant-colonel and chief of staff of General Longstreet), under the orders of his chief, took Mahone's, Wofford's and G. T. Anderson's brigades, and, swinging around to the right, the Confederates carried everything before them. For his gallantry on that occasion, Colonel Sorrel was made a brigadier-general on the recommendation of General Longstreet, in the subjoined letter:

LYNCHBURG, VA., May 19, 1864.

GENERAL R. E. LEE, *Commanding, etc.*

SIR: The peculiar character of the position occupied by the enemy in my front on the 6th inst. was such as to render a direct assault impracticable. After a brief consultation with the commanding general, a move was agreed upon, turning and attacking the enemy's left flank. Lieutenant-Colonel Sorrel, my chief of staff, was assigned to represent me in this flank movement, with instructions as to the execution of it. The flank attack, made by three brigades, was to be followed by a corresponding movement of the other brigades of the command. This attack, made under the supervision of Lieutenant-Colonel Sorrel, was executed with much skill, promptness, and address, and the enemy was driven from his position in haste and some confusion.

It occurs to me that this is one of the instances of skill, ability and gallantry on the battle-field which should commend itself to the high approval of the Executive.

I, therefore, take great pleasure in recommending Lieutenant-Colonel Sorrel's promotion to brigadier-general for distinguished conduct on this occasion. I should have reported this case much earlier and asked for promotion upon the spot, but that I was struck down by a painful wound a few moments after the execution of the movement. I am still unable to write and hence must ask the privilege of signing this by my aide-de-camp.

I am, General, very respectfully, your obedient servant,

(Signed.) J. LONGSTREET,
Lieutenant-General.

(Signed.) By T. J. GOREE,
Aide-de-Camp.

Hancock said long after to Longstreet, "You rolled me up like a wet blanket and it was some hours before I could reorganize for battle."

Many years after this great struggle, opportunity was given me of placing with Hon. John Wadsworth, M. C., son of the general, the map before referred to as taken from his father when he fell.

In making his acknowledgments it was gratifying to learn that nearly all the other belongings of this gallant officer had gradually, by kindness of friends, found their way back into the family possessions.

Some coincidences in the fall of Jackson and Longstreet are not without interest.

On *May* 3, 1863, Lieutenant-General Jackson, great corps commander of the Army of Northern Virginia, was struck down by the fire of his own men while executing a successful flank movement in the Wilderness at the battle of Chancellorsville. On *May* 6, 1864, just one year later, Lieutenant-General Longstreet, the other great corps commander of the Army of Northern Virginia, was also struck down by the fire of his own men while conducting a successful flank movement, and this on almost the same ground.

While one fell (unhappily mortally wounded) at Chancellorsville and the other at Wilderness, both names apply to that singular district, and the two points were not very wide part.

At sunrise, on the 7th, I was summoned to the Commander-in-Chief and promptly reported. General Lee received me most kindly and at once withdrew under a neighboring tree. "I must speak to you, Colonel," he opened, "about the command of the First Corps." He then in substance went on to say that the two major-generals of the corps present were too recent for the command (Pickett does not appear to have been thought of) and an officer must be assigned. He had three in mind: Major-Generals Early, Edward Johnson, and Richard H. Anderson, and did me the honor to invite my opinion. "You have," he said, "been with the corps since it started as a brigade, and should be able to help me."

At once I saw the need of giving all the assistance possible and that I must use every care in judgment.

Thanking the General for his unprecedented confidence, I said that probably Early would be the ablest commander of the three named, but would also be the most unpopular in our corps. His flings and irritable disposition had left their marks, and there had been one or two occasions when some ugly feelings had been aroused while operating in concert. I feared he would be objectionable to both officers and men. "And now, Colonel, for my friend Ed. Johnson; he is a splendid fellow." "All say so, General," was my answer—and I fully believed it—"but he is quite unknown to the corps. His reputation is so high that perhaps he would prove all that could be wished, but I think that some one personally known to the corps would be preferred."

This brought the commander to Gen. Richard H. Anderson, and I was led to say, without presuming to criticize him or point out his merits or demerits (there are probably plenty of both), "We *know him* and shall be satisfied with him." He was long a brigadier with us, tried and experienced; then a major-general until withdrawn to make up the Third Corps.

"Thank you, Colonel," said General Lee. "I have been interested, but Early would make a fine corps commander." Being dismissed, I hastened back to camp, full of thoughts as to who was to command us. It looked from the General's closing words as if it would be Early (I am sure he preferred him), but no, Anderson was the man. Later, the same day, came the order assigning chivalrous, deliberate "Dick" Anderson to the command of the First Army Corps and it was not very long before he was made lieutenant-general.

CHAPTER XXXII

Battles of Spottsylvania C. H., May 10 and 12, and Cold Harbor, June 3, 1864.

The night's horrors—The forest on fire—Sufferings of the wounded—On same ground May 7th—Anderson in command of First Corps—Characteristics—The great strategic contest between Grant and Lee—Grant moves for Spottsylvania Court House—Lee follows in time—Both sides entrench—Union attack of 10th checked—Not so on the 12th—Edward Johnson's division suddenly assailed—Is captured with guns and colors—A serious loss keenly felt—Salient was exposed—New line established—Terrific fire for its possession by Gordon's fresh troops—We hold the new ground after heavy losses—Sedgwick killed on 10th—Stuart, our cavalry leader, shot on May 12th—General Lee not in good health—Attack by Grant at Cold Harbor—Great slaughter of Union soldiers—Assaults abandoned—Grant asks for truce to bury dead—Lee in doubt as to enemy's movements—Grant stole a march and nearly had Petersburg—Saved by Beauregard—Reinforcements and losses—An accident by falling chimney—Death of Colonel Edward Willis—General Hampton assigned to command of cavalry—Sketch.

The night was hideous. The brush and undergrowth had taken fire from the musketry and flames and smoke were obscuring everything. The numerous parties out for burying the dead and gathering the wounded were much impeded and many wounded must have perished, hidden from sight of man in that awful burnt tangle. These duties and close search continued all next day.

Our new commander, General Anderson, took the corps early on the 7th, during which the armies lay quiet after the battle. Grant was not aggressive, nor were we. The Federal commander's reflections may have been sombre. Expecting only a march, he had found bloody battles, for the Army of Northern Virginia was always in front of him. On the other hand, Lee was doubtless in the full gravity of the immense responsibilities before him and his severe losses.

It was from now until June 14th, when Grant reached his pontoon bridge over the James on his way to the new scene of action at Petersburg, a game to the death for the possession of Richmond. His able and powerful movements were to throw his army between Lee and our capital. He found Lee always, not the capital, and the movements, which shall not be detailed too much, were steadily on that line. Our General invariably penetrated his adversary's design and objective and was there—perhaps in a hurry and breathless, but there; and enough of us were ready to make necessary another march of the Union left.

Following then his original plan, Grant, on the night of the 7th, made a rapid flank movement to secure Spottsylvania Court House. Immediately part of our corps moved with General Anderson and arrived at the Court House contemporaneously with the Northerners.

The march through the scorched and smoking Wilderness was most painful. The Union men, a little in advance, had seized the best strategic point, but were driven off by our arrival, and on the 9th we found each other in line of battle, both sides entrenching wherever they might stand.

On the 10th the enemy made a handsome dash at Ewell's left and dislodged it, taking two guns. General Lee wanted to lead for recovery, but was dissuaded. The enemy being attacked was made to give up the line and the guns.

It was in this affair that Maj.-Gen. John Sedgwick, commander of Grant's Sixth Corps, was killed. A bullet pierced his head from a great distance. He and Lee had been warm friends, and the latter expressed many regrets.

There was a salient on Ewell's line, occupied by Edward Johnson's division, that Lee rightly considered dangerous to our security. Another line across the base was ordered constructed and the exposed artillery transferred to it. Before arrangements could be completed and before the artillery could be pushed forward again, Johnson was fiercely assailed at sunrise on the 12th by a heavy column massed for the purpose during the night. Most of the division was captured, including Major-General Johnson and Brigadier-General Stewart.

Lee's position instantly became perilous. He was cut in twain and fully realized it. Good work was done in repairing the break and strong bodies of troops moved from right and left to check the enemy's further advance. General Lee was under intense anxiety, plainly evinced, and was quite on the point of leading his fresh troops for restoring the line. Gen. J. B. Gordon, however, came on the scene, got the General back in his right place, and after a short, impassioned address to the troops, attacked most vigorously with the other generals. Truly it was the center of a fire from hell itself!

The Federals lining the two sides of the captured salient and the Confederates at the base poured forth a fusilade that could not be exceeded. Nothing uncovered could live in such a fire—trees were felled, trunks cut by small-arm bullets! The Union advance was checked, but we failed to recover our first lines and rested with a new one better drawn.

The army felt keenly the loss of Johnson's division and guns, but our lines were not again forced in the field. Reinforcements poured into the Union army, Grant waiting quietly until the 18th for assembling them from Washington, occasionally also doing some maneuvering. Our own army was likewise in quiet inaction, but unhappily receiving no such reinforcements.

General Anderson, as already stated, was well known to us, and fell easily into position as corps commander. During the events just sketched he had shown commendable prudence and an intelligent comprehension of the work in hand. He was a very brave man, but of a rather inert, indolent manner for commanding troops in the field, and by no means pushing or aggressive. My relations with him were uniformly pleasant. He seemed to leave the corps much to his staff, while his own meditative disposition was constantly soothed by whiffs from a noble, cherished meerschaum pipe in process of rich coloring. He was a short, thick, stocky figure, with good features and agreeable expression. I sometimes found myself sleeping in the same tent with him. He had a way on waking of sitting on his bed and proceeding to mend and patch his belongings out of a well-filled tailor's "necessaire" he always carried—clothing, hats, boots, bridles, saddles, everything came handy to him. He caught me once watching this work, and said, smiling: "You are wondering, I see; so did my wife when first married. She thought she should do the mending, but I told her I ought to have a little recreation occasionally."

We heard of Stuart's death near the Yellow Tavern on May 12th. It caused indescribable feeling in the army.

The great cavalry leader was so known to us all, officers and men; had passed through so much without hurt; his devotion to Lee was so thoroughly appreciated, and our sense of security against surprise so confident with him in the saddle that deep was our grief. His disposition so happy and sunny, his enterprise so untiring, his soul so valiant, all sprang to our memories. It was really after the battle that he fell, by an outpost bullet, when he should have been safe.

Long years after, on a glorious day in May, Confederate veterans thronged Richmond to dedicate the statue of their beloved commander.

The flower-strewn city—grim war having long since given way to gentle peace—was gay with lovely women and their happy smiles; while bright bunting, our own starry cross and the stars and stripes, conspicuous with flags of all nations, made the streets a mass of flaming color.

It was as one of the marshals that I was assisting on the memorable occasion, and dear friends at the fine old Virginia estate, the Stewart's hospitable "Brook Hill," near the city, had made me their guest. The gracious hostess, growing if possible more lovely with advancing years, recalled from far back that historic toast and beauty of old Virginia, Evelyn Byrd, from whose family she descended; there this pictured chatelaine of Brook Hill, encompassed by accomplished daughters, dispensed a charming hospitality.

On one of those days Miss Stewart drove me to the spot where Stewart fell, about half way between their residence and the old Yellow Tavern. A small stone shaft by the roadside marked it. There we feelingly recalled his deeds and fame, and placed upon it our flower tokens. It was pleasant to see, too, the young people and children of the countryside tenderly placing their own remembrances on the hero's column. The valiant rider was not forgotten!

On the 18th we sustained on our lines another attack. It was easily resisted, and then Grant, two days after, started toward Bowling Green. Lee was quick to move for Hanover Junction and offered battle there. Grant declining, moved about May 25th on a detour to the east—Lee always parallel and Richmond behind him.

Our Commander-in-Chief was far from well physically. Colonel Taylor, his adjutant-general, says the indisposition was more serious than generally supposed. Those near him were very apprehensive lest he should be compelled to give up. General Early writes: "One of his three corps commanders had been disabled by wounds at Wilderness. Another was too ill to command his corps, while he himself was suffering from a most annoying and weakening disease." Only his indomitable will and devotion could keep him in the field. To them we owe his patriotic adherence to the command of his unexampled army.

About the 30th the Confederate army was in battle order near Atlee's Station, but General Grant continued his flank movement, Lee by him, in an easterly direction, and on June 3d the two armies confronted each other at Cold Harbor, the Confederates hastily entrenching, as usual.

It was historic ground. We had fought on part of it on the eventful days of June 26, 27, 28, 1862. Here the Federal commander, weary of Lee and the oft-repeated march, made up his mind evidently to finish things. He attacked us with the utmost ferocity, but in vain. The assaults were delivered repeatedly but always repulsed with frightful carnage, and finally men could do no more. The officers with drawn swords pointed the way, but the men stood motionless in their ranks, a silent, effective protest against further "attrition."

Our men were steady in their field works and suffered but little loss. A section of a Savannah battery, commanded by Lieutenant Ross Faligant, was on our line and conspicuous for its brilliant work. Swinton, the historian, says, "The loss on the Union side in this sanguinary action was over 13,000, while on the part of the Confederates it is doubtful if it reached that many hundreds."

General Grant was late in asking for a truce to bury his dead, but finally did so. The sight in our front was sickening, heartrending to the stoutest soldier. Nothing like it was seen during the war, and that awful mortality was inflicted in but little more than an hour! The Union commander afterwards announced in general orders that no more assaults on entrenched lines should be made. He then continued his movement eastward. Lee was for a short time in painful doubt whether Grant would cross the river or hold his route up the north side. It was solved by Grant's bridge and rapid crossing, Lee having barely time to throw his van into Petersburg. Grant had nearly stolen the march on him.

The latter had expected to capture the town by surprise, a coup de main. He was foiled by Beauregard and Wise and some brave militia and home guards. They defended the position until succor came, by the head of Lee's column hastening to the rescue. Beauregard's conduct on this occasion was admirable, and much was owing to him, for which I doubt if full acknowledgment has been made.

According to official returns the Union losses since May 5th had been 6,700 killed, wounded and missing—3,000 more than Lee numbered at the opening of the campaign. Grant had received in reinforcements 51,000 muskets, including Smith's four brigades. Lee's were 14,000.

From Wilderness to Cold Harbor: Lee's aggregate, 78,400; Grant's aggregate, 192,600.

I place here an incident less dismal than the reflections brought up by the foregoing gruesome figures.

At one of the small rivers in the sharp campaign just ended we were in line on the south side inviting battle. The enemy were on the other side, but with no intention of crossing. He contented himself with abundant artillery practise, and made everything uncomfortable in range of his shell. We found no need of making reply and saved our ammunition. Our corps headquarters had made halt for the time in a beautiful grove, where stood a large, old-fashioned Virginia residence, a great house of wooden framing, with two immense brick chimneys at each gable, the chimneys stretching far above the roof apex.

The shelling was so frequent and the small fragments flying everywhere so annoying that most of us got under the lee of a gable. We knew it would not resist a shell, but could fend off the offensive fragments. General Anderson was coolly walking about the grove, sucking his big pipe, and warned us that if a shell struck one of the chimneys there might be trouble. We were perhaps two dozen sitting there, officers, orderlies, and some horses held by the bridle. Anderson was right. A crash, a bursting roar, and down came bricks and mortar on those not quick enough to skip out of the way. I myself lost no time, and was unhurt, as also were the others of the staff. But two of the couriers had a bad time of it. Hardy, my Chickamauga man, and Tucker, from Milledgeville, had, one a broken leg, the other a fractured arm. Both were put into and ambulance and, cursing and reviling at being wounded by loose brick-bats instead of honorable bullets, were carried to the rear. The laugh was decidedly on us.

A loss, personal to me as well as to the army, happened during the marches, in which there was sometimes severe fighting by parts of the armies not mentioned in the narrative. General Early, a most enterprising, resourceful officer, was much given to forced reconnaissances. They usually seemed to me unnecessary and wasted men by death and wounds. Their intention was to ascertain accurately the positive strength and morale of the enemy, and generally a brigade was told off for the service. It appeared to me that the information could be gathered by scouts and picked men without sacrificing the ranks, but General Early thought differently. On one of these movements the Virginia brigade of Pegram (who was absent, wounded) was commanded by Col. Edward Willis, of the Twelfth Georgia Infantry. His was a fine character. Just from West Point at the outbreak of the war, he threw himself into the army with ardor, became colonel of the fine Twelfth Georgia Infantry, worthily succeeding Ed. Johnson, and was about to be made brigadier-general when ordered to the reconnaissance in force. He was shot down, mortally wounded—the gallant, fair-headed, white-skinned, slight young colonel (he was very young), valiantly leading the brigade.

Our position was at some distance, but I was immediately sent for. Our families had long been neighbors and friends in Savannah, and young Willis was soon to be one of us by a still closer tie. I was quickly by his side. He died on my arm, but not before whispering loving messages for home and to that one he bore on his brave heart to its last beat. The remains of this brilliant young soldier were sent home, accompanied by a guard of honor picked from the brigade by his division commander.

Major-General Hampton succeeded Stuart in command of the cavalry. This officer had served from the very beginning of the war with high distinction, had proved himself a careful, vigilant, as well as enterprising cavalry leader, and possessed the confidence of the cavalry troops. General Lee gave him his own without reservation and his hearty support in every situation.

General Hampton was of fine presence, a bold horseman, a swordsman, and of the most undaunted courage. He had received several wounds, but was now in robust health.

His family were identified with South Carolina from its earliest settlement, and grew to be of commanding importance and wealth.

He rose to the rank of lieutenant-general, and after the war performed great political services to his State within her borders and as her Senator at Washington.

CHAPTER XXXIII

The Siege of Petersburg, June, 1864, to March, 1865

Siege of Petersburg—Lines closely drawn—Attacks on Lee's right—Mahone's defense—Mining for an explosion—North side threatened—Troops sent—Capture of Battery Harrison—Lee's attempt to retake it—The repulse—General Lee and General Pemberton—Attack on Fort Gilmer—Negroes in the van—General Lee's activity—His headquarters—Enemy's fire on Petersburg—Meeting with Twelfth Virginia Infantry—Lee attacks in front of Richmond—Beats Kautz and takes his cannon—Kautz retreats to a fort—Lee attacks and is repulsed—Union troops armed with Spencer rifles—General Lee's quick eye for horses—Ewell's fall from his horse—Kershaw's Division sent to Valley—Destruction of barns and houses—Kershaw returns—Capture of a remount—The crater—Intercourse between pickets—Continuous firing—General E. P. Alexander's love of shooting.

The siege of Petersburg had now begun. It is certain that Lee had had a narrow escape in getting there in time. Grant had nearly beaten him and indeed should have taken the place, notwithstanding Beauregard's boldness. The Union generals had been explaining with some heated recriminations how they failed to be in possession before Lee came up. The latter on the north side had been for hours under intense anxious uncertainty in discovering Grant's move, whether a crossing or continued march on the north side.

The lines were closely drawn and severe fighting ensued. Digging began in earnest on both sides.

Salients, traverses, bastions, forts, trenches, covered ways, parallel, zig-zags, and all the other devices for the taking and defense of fortified cities were resorted to. Our left rested on the Appomattox River and was so close to the enemy's line that a biscuit could be thrown across, and conversation went on constantly between the fighters, who the next minute were firing at any head or arm that might be incautiously exposed. Our works stretched from the left around the town to the Weldon Road on the right, and this was an object of Lee's constant solicitude. It was our direct railroad to the South, and Grant in possession would have our communications cut and supplies broken off. For months it was the Federal General's incessant effort to accomplish it. His great numbers made it possible, but Lee always managed, notwithstanding, to have a defense.

At Reams Station Major-General Mahone performed great service in beating back the force sent to seize the road at that point. Later in the siege, mining began by the enemy. The result was the appalling hour of the crater explosion by which very many Confederates perished, and then in the great combat that followed for recapturing the ground, hundreds of Federals fell. Mahone was conspicuous in restoring the broken lines.

But the story of the siege of Petersburg—eight months—is not to be told in a few pages. It was a struggle from day to day, night to night, and filled with picturesque scenes of individual daring and valor, sorties and strategems. There was often quiet massing of columns for heavy assaults on points supposed to be relatively weak. We sustained many of these but the lines were maintained. Lee also made some hard drives at his opponent with varying success. All, however, pointed to only one thing—the wasting of our unrecruited strength and the apparently limitless numbers available for the Union Army.

While such operations were carried on south of the James, General Grant was not idle on the north side. A strong force was held there threatening Richmond, and our commander had to provide for it out of his thin ranks and keep some show of strength in front of our capital, immensely aided, however, by the excellent lines of field works that environed the city. These conditions brought about considerable shifting of our two divisions. Field and Kershaw were between the Petersburg lines and the north side, and Pickett's division was defending what was known as the Chesterfield lines between Petersburg and Richmond, but was not threatened.

A strong force of the enemy had massed north of the James and captured a powerful earthwork known as Battery Harrison on our extreme right. General Lee had come on the scene with one of the First Corps divisions and other troops. He decided to retake the fort, attaching great importance to its possession. An assaulting column of three good brigades was organized, Bratton's South Carolina regiments among them. Captain Sorrel, then adjutant-general, shook hands with me as they started forward, almost "a forlorn hope," and I thought never to see him alive again. But he came out safe among many killed and wounded, the assault being repulsed with great loss. A new line was entrenched and fortified, thrown back to right and rear.

General Lee, when he liked, could sit down pretty hard on words not agreeable to him. An example was given that night. With his staff and several general officers he was at the Chaffin farm-house on the James, reviewing the serious events of the day. General Pemberton, after the fall of Vicksburg, being without assignment, had assumed his rank of lieutenant-colonel in the Regular Army, and as such was on engineer duty on the Richmond line of defenses. He was present and, speaking of Battery Harrison, said with something like superior confidence, "I presume, General, you will retake the fort, coûte que coûte." Lee's sad, steady eyes rested on that unfortunate officer as he slowly said: "General Pemberton, I made my effort this morning and failed, losing many killed and wounded. I have ordered another line provided for that point and shall have no more blood shed at the fort unless you can show me a practical plan of capture; perhaps you can. I shall be glad to have it." There was no answer from Pemberton.

General Lee had had an anxious day; all of it was occupied in meeting the enemy's attacks. There was an especially severe one on Fort Gilmer by Ben Butler's command, with negro regiments pushed in front of the assailing whites. Fortunately we had a staunch regiment in the fort, which beat back the attacking column.

A hundred or two of the negroes, half crazed with whiskey, got into the ditch of the fort and refused surrender.

Our men lighted some shells, rolled them over the parapet and quickly brought the darkies to subjection. It was an ugly affair all through.

And so the siege passed. One day strong detachments must be made to meet powerful movements against our extreme right flank, and requires the leaders' presence. Truly never was a leader called on for greater performance. General Lee's health was now fortunately stronger and his activity most wonderful.

He was in comfortable quarters at the Turnbull House, offered for his use by the owner. Our own were not far distant, and quite comfortable in tents and small houses. The routine life of the town passed from day to day without excitement. The people had become accustomed to shell and bullets and made no ado when they whizzed about their heads.

I do not think the enemy's fire was directed especially at the non-combatant part of the town, but much of it got there all the same. A new accession to our staff was Captain Dunn, of Petersburg, an excellent gentleman, with us now for several months. A shell burst on him while bathing in his house, and smashed things all around, but the A. D. C. and his family escaped. A bullet had found his leg before this good luck.

The citizens were very hospitable and very self-sacrificing. Too much could not be done for the soldiers. But this was the feeling and the practise all over Virginia.

As we entered Petersburg I came up with the regiments of Mahone's brigade, the Twelfth among them. They had not forgotten the Wilderness, gave me a rousing cheer, and cried out that we must again together charge these fellows in front of Petersburg.

Their brave survivors keep me in mind still, after these many years.

General Lee, always aggressive, was quick to find opportunity of attack. He saw his enemy rather exposed at a point in front of Richmond, quickly got some troops in position, and made a dash at them in great style. It was a strong force of infantry and cavalry under General Kautz, and he left eight or nine guns, many prisoners, and some colors in our hands, retiring to a strong fort and defenses about a mile in his rear. Our General decided to have it and follow up his first success. Gregg's Texas Brigade and two others—seasoned troops—were thrown at Kautz's fort. We could not live against its fire—no troops could. His men were armed with the Spencer magazine rifles and such a fire had never before jarred and stunned us. We had to retire and resume our positions. Losses were considerable, among them Brig.-Gen. John Gregg, commanding the Texas Brigade—a very able officer.

General Lee was fond of horses and had always an eye to them. When the first attack was made my brother, Captain Sorrel, was mounted on a nice young mare I had just given him. At the first onset she was shot, and horse and rider were both in the mud. It happened almost under General Lee's eyes.

Some days after, the General meeting Sorrel on the road kindly asked if he were hurt, and was sorry for the loss of the mare. "But I have got another, General," said the Captain. "Yes, two it seems," the General answered as he rode off, smiling. Sorrel's bewilderment was removed when later on it became plain that the new purchase was in foal.

When Ewell, one leg gone, was forced to relinquish field work and take leave of his corps, the old warrior insisted on other duty, and was assigned to command of the inner line of defenses about Richmond. General Lee, with Ewell, Anderson, and a number of other officers, and some of our staff, was examining a new line of defense with that trained engineer's eye of his, Ewell riding by him. The latter was so good a horseman that his one leg was equal to most riders' two, but his horse stumbling, down came both—an awful cropper. I made sure the General's head and neck were cracked. He was picked up, no bones broken, but an "object" about the head; scratched, bruised, torn and bloody. Lee instantly ordered him back to Richmond and to stay there until completely well.

In two or three hours he was again on the lines, and such a sight! Painfully comical it was. He had gone to the hospital, where the bald head and face were dressed. He returned swathed in bandages from crown of head to shoulders. Two little apertures for his piercing eyes and two small breathing spaces were all that was left open for the Lieutenant-General. Quite indifferent, however, to such mishaps, he was sharp about his work and lisping out directions as usual.

General Lee thought to weaken the pressure on him at Petersburg and Richmond by transferring some of it to the open field of the Valley, where skilful maneuvering might offset inferior numbers. He had the temerity to detach part of his army for the purpose, and with some other commands sent General Anderson with Kershaw's division across the mountains. Most of the staff went with the expedition and had opportunity of witnessing Sheridan's work in destroying all the resources of that fighting-ground.

As we marched forward, the enemy slowly retiring, smoke was seen ahead on a wide range from the burning barns and granaries of the noncombatant people. Sheridan was arranging for his "crow" to carry his own rations should he venture into the Valley.

General Lee's ingenious and bold attempt did not result as he hoped. Grant could not be tempted that way. His business was at Petersburg and Richmond, and besides there were already enough of his troops in the Valley and covering Washington to answer for the safety of that capital. Our expedition was therefore soon terminated and came back to the James. The division had but two encounters in the Valley. One at Charlestown, a small affair, in which General Humphreys, commanding the Mississippi Brigade, was wounded. Another was at Front Royal, in which Wofford's brigade got caught in a bend of the river and was beaten off with loss in killed, wounded, and prisoners. A dear friend, Colonel Edward Stiles, Sixteenth Georgia Regiment, was killed.

I had chance, however, before marching, after a sharp night's ride, to pay a flying visit at their home to the good ladies Hamtrammock, who had cared for me wounded at Sharpsburg. They were as pleasant as ever and the hour seemed all too short. While in the Federal lines they had supplied themselves with all sorts of little things for soldiers in the field, as tokens of remembrance, and I had pressed on me a pair of fine gauntlets, which seemed about everything that I wanted at the moment.

On our way back to Lee the division (Kershaw's) suddenly came up with a Union regiment of cavalry foraging at the foot of the mountains. It was a surprise to the riders, and they at once took to their heels, pressing up on the side of the mountains for escape. We had nothing but food with us, and most of the mounted regiment got safely away in small parties. Two fully-equipped ambulances, however, could not follow the riders, and were overturned in a mountain gulley. One of them furnished me with an excellent mount. Two soldiers were going through its beautiful equipment, and coming among the medicines to a large vessel labeled "Spiritus frumenti" it was tossed aside with the rest of the pharmacœpia. But some one suggested that "Spiritus frumenti" might be another way of spelling whiskey—and then to see those fellows go for it!

While the commander and most of the troops of the First Corps were on the north side, the enemy's mines at Petersburg were "spring making." "The Crater" was a frightful affair, and should, it appears to me, have been prevented. We knew they were mining. Our shaft had been sunk and short galleries run out. Their working parties could be heard. Should we not have countermined actively and fought their men off in their own galleries? However, it was not done, and the "blow up," considered only barely possible, was upon us. When it came it was all that the enemy could wish. His plans were excellent, but miscarried by the conduct of one or more of his leading officers. The crater was at once filled with their men, many negroes among them—negroes who, as usual, primed with whiskey, had been pushed to the front and into the breach, but support failed them.

Then came the Confederates' great work of destroying these men and recovering their mutilated line. Mahone did brilliant service. His division of five brigades was thrown at the invaders, and with other forces seized the "hole," captured or killed the unfortunates in it, and the day was ours with the works and integrity of the line restored.

I had heard much of this remarkable fight from the Georgia Brigade (it had been very conspicuous in it) that I took command of some days after.

This amusing story was told me by one of its men. Exhausted in the crater fight, he sank wearily on a log for a short rest. It moved gently and an old-fashioned negro's voice came from the log-like darky, "Please, Marster, don't shoot; I'se doin' nuttin'." The rascal had doubtless been one of the first in the crater, wild with liquor; but the Southerner was merciful and sent him to the rear.

Of course the men on both sides behind the works, so close sometimes, got tired of "potting" at each other, and taking a rest became altogether too friendly. Firing would cease and individuals and small parties appear in front bartering and chaffing with the boys in blue.

Our tobacco was always good for coffee and a Northern paper. It got to be too familiar and led to desertions of our men. Their rations were of the poorest (one-half pound of bacon and three-quarters of a pound of cornmeal), their clothing and shoes worn and unfit for the field, and their work and duties of the hardest on our attenuated lines. Reliefs were few and far between. No wonder they sometimes weakened to better themselves, as they supposed, and stayed with the fat-jowled, well-clad, coddled up masses opposite them. But we had to stop the desertions at any price, so at night steady, continuous musketry firing was ordered, sweeping the glacis in front of our entrenchments. It cost a lot of lead and powder, but did something in holding back the weaklings in our command.

The enemy, nothing loth, returned the fire, and were good enough to send plenty of their own lead. There was considerable to be gathered during the day, and this got my friend, Gen. E. P. Alexander, into trouble. He was a many-sided character—an engineer of the highest abilities, an artillerist of great distinction, a good reconnoitering officer and an enthusiastic sportsman besides. In the early days of the war I one day met him, mounted as usual on a very sorry, doubtful-looking beast, with a pair of enormous holsters on his saddle-horn. "And what have you there, Alexander?" I asked, thinking possibly of some good edibles. "These," he said, and drew out his long telescope for reconnaissance—a very powerful glass—and from the other an enormous old-fashioned horse-pistol of immense calibre, some tiny cubes of lead, cut from bullets, and a pinch or two of gunpowder. "Quail," he said, "are eating up this country and I like them. This old pistol gives me many a mess of birds." At

Petersburg his only want for his private gunning was lead to melt into small shot, and gathering some (after working his big gun) he received an unexpected contribution—a bullet in his shoulder, hot from the enemy, which made him a very uncomfortable wound.

CHAPTER XXXIV

LONGSTREET'S RETURN—FAREWELL TO LEE

Return of Longstreet—Am promoted brigadier-general—Parting with the First Corps—Report to A. P. Hill and Mahone—Sketches—Assume command of brigade of Georgians—its staff—Drill and exercises—Laying out a camp—General Lee's encouragement—Want of field officers—Captain H. H. Perry—Mahone's bread ovens—Christmas, 1864—Sherman's march in Georgia—Grant's Virginia strategy—Our division moves out in bitter cold—Demonstration on our extreme right against the railroad—Brigade forms line—No close firing—Enemy rejoins his main command—Received a slight wound—The return to camp—Its bad condition in our absence—Valuable boots burnt in bivouac—In February again ordered out to right—Serious collision with enemy in force at Hatcher's Run—General Pegram killed—Am shot in lung and borne from the field—Moved to Richmond and thence to Colonel Watts's, in southwest Virginia for convalescence—My recovery—Marriage of Doctor Sorrel—At Lynchburg—Hear of Lee's surrender—Take to the mountains—Again at Colonel Watts's—Hunter and Crook—Homeward bound—Lady Godiva—Farewell to Lee and the Army of Northern Virginia.

It was in October, our corps (two divisions) being on the north side, that we had the happiness of welcoming our chief back to his command.

His right arm was quite paralyzed and useless. He had taught himself to write legibly and easily with his left. Following the advice of his doctor, he was forever pulling at the disabled arm to bring back its life and action. He succeeded, for, though never strong, its use was partially restored in later years and his pen went back to it.

I was with him but a few days. My commission as brigadier-general came unexpectedly, a note from my friend Burton Harrison, the President's Secretary, to the effect that it had been signed, reaching me the evening before. This was the first inkling I had of the promotion. Elsewhere it has been told how it came about, and I began preparing to move, my orders being to report to Lieut.-Gen. A. P. Hill for command in Mahone's division. Hill's corps was on the south side in front of Petersburg. Lieut.-Col. O. Latrobe succeeded me as A. A. G. and chief of staff; an excellent assignment. A brigadier going to an organized command carries no staff with him. That is attached to the brigade, not to the general. He has one appointment, that of A. D. C. (captain's rank), personal to himself. There were many applications for the place, but sending for Spencer, private, Fort Alabama, my sergeant of couriers for several years. I almost floored the modest fellow by asking if he should like to go with me as captain. "Of course" he should, and did, and was part and parcel of that brigade of Georgians in no time until Appomattox dispersed us. I had made no mistake in him; an exceedingly useful staff officer.

Few can know how painful it was to part with my corps and its chief. I had started with them at the opening battle, handled its growing battalions into brigades and divisions, and shared its battles, expeditions, and campaigns; was proud of its renown; was known to officers and men of every regiment and had, I believe, their confidence and respect. It was much to give up, but the duty called, and on a fine morning I mounted with my A. D. C. to cross the river and take up my new billet. I shall be excused, I hope, if a little homesickness is confessed.

My comrades did not let me go easily. The night before there was a farewell party of many officers at headquarters. A goodly quantity of apple-toddy was consumed, but not to hurt, and the party, General Longstreet with us for a time, was full of feeling, touching me keenly by its spontaneous demonstration.

Here ended the staff officer's duties, but his recollections will yet carry him a little way forward while commanding his brigade. The end was fast approaching, and my concluding jottings seem to belong to what has gone before.

Turning my back, then, for the first time on the glorious old First Army Corps, I reported next day at A. P. Hill's quarters. Nothing could exceed his kindness in receiving me; it continued all through my service in his corps and I had every evidence of the good feeling of this distinguished officer. I was to report next to General Mahone for command of his Georgia brigade. This remarkable man was at breakfast when I entered and immediately had me seated with him.

Maj.-Gen. William Mahone was a Virginian, about forty years of age. His appearance arrested attention. Very small both in height and frame, he seemed a mere atom with little flesh. His wife said "none." When he was shot (slightly) she was told it was only a flesh wound. "Now I know it is serious," said the good lady, "for William has no flesh whatever." Sallow of feature, sharp of eye, and very active in movement was the General; in dress quite unconventional, he affected jackets rather than coats, and on a certain hot summer's day that

I recall he was seen, a major-general indeed, but wonderfully accoutered! A plaited brown linen jacket, *buttoned to trousers,* of same material, like a boy's; topped off by a large Panama straw hat of the finest and most beautiful texture, met our eyes, and I must say he looked decidedly comfortable. But not always was he thus attired. He could be strictly uniformed when he chose.

He had been president of the railroad between Petersburg and Norfolk, and retaining the office, managed the road all through the campaigns. Finally the enemy captured his wagon-load of railroad papers, records, etc., and Mahone was raging. It was that railway, when hostilities ended, that he combined with others connecting and gained a start into the political power and mischief he exercised in Virginia. His brigade of Virginians had not seen much hard fighting until the Wilderness, and there they did well. It was at Petersburg, in command of his division of five brigades from Virginia, Georgia, Alabama, Mississippi, and Florida that he justly won great reputation for brilliant achievements in defense of the beleaguered city. He was undoubtedly a general of very uncommon ability.

While we sat, I enjoyed his breakfast. A high liver, nothing could excel it, and he was never without the materials. A cow was always by his quarters and laying hens cackled loud, besides many luxuries. Delicate in physique, he had to nourish himself carefully.

I received his orders to take command of my Georgians, and mounted on my way to them. Mahone was said to be irritable and in some instances tyrannical, but for myself I had invariably nothing but consideration, and often good help from him.

The brigade was in trenches far on the right, not in very close touch with the enemy, and was having a quiet time of it with Col. William Gibson in command. He was well known in Georgia politics for some years, and a very brave officer; repeatedly wounded, but without discipline or organization. Leave of absence was allowed him to return to Georgia.

On assuming command, Captain Evans, a line officer detailed as A. A. G., supposing that I was bringing an officer of the staff department with me, suggested that probably I should wish him to rejoin his regiment.

But I wanted him with me. He had long filled the post, was acquainted with almost every officer and man of the brigade, and was a brave and qualified officer. The command consisted of the Second, Twenty-second, Forty-eighth, and Sixty-fourth Regiments and Second and Tenth battalions, Georgia Infantry. The Sixty-fourth and Tenth battalions were late levies and had not made the great reputation of the others, while serving under Wright and Girardy. The latter was a most promising officer, promoted from captain in the brigade, and was killed at the head of it two weeks after taking command.

The Third Georgia enjoyed a reputation excelled by none in the army.

My first thought was to get supplies of clothing and shoes for the men and have the command relieved from trench duty, to which it was entitled by the length of service in them. Our work strengthening the defenses always went on, and there was no time for much-needed drill and military exercise.

General Lee, taking his daily ride about the lines, came on me while the working parties were digging and spading. His greeting was, "Good-morning, my young friend; I feel sorry for you." "Why so, General?" "Because you have so much to do," answered the commander, the gleaming white teeth showing his pleasant humor as he continued his ride. He generally had some such words to let one know he expected a lot of work out of him.

I was not unsuccessful as to my wants. A fair quantity of supplies were issued and orders came for relief from the trenches and to pitch good winter camps a little in the rear. It was great joy to the troops.

A good piece of woods was selected and a fine camp of winter huts laid out and built according to regulations, with battalion fronts and company streets and all the rest in good soldierly form. Once settled, drill became the order of the day in good weather. There were fine open fields near by furnishing good ground, and company drill, battalion drill, and evolutions of the line by the brigade were followed up vigorously, as well as all military exercises and street duties practised and perfected. The men were in much need of the instruction. Decided neglect in these respects had fallen on this fine brigade after the stern and gallant Wright left it, and the good effects of the efforts now working out were soon apparent.

The greatest want was in field officers; so many had been wounded and left with the enemy at Gettysburg, besides others sick at home or in the hospital, that the regiments suffered thereby.

I wrote urgently and personally to Mr. Ould, our commissioner for exchange, to get back to me certain officers whom I wanted badly. He managed to get only one, Colonel Snead, of the Third Georgia, and him I was glad to have.

The brigade was well equipped with staff officers of the subsistence, quartermaster, ordnance, and medical departments. The commissary, Major Hughes, an excellent fellow, was the same who had sold me those two sorry mounts that broke down in the Chickamauga Campaign. On reporting, he evidently thought I might recall him unfavorably and was a bit uneasy, until shown that no ill feelings were harbored against him. In horse dealing it is "caveat emptcr"—the buyer must look sharply to himself.

It was not long before Capt. H. H. Perry, of the Adjutant-General's Department, was transferred from Benning's brigade to report to me as A. A. G. There being two of that department with Benning and none with me, Perry was summarily transferred without any question. He had always performed inspection duty, and preferring it, was assigned to that branch of his department in my brigade, thus retaining Evans as A. A. G. "Old Rock" (General Benning) always believed I was at the bottom of the whole business and never forgave me.

I was surely fortunate in securing so excellent a staff officer. Highly educated, experienced with troops, active and resourceful, he soon became prominent and strong in the brigade as well as attached to his brigadier. He is still with the living in Georgia, numbered among my dear friends.

At times the soldier's ration was execrable, really unfit. Some bacon from Nassau was coming through the blockade, and it would not be incredible for the blockading fleet to allow it to come through in hope of poisoning us. A third of a pound of this stuff and some corn-meal was often the full extent of the daily ration.

Sometimes we got better allowances of wheat flour, and then General Mahone took a notion to improve on it by baking. The brigade commissaries were ordered to set up ovens—plenty of bricks and material lying about—and issue the flour baked in good loaves. There is, too, a slight gain in weight in baking. But the men would none of such food, it was too light and wholesome. Their stomachs wanted the flour stirred with grease in a skillet and cooked solid and hard. When a chunk was eaten it stayed with the soldier and kept his appetite partly appeased. But these new-fangled loaves—so easily digested! Hunger came again, almost before finishing one of them. Not for Johnny Reb was this thing; he wanted, like Tommy Atkins, "some bulk in his inside," and one fine morning Mahone's ovens were found completely demolished. The soldiers took again to their old-time toothsome and staying morsels out of the skillet.

Christmas of 1864 was now at hand. The birth of the Prince of Peace was given such honor amid the warlike scenes of the siege as our small resources permitted. Some boxes came from loving hearts at home, the commissaries did all they could, and the Army of Northern Virginia actually feasted, trying to forget for an hour or two the perils and hardships that beset it.

At Christmas General Sherman was in Savannah, his march to the sea a complete success. My people at home suffered no great annoyance. Sherman as a young lieutenant had shared my father's hospitality and had not forgotten it. The old gentleman, however, persistently fastened on him the crime of burning his comfortable country establishment in Virginia.

Sherman's march and other movements in the West were in Grant's strategic combination for the destruction of Lee's army and should be considered in estimating his abilities outside of operating in Virginia. Indeed, it might be said that Sherman contributed to the fall of Richmond almost as much as did the Army of the Potomac.

Early in January it came on to be very cold, and during the worst of it our division was ordered out to meet a threatening demonstration against our right at a considerable distance. My brigade marched instantly, our camp being occupied by Gen. C. A. Evans's Georgia Brigade to fill our position on the line. Evans was in luck to get his men into such well-prepared camps. We moved rapidly and in two days came up with a large force of the enemy, formed in line and prepared for battle. It appears, however, that he was not ready this time, or that he overestimated the Confederate strength sent against him. Some shelling was indulged in and small-arm long-distance firing. It seems that but two or three of us were touched, among them myself. I was sitting on the white mare (my other mount gone suddenly lame) in front of the line, with no thought of firing then, so distant was the enemy,—quite out of range,—when a long-range rifle sent a bullet through many folds of thick clothing and striking on the hip bone knocked me out of the saddle. It proved to be nothing serious. The ball had glanced off, stiffening and bruising the leg rather painfully, so that remounting after some bandaging, it stuck out like a wooden leg. I did not think that just such a hit could unhorse me.

My men said the brigade was unlucky for its commanders. General Wright had been repeatedly and dangerously wounded; several colonels commanding, wounded or killed, and General Girardy killed. I began to think there might be something in it. The enemy took up the march, and leisurely rejoining their main body to the right, Mahone's division began moving for the camps just vacated. It continued very cold, much ice and snow lying about the roads. At our last bivouac some miles from camp I suffered a loss, nothing less than a noble pair of riding-boots, a present, kept for extra work.

At the bivouac the negro servant had taken them out of the blanket roll and failed to replace them. As soon as they were missed, back he went and returned with the precious leathers burned to a crisp! Our campfires had spread through the forest. At this period boots cost five or six hundred dollars of our currency, if to be had at any price.

On starting back I sent word to General Evans of our approach so that my camps could be vacated in good order. The men were utterly disgusted and indignant when they re-entered their quarters. They were little like the well-kept camps they had temporarily vacated. Evans's officers had not properly restrained the careless, reckless soldiers. I made vigorous complaint at headquarters, but at this date there was perhaps too much else to think of. General Evans is now chief of the veterans in Georgia and held in great respect by their dwindling numbers.

Mahone's other brigades were efficiently commanded by Finnegan, Florida; Harris, Mississippi; Weisiger, Virginia; Sanders, Alabama.

In the first days of February another demonstration was made against Lee's extreme right, this time in great force and meaning business. Our division and other troops with cavalry at once pushed out to meet it, with Finnegan in command of division (Mahone was absent, sick). The collision came at Hatcher's Run by some preliminary skirmishing on February 5th, a sanguinary action on the 6th, followed up by the enemy feebly on the 7th. On the 6th, my Georgians were hotly engaged in the afternoon and made a handsome, successful charge, which dislodged and forced back the Federals. The contest went on until darkness stopped it, and the night passed entrenching where we stood, caring for wounded and burying dead.

Early next morning the enemy, driving back my pickets, got too close to us, and a rifleman put a bullet through my right lung, smashing the ribs front and rear. I was down this time for good, I supposed, the breath gushing through the orifices instead of its natural channel. The surgeon, Dr. Wood, however, soon relieved that by plastering the holes, and sent me back that night. The roads being frozen and very rough, my brave fellows made two relief gangs and bore their commander by litter on their shoulders eight miles to a small shanty, where rest was taken.

All through the night, while passing stray troops on the road, I could hear the question, "Who have you there?" "General Sorrel." "Is he badly hurt?" "Yes, mortally wounded." The soldier habitually takes a gloomy view of things.

Very soon I was in comfortable quarters near Petersburg, in the hands of my excellent brigade surgeon, Dr. Sampson Pope, and progressed so well that in a fortnight I could be moved to Doctor Sorrel's quarters in Richmond, under treatment of my friend Dr. J. B. Reid, and with that ended the staff officer's soldiering. A few closing words will bring me to the end of these "Recollections" nearly forty years behind us.

My wound healing satisfactorily, Doctor Sorrel proposed in March taking me to "The Oaklands," the beautiful estate in Roanoke County of Colonel Wm. Watts, who had kindly sent me an invitation to visit him. He was the invalided colonel of the Twenty-eighth Virginia, of the First Corps, a fine officer and most hospitable, the leading man of the county. To him we went, the change being very beneficial. Then the railroad station was Big Lick, a post-office, shop, and tavern. It is now grown to be Roanoke, a prosperous city of 25,000. Colonel Watts's widowed sister, Mrs. Rives, presided over the delightful old Virginia establishment. Her lovely character won all hearts. The stately figure and attractive features were known and admired widely over the countryside. To me she was kindness itself, and no marvel is it that I mended rapidly.

There was an engagement of a few months' standing between Doctor Sorrel and Mrs. Rives, and soon after our coming the uncertain future was considered. They decided to wed without longer waiting, and the ceremony, quite private, was performed at the residence, myself in full uniform as the Doctor's best man, propped on my feet by the dignified, silver-haired black major-domo.

While in this part of the country I heard much about Hunter's expedition into it the previous year and the devastation he had brought in the region round about. Truly Maj.-Gen. David Hunter, of the United States Army, was a torch bearer if nothing else. He had no military distinction, but had served against the Indians, it is said, with the same cruelties it was now his delight to apply to non-combatant dwellers in southwest Virginia and the head of the Shenandoah Valley. No property within reach of his destroying hand seemed safe from him. His fame lay not in the soldier's hard-fought battles, but in burning farmers' houses and barns. The extensive schools at Lexington aroused his hate and were laid in ashes by his torch.

General Crook, the fine soldier then serving with him, said, "He would have burned the Natural Bridge could he have compassed it." Marvel it is that Hunter did not blow it up. He was, however, beaten off by Early's forces and the home guards, and the country cleared of that devastator. There was little more heard of him as a soldier.

Maj.-Gen. George Crook was altogether a different character. He was a soldier of high training and tried courage, making no war on women and children, houses and barns.

Some time later, one of our daring rangers, McNeil, with a small following, achieved a bold exploit. While Crook was commanding a department at Cumberland, Md., the ranger penetrated many miles within the blue lines, took the General out of bed, mounted him well, and landed his distinguished prisoner safely in Richmond.

There Doctor Sorrel, who had served with him in the old Army, called to see to his comforts. Crook as a thorough-going Indian fighter was not without some admiration for the way McNeil had gathered him in. "But, Sorrel," said he, "I shall get even with that fellow at his own work. Just as soon as I get out of this my commission will drop for a few weeks, while I raise a hundred men with whom I undertake to beat Master McNeil at his own game."

Such was perhaps his intention then, but, exchanged soon after, there was other and more important work awaiting this gallant and respected officer.

Early in April, after grateful farewells to my host and new sister, we started to rejoin the army. At Lynchburg came to us the accounts of the surrender at Appomattox, with all the pathetic, harrowing details attaching to that event; the feeling of the soldiers, their overflowing affection for Lee and sympathy with him and his own hidden but overwhelming grief—I pass them by. My brigade was on hand in good shape, with Captain Perry looking after it, and paroled stronger than any brigade in the army. (See Appendix.)

The commandant at Lynchburg, General Lomax, placed at my disposal an ambulance and mules to get out of reach of the Union forces. We could not yet realize that the war was ended with the life of Lee's army. I took to the mountains for some days, and then finding things really ended and my troublesome wound breaking out afresh, ventured again on Colonel Watts's hospitality. It was as generous as the day. But it was time to move, and after farewell to hospitable Oaklands the Doctor and I started on our return home. The rails were sufficiently repaired to take us to Lynchburg, where we were paroled by the United States officer. Between us we had just fifteen dollars good money, and it came to me in this way. When I was last in Lynchburg, as already described, one of our quartermasters pressed on me $20 in gold, four half-eagles; "A barrel of Confederate money not good," as he said, "for the price of a dinner."

Some time after I came up with a young Maryland cavalryman making his way back to Baltimore. He had no coat or jacket, although the rest of him was good, and I wanted to know why. "Well," said young Latrobe (it was my friend's brother), "my horse wanted a set of shoes. The farrier would not look at my money, but took the jacket, and I got my shoes." It was quite certain the young fellow would part with his remaining outfit, piece by piece, with the same easy nonchalance, if need be, and I insisted on his taking one of my half-eagles. But for that the "Peeping Toms" of Baltimore might possibly have seen a new Godiva, "clothed only with chastity," riding through their streets fresh from the Southern armies. Their blushes and the young cavalryman's were saved by that golden half-eagle.

From Lynchburg to Richmond the route was tedious and wearying. It was partly by rail, partly in an army wagon, and partly on foot. On arriving at the Confederate capital we were amid the ruins of the great fire that nearly destroyed it. The army of occupation was in force, everywhere the Union army filled one with wonder. It was like the ant in numbers, and I really could not take in its unstinted equipment in wagons, ambulances, mules, draught horses, light artillery, and horse furniture, all apparently new and of the best class for field work. The contrast with our own inadequate equipment was very decided, and still greater was the splendor of their officers, mounts and uniforms, and the good clothing of the soldiers, with what on our part had contented us. In Richmond, nursing our dwindling cash, we found a frugal but cheerful hospitality while preparing for the next move to Baltimore, where we were sure of meeting my good father's provision for us. My weak condition would not permit me making the journey home on horseback; it must be by sea.

At Richmond we took the oath, as prescribed, to the United States Government, the courteous Federal officer asking pleasantly if it "tasted bad?" This done we hoped to get a permit to leave by boat for Baltimore, but were refused. No movements of Confederate officers, except Marylanders returning, were suffered in that direction. The decision was then forced on us that we must go, "coûte que coûte." It was managed successfully with some little risk. By the help of friends we were smuggled on board just as the boat was starting. The Doctor was in mufti and I had doffed as much military attire as I could. We kept very quiet and secluded on the main deck of the boat as she glided down the river of so many warlike scenes of the preceding years! past frowning Drewry's Bluff, past bristling Chappin's farm, City Point, Westover, and Harrison's Landing, Turkey Bend and Butler's Dutch Gap Canal—all saddening and depressing in the retrospect, crossing thoughts of the misty future. At the fortress a short stop was made, and then the voyage up the noble Chesapeake resumed. One of the coal passers here recognized me with a wide, astonished grin. He was one of my brigade fellows, in now for a job at anything. The night was passed on the bay and could have been very comfortable with a trifle more cash. We had, however, just about enough to pay for passage, without bed or meals. So we stood out the long night and could provide some small refreshments. When morning came we were moored to the wharf, and I soon found my good Baltimore relatives most hospitably inclined, and our troubles for the time were done with.

There were many Confederate officers and soldiers about the city, all watched quite closely by the Federal authorities. General Hancock was in command of the department, and from his adjutant-general I received an order to report in person. Upon so doing I was questioned as to my reasons for being in Baltimore and my intentions. Upon explaining why I was returning home by that route and that I should have to go to New York to find a steamer for Savannah, he was civil and obliging; allowed a stay of a week in Baltimore; but I was required to report once in every twenty-four hours. The next day this considerate officer dispensed with such visits, adding, "You shall not, General, be troubled in any way while you are stopping here." Here Doctor Sorrel left me. Deciding to defer his visit home, he returned at once to Virginia. A few days later I was in New York at the New York Hotel, Mr. Cranston the proprietor, and for years past, as then, the resort of everything Southern. There were many officers in the hotel, some I suspect by Cranston's good nature and kindness. After a visit to some relatives and friends, who had only thought of me as one dead, I took passage for Savannah on a small, crowded, most uncomfortable little steamer. The rough voyage was safely made, and I landed on my own shores in dear old Georgia, greeted by kindred and friends, with hands outstretched in a hearty welcome home.

And now these recollections approach their close. There are many more thronging, pulsing memories that could interest, perhaps instruct. What is here gathered has been an inexpressible comfort and occupation in the colorless hours of recent tedious convalescence, and could be extended, but the parting word must be spoken.

It is farewell to the Army of Northern Virginia and its ever-glorious commander.

His name, his fame shall forever live! His sword, unstained, be ever a soldier's shining light and bright example!

> "Ah Muse! You dare not claim
> A nobler man than he,
> Nor nobler man hath less of blame
> Nor blameless man hath purer name,
> Nor purer name hath grander fame,
> Nor fame, another Lee!"

His army incomparable holds, after long years, the abiding love of its surviving veterans. Who that marched with it, fought with it, took part in its victories and its defeats, shared its sufferings and its joys, shall ever be deaf when its deeds are sung or mute when ring out its plaudits!

For my part, when the time comes to cross the river like the others, I shall be found asking at the gates above, "Where is the Army of Northern Virginia? For there I make my camp."

APPENDIX

"HEADQUARTERS NEAR BEAN'S STATION,
"December 17, 1863.

"Special Orders No. 27.

"Major-General L. McLaws is relieved from further duty with this army, and will proceed to Augusta, Georgia, from which place he will report by letter to the adjutant and inspector-general. He will turn over the command of the division to the senior brigadier present.

"By command of Lieut.-General Longstreet.

"G. M. SORREL,
"Lieut.-Col. and Assistant Adjutant-General.

"Major-General McLAWS,
"Confederate States Army."

"CAMP ON BEAN'S STATION GAP ROAD,
"December 17th, 1863.

"Lieut.-Col. SORREL,
"Assistant Adjutant-General.

"I have the honor to acknowledge the receipt of Special Orders No. 27 from your headquarters, of this date, relieving me from further duty with this army. If there is no impropriety in making inquiry, and I cannot imagine there is, I respectfully request to be informed of the particular reason for the order.

"Very respectfully,
"L. McLAWS,
"Major-General."

"HEADQUARTERS NEAR BEAN'S STATION,
"December 17th, 1863.

"Major-General MCLAWS,
"Confederate States Army.

"General: I have the honor to acknowledge the receipt of your note of to-day, asking for the particular reason for the issue of the order relieving you from duty with this army.

"In reply I am directed to say that throughout the campaign on which we are engaged, you have exhibited a want of confidence in the efforts and plans which the commanding general has thought proper to adopt, and he is apprehensive that this feeling will extend more or less to the troops under your command.

"Under these circumstances the commanding general has felt that the interest of the public service would be advanced by your separation from him, and as he could not himself leave, he decided upon the issue of the order which you have received.

"I have the honor to be, general, with great respect,

"G. M. SORREL,
"Lieut.-Col. and Assistant Adjutant-General."

From *The Savannah News,* 1899.

"During the siege of Petersburg, Va., there was a severe combat at Hatcher's Run, resisting one of Grant's attacks on Lee's right flank.

"Brig.-Gen. John Pegram was killed and Brig.-Gen. Sorrel was, for some time, thought to be mortally wounded.

"The action took place on February 6, 1865. A time-stained clipping from the *New York Herald,* a few days later, gives 'Sketches of the Dead Rebel Generals,' with some detail, indicating considerable acquaintance with the Confederate personnel.

"We print what it had to say of our townsman, who, still with us, is thus permitted to read his own obituary from the *Herald's* columns:

" 'BRIGADIER-GENERAL G. M. SORREL

" 'The rebel Gen. Sorrel, reported seriously wounded in the battle on Hatcher's Run, has been permitted to enjoy his rank but a short time. He has been but lately appointed to the rank and assigned to duty.

" 'Gen. Sorrel was a native of Georgia, and, at the commencement of the war, was a teller in the Central Railroad Bank in Savannah. He had no military education. To his established character as a quiet, taciturn business man and accountant and to some influence from an extensive family to which he belongs, he owes his appointment on the staff of Gen. Longstreet at the beginning of the war. He served in the capacity of assistant adjutant-general to Gen. Longstreet, at Bull Run, July 21, 1861, was wounded at Antietam, September 17, 1862, and since followed the varied fortunes of Longstreet. He has been advanced from a lieutenancy to a lieutenant-colonelcy in the adjutant-general's department of the rebel army.

" 'During the battle of the Wilderness, fought in May, Lieut.-Col. Sorrel displayed great gallantry and evinced much ability in directing and managing a division whose commander had fallen, and of which he was placed in command by Longstreet. Generals Lee and Longstreet awarded him high praise for his conduct, and recommended him for promotion. He was in consequence appointed brigadier-general, November 1, 1864, and assigned to the command of the brigade formerly commanded by Gen. Wright. In relieving him from duty as his assistant adjutant-general, Gen. Longstreet paid the following compliment to young Sorrel:

" ' "General Order No. 15—Headquarters First Army Corps, November 4, 1864. Col. G. M. Sorrel, assistant adjutant-general, having been promoted to the rank of brigadier-general, and assigned to the command of a brigade in the Third Corps, is relieved from duty as assistant adjutant-general of this corps. The loss of this officer to the First Corps, with which he has been so permanently connected since its organization, will be severely felt. Distinguished alike for gallantry in the field and for energy and skill in the administration of his department, his value cannot be over-estimated. He will carry with him to his new command, so richly won, a sure promise of success in the record of the past.

" ' "By command of Lieut.-Gen. Longstreet.

" ' "Official:

" ' "O. LATROBE,

" ' "*Assistant Adjutant-General.*"

" 'The rebel papers of February 9th report Gen. Sorrel dead of the wounds received on the 6th inst.' "

From an address delivered by Comrade John R. Turner before A. P. Hill Camp of Confederate Veterans of Petersburg, Va., on the evening of March 3, 1892.

"My letter to General Sorrel I mailed to Savannah, Ga., and was as follows:

" 'PETERSBURG, VA., January 13, 1892.

" 'GEN. G. M. SORREL,

" 'Savannah, Ga.

" 'DEAR GENERAL: Being anxious to know if your recollection and mine accorded, as to certain movements made at the battle of the Wilderness, May 6th, 1864, in which we both participated, I take the liberty of addressing you this communication, and hope (if not trespassing too much upon your time) you will do me the kindness to favor me with a reply.

" 'You will remember Mahone's brigade of Anderson's division was quartered near Madison Run Station. We broke camp on the morning, I think, of the 4th, and bivouacked near Rapidan Station that night. In the early morning of the 6th we made a forced march to the battlefield, which we reached about 10 o'clock.

" 'Mahone's brigade was ordered very soon afterwards to the right in the Wilderness. After going some distance through the thicket, we encountered the enemy apparently bivouacking, and little expecting any attack from that direction. They fled pell-mell before us, leaving their light camp equipage scattered in every direction, making scarcely any resistance until they reached the Orange Plank Road; when, having a natural fortification, strengthened hurriedly by them, they stoutly resisted us. Just at this point you dashed up to the front of my regiment, the Twelfth Virginia, and approaching our color-bearer, Benj. H. May (as gallant a soldier as ever carried a flag or shouldered a musket, and who was killed at Spottsylvania Court House the 12th of May), asked him for his colors to lead the charge. He refused to give up his colors, but said: "We will follow you." With great enthusiasm we followed you in the direction of the Plank Road. The enemy broke and fled before us. I remember seeing you then dash with great speed up the road in the direction, I suppose, of General Longstreet, to inform him that the way was clear. Our color-bearer, in the excitement of the moment, failed to observe that the other regiments of the brigade had halted at the Plank Road. We became detached and passed over the road forty or fifty yards before halting. Our colonel, D. A. Weisiger, observing that we were in advance of the brigade, ordered us to fall back in line with the brigade. In doing so the other regiments, mistaking us for the enemy, fired into us, killing and wounding several of our men, and I always thought the same volley killed General Jenkins and wounded General Longstreet, this apparently putting an end to all operations for the day, as there seemed to be very little done afterwards during the day.

" 'I had the pleasure of a short conversation with General Longstreet returning from Gettysburg three years ago, and he told me that, while he knew he was wounded by his own men, he never knew exactly how it occurred. He said everything was working beautifully up to this point, and what seemed to be an opportunity for a brilliant victory was lost by this unfortunate circumstance.

" 'I have often thought of your bravery and gallant bearing as you led us through the woods up to the Plank Road. I feel that I would like to know with certainty whether or not my recollections are correct as to the part you took in that charge.

" 'Wishing you a long life, much happiness and great prosperity, I am very truly, your comrade,

" 'John R. Turner.'

"To this letter General Sorrel replied as follows:

" 'New York, January 19, 1892,
" 'Lee's Birthday.

" 'John R. Turner, Esq.,
" 'A. P. Hill Camp, C. V.,
" 'Petersburg, Va.

" 'Dear Sir: Your letter of January 14th was forwarded to me from Savannah, and I am very glad to hear from you. The events you describe are so long ago, that one's memory may be pardoned if slightly treacherous as to details, but I may say at once that your recital of the incident and the movements of Mahone's brigade at the battle of the Wilderness conform accurately to my own recollection of it, excepting, of course, the too-partial and flattering view you take of my own personal service there. But I will give you briefly my own version of it, which really is near your own.

" 'Longstreet's corps had to move at the earliest hour in the morning of the 6th of May, and arriving at the battlefield was just in time to be thrown across the Plank Road and check the enemy, whose attack had begun on A. P. Hill's corps. This of itself was a magnificent performance of the corps to form line in the dense thicket after a hasty march, in the midst of troops suddenly attacked and retiring from the front in disorder. Being done during the enemy's attack it displayed the steadiness characteristic of Longstreet's famous corps. This checked that attempt and for some time there was some quiet. It was then, too, you will recollect, that General Lee was about to lead the Texas Brigade into action, so threatening was the situation. He was almost forcibly stopped by his officers and the entreaties of the soldiers. It was soon after this that General Longstreet said to me that if I were to collect some troops over on the right, get them in good line and in touch with each other, and make a strong movement forward, swinging by the right, he felt sure a splendid success would follow. I proceeded to follow out these directions, with full authority to control the movement. There were three brigades, in addition, perhaps, to other troops, that I succeeded in getting into good form and ready to move. These were Mahone's, Wofford's, and Anderson's. The movement soon began, at a given signal, our right swinging swiftly around, driving everything before it. The lines in front of us made some sharp resistance, but they were quickly overcome, and our troops, Mahone's brigade notably distinguished in the affair, rushed forward through the dense undergrowth, carrying everything before them. It was then that the incident occurred of which you speak, about poor Ben May. He was doing all that man could do with his colors, but seemed to be somewhat embarrassed by the bushes, and I thought perhaps I might help to get them forward, mounted as I was. As you say, he positively refused to let them leave his own hands. I was filled with admiration of his splendid courage. I think it was on the 12th that poor May was shot, and I received from a member of the Twelfth Virginia an affectionate message that he sent me. I have always remembered him as one of the bravest of Confederate soldiers. The Twelfth Virginia did splendid service that day, and the regiment and myself became great friends. Till the end of the war, whenever in marches or elsewhere I met it, I was always honored with its friendly greetings. As our troops reached the Plank Road, you will recollect that a volley was given to the enemy, who were trying to rally on the opposite side. By this volley General Wadsworth and his horse (while trying to rally his men) were both killed, and his soldiers could make no stand against us. Our rapid movements through the woods had disordered our line, as you correctly describe it. Leaving them for a moment, while recovering good order. I hastened to General Longstreet with a view to bringing up supports to follow up our splendid success. I met the General near by, Jenkins's brigade immediately behind him. He had heard the sound of our rifles, and, with the quick instinct of the general that he was, was following us up with a strong and powerful support to pursue his victory. I had scarcely taken more than a few steps with him when a sudden and unexpected fire, at first scattering, then heavier, broke out from our men. The General was shot down by my side, and at the same time General Jenkins, one or two staff officers, and several couriers. I have never known accurately who started this fire; there is yet some confusion about it, but it was fatal, and had the effect, by disabling the General, of putting a stop to the heavy blow he was about inflicting on the disordered enemy. Later in the day, you will remember, we made another attack, rather more direct, with a strong force, on the enemy, who had got behind some entrenchments; but we there sustained a repulse, and that about closed the principal features of the battle of the Wilderness on the 6th of May.

" 'The importance of our flank attack, which I have described here so briefly, was not under-estimated by the enemy in his subsequent reports. The official report of the battle by General Grant, or his immediate subordinate, describes the tremendous attack of these three brigades, which turned his own left flank and nearly brought about a widespread disaster to the Federal army. I cannot but think it would have ended so, had not General Longstreet, in the flush of his success, and with ardent, fresh troops in hand, been struck down in the very act of delivering this blow.

" 'I am sketching this off to you hastily, and entirely from memory, and while there may be some omissions or inaccuracies as to detail, I think the account is not far from wrong.

" 'With best wishes, I am, yours very truly and sincerely,

" 'G. M. Sorrel.' "

From Colonel Freemantle's (Coldstream Guards) "Three Months in the Southern States."

"30th June, Tuesday.—This morning before marching from Chambersburg, General Longstreet introduced me to the Commander-in-Chief. General Lee is, almost without exception, the handsomest man of his age I ever saw. He is 56 years old, tall, broad shouldered, very well made, well set up, a thorough soldier in appearance, and his manners are most courteous and full of dignity. He is a perfect gentleman in every respect. I imagine no man has so few enemies, or is so universally esteemed. Throughout the South, all agree in pronouncing him to be as near perfection as man can be. He has none of the small vices, such as smoking, drinking, chewing or swearing, and his bitterest enemy never accused him of any of the greater ones. He generally wears a well-worn long gray jacket, a high black felt hat, and blue trousers tucked into Wellington boots. I never saw him carry arms, and the only mark of his military rank are the three stars on his collar. He rides a handsome horse which is extremely well groomed. He, himself, is very neat in his dress and person, and in the most arduous marches he always looks smart and clean.

"In the old Army he was always considered one of its best officers; and at the outbreak of these troubles he was lieutenant-colonel of the Second Cavalry. He was a rich man—but his fine estate was one of the first to fall into the enemy's hands. I believe he has never slept in a house since he has commanded the Virginian army, and he invariably declines all offers of hospitality for fear the person offering it may afterwards get into trouble for having sheltered the rebel General."

From Viscount Wolseley.

"Office of Commander-in-Chief,
"London, 10th July, 1899.

"My Dear General Sorrel: I have great pleasure in complying with your request, and hope Mrs. Sorrel will do me the honor of accepting the enclosed latest photograph I have had taken.

"I am a collector of autograph letters, but I lack letters from the Confederate commanders. I am very glad to have your letter to add to my collection. If you happen to have any letters from the Southern generals that you could spare me I should esteem it a great favor.

"Believe me to be, with a very keen and pleasant remembrance of all the kindness I received when in the Southern States,

"Sincerely yours,
"Wolseley.

"To General Sorrel,
"New York."

Thanks of the Confederate Congress to Lieutenant-General James Longstreet and his Command.

"Resolved by the Congress of the Confederate States of America.

"That the thanks of Congress are due and hereby cordially tendered to Lieutenant-General James

Longstreet and the officers and men of his command for their patriotic services and brilliant achievements in the present war, sharing as they have, the arduous fatigues and privations of many campaigns in Virginia, Maryland, Pennsylvania, Georgia, and Tennessee, and participating in nearly every great battle fought in those States, the commanding general ever displaying great ability, skill, and prudence in command, and the officers and men the most heroic bravery, fortitude, and energy in every duty they have been called upon to perform.

"*Resolved,* That the President be requested to transmit a copy of the foregoing resolution to Lieutenant-General Longstreet for publication to his command.

"Approved February 17, 1864."

J. Longstreet to Secretary of War.

"HEADQUARTERS NEAR CHATTANOOGA,
"September 26th, 1863.

"HON. J. A. SEDDON, *Secretary of War.*

"SIR: May I take the liberty to advise you of our condition and our wants. On the 20th instant, after a very severe battle, we gained a complete and glorious victory—the most complete victory of the war, except perhaps the first Manassas. On the morning of the 21st General Bragg asked my opinion as to our best course. I suggested at once to strike at Burnside and if he made his escape to march upon Rosecrans's communication in rear of Nashville. He seemed to adopt the suggestion and gave the order to march at four o'clock in the afternoon. The right wing of the army marched some eight or ten miles, my command following next day at daylight. I was halted at the crossing of the Chickamauga, and on the night of the 22d the army was ordered to march for Chattanooga, thus giving the enemy two days and a half to strengthen the fortifications here already prepared for him by ourselves. Here we have remained under instructions that the enemy shall not be assaulted. To express my conviction in a few words, our chief has done but one thing that he ought to have done since I joined his army—that was to order the attack upon the 20th. All other things that he has done he ought not to have done. I am convinced that nothing but the hand of God can save us and help us as long as we have our present commander.

"Now to our wants. Can't you send us General Lee? The army in Virginia can operate defensively, while our operations here should be offensive, until we have recovered Tennessee, at all events.

"We need some such great mind as General Lee's (nothing more) to accomplish this. You will be surprised that this army has neither organization nor mobility and I have doubts if this commander can give it to them. In an ordinary war I could serve without complaint under any one whom the Government might place in authority; but we have too much at stake in this to remain quiet under such distressing circumstances. Our most precious blood is now flowing in streams from the Atlantic to the Rocky Mountains and may yet be exhausted before we have succeeded. Then goes honor, treasure, and independence. When I came here I hoped to find our commander willing and anxious to do all things that would aid us in our great cause and ready to receive what aid he could get from his subordinates.

"It seems that I was greatly mistaken. It seems that he cannot adopt and adhere to any plan or course whether of his own or some one else. I desire to impress upon your mind that there is no exaggeration in these statements. On the contrary I have failed to express my convictions to the fullest extent. All that I can add without making this letter exceedingly long is to pray you to help us and speedily.

"I remain, with the greatest respect, your most obedient servant,

"J. LONGSTREET,
"Lieutenant General."

Captain H. H. Perry, A. A. G., Sorrel's Brigade, writes of Grant's first demand for Lee's surrender at Appomattox.

"THE EVENTFUL NIGHT.

"It was night, April 7th, 1865. We had crossed the river, near Farmville, and had taken up a position about, as near as I can remember, a mile from the crossing, which the Confederates had attempted to burn, but unsuccessfully. General Miles, commanding a Federal brigade, made a mad attempt to throw the Confederates into confusion on their left by a flank movement (perhaps that was his purpose), but it was a very unfortunate move, for his lines were in a few minutes nearly cut to pieces and his brigade placed hors de combat. A furious picket firing and sharp-shooting began on both sides, while the wounded and dead Federals lay between the two lines.

"Mahone's division was now the rearguard at this point of General Lee's army. General Lee's forces were reduced now to their minimum strength, but a fiercer, more determined body of men never lived. They simply waited for General Lee's orders.

"About five o'clock p. m. a flag of truce appeared in front of General Sorrel's brigade (General Wright's old brigade), of which the writer of this account was the adjutant-general. A courier was sent to division headquarters to announce it. Colonel Tayloe, a splendid young Virginian, had been assigned temporarily to the command of General Sorrel's brigade, General Sorrel having been almost mortally wounded near Petersburg. In a short while Colonel Tayloe was ordered to send a staff officer to answer to the flag of truce.

"The writer was assigned to this duty at the Confederate front lines. As the top of the earthworks was reached, a number of Federal sharpshooters fired at me, and two balls passed through the uniform coat I wore, and one ball wounded a Confederate soldier in the hand, who had risen up with others from behind the works, out of curiosity to see what was going to take place. That ended the truce business for that afternoon. After nightfall and after everything on both sides had lapsed into silence, pickets were put in front of our lines about one hundred yards. Captain James W. English, one of the bravest, coolest, most faithful and vigilant officers in the Confederate Army, was in charge of the line in front of our brigade. I had selected him for the reason that I knew that he would not fail me if I depended on his courage and faith. Colonel Tayloe knew nothing of our command or its officers, and the responsibility rested on me to select the right man in the crisis there was now upon us. We apprehended a night attack.

"About nine o'clock at night, as soon as the moon was about to rise, Captain English reported that a flag of truce was again offered on the Federal lines on our front. It was reported again at our division headquarters and I was again sent out to answer it as before. I put on an army revolver, put aside my sword, and advanced about fifty yards from our pickets, halted, and called for the flag. Where I stood there were scattered around several Federal dead and wounded.

"One of the latter asked me to do something for him. I told him I would very soon, making this promise only to encourage him, for I could really do nothing for lack of authority, as well as lack of means. I asked his name and was rather astonished when he said he was General Miles's adjutant-general and that his name was Boyd, as I now remember it. A response to my call in front took my attention, though I remember that the wounded officer said he had been shot through the thigh.

"I advanced some distance and met a very handsomely dressed Federal officer. We stepped in front of each other about seven or eight feet apart. I soon recognized the fact that my worn Confederate uniform and slouch hat, even in the dim light, would not compare favorably with his magnificence; but as I am six feet high I drew myself up as proudly as I could, and put on the appearance as well as possible of being perfectly satisfied with my personal exterior. The officer spoke first, introducing himself as Gen. Seth Williams, of General Grant's staff.

"After I had introduced myself, he felt in his side pocket for documents, as I thought, but the document was a very nice-looking silver flask, as well as I could distinguish. He remarked that he hoped I would not think it was an unsoldierly courtesy if he offered me some very fine brandy. I will own up now that I wanted that drink awfully. Worn down, hungry and dispirited, it would have been a gracious godsend if some old Confederate and I could have emptied that flask between us in that dreadful hour of misfortune. But I raised myself about an inch higher, if possible, bowed and refused politely, trying to produce the ridiculous appearance of having feasted on champagne and pound-cake not ten minutes before, and that I had not the slightest use for so plebeian a drink as 'fine brandy.' He was a true gentleman, begged pardon, and placed the flask in his pocket again, without touching the contents in my presence. If he had taken a drink, and my Confederate olfactories had obtained a whiff of the odor of it, it is possible that I should have 'caved.' The truth is, I had not eaten two ounces in two days, and I had my coat-tail then full of corn, waiting to parch it as soon as opportunity might present itself. I did not leave it behind me because I had nobody I could trust it with.

"As an excuse which I felt I ought to make for refusing his proffered courtesy, I rather haughtily said that I had been sent forward only to receive any communication that was offered and could not properly accept or offer any courtesies. In fact, if I had offered what I could it would have taken my corn.

"He then handed to me a letter, which he said was from General Grant to General Lee, and asked that General Lee should get it immediately if possible. I made no reply except to ask him if that was all we had to transact, or something to that effect. He said that was all. We bowed very profoundly to each other and turned away.

"In twenty minutes after I got back in our lines, a Confederate courier riding a swift horse had placed in General Lee's hands the letter which was handed to me, the first demand for surrender of his devoted army. In an hour's time we were silently pursuing our way toward the now famous field of Appomattox. We marched all day of the 8th of April and slept in bivouac not more than three or four miles from Appomattox, where the demand was made again and was acceded to, and the Confederacy of the South went down in defeat, but with glory.

"We arrived on the field of Appomattox about 9 o'clock on the 9th day of April, the day of capitulation. The negotiations lasted during that day.

The general order from General Lee was read to the army on the 10th of April. That is, as I remember it, General Lee published his last order to his soldiers on that day. I sat down and copied it on a piece of Confederate paper, using a drum-head for a desk, the best I could do. I carried this copy to General Lee, and asked him to sign it for me. He signed it and I have it now. It is the best authority along with my parole that I can produce why, after that day, I no longer raised a soldier's hand for the South. There were tears in his eyes when he signed it for me, and when I turned to walk away there were tears in my own eyes. He was in all respects the greatest man that ever lived, and as an humble officer of the South, I thank Heaven that I had the honor of following him.

"Waynesboro, Georgia, 1896."

Some extracts from Colonel Freemantle's "Three Months in the Southern States."

"GETTYSBURG—PICKETT'S CHARGE.

"I determined to make my way to General Longstreet. It was then about 2.30. After passing General Lee and his staff I rode on through the woods in the direction in which I had left Longstreet. I soon began to meet many wounded men returning from the front; many of them asked in piteous tones the way to a doctor or an ambulance. The farther I got the greater became the number of the wounded.

Some were walking alone on crutches composed of two rifles, others were supported by men less badly wounded than themselves, and others were carried on stretchers by the ambulance corps; but in no case did I see a sound man helping the wounded to the rear, unless he carried the red badge of the ambulance corps. I saw all this in much less time than it takes to write it, and although astonished to meet such vast numbers of wounded, I had not seen *enough* to give me an idea of the real extent of the mischief.

"When I got close to General Longstreet I saw one of his regiments advancing through the woods in good order; so thinking I was in time to see the attack I remarked to the General that *'I wouldn't have missed this for anything.'* Longstreet was seated at the top of a snake fence at the edge of the wood and looking perfectly calm and unperturbed. He replied: 'The devil you wouldn't! I would liked to have missed it very much; we've attacked and been repulsed; look there!'

"For the first time I then had a view of the open space between the two positions and saw it covered with Confederates slowly and sulkily returning toward us in small, broken parties under a heavy fire of artillery. The General told me that Pickett's division had succeeded in carrying the enemy's position and capturing the guns, but after remaining there some minutes it had been forced to retire. No person could have been more calm or self-possessed than General Longstreet under these trying circumstances, aggravated as they now were by the movements of the enemy, who began to show a strong disposition to advance. I could now thoroughly appreciate the term 'Bulldog,' which I had heard applied to him by the soldiers.

Difficulties seemed to make no other impression upon him than to make him a little more savage.

"Major Walton was the only officer with him when I came up—all the rest had been put into the charge. In a few minutes Major Latrobe arrived on foot, carrying his saddle, having just had his horse killed. Colonel Sorrel was also in the same predicament and Captain Goree's horse was wounded in the mouth.

"The General was making the best arrangements in his power to resist the threatened advance, by advancing some artillery, rallying the stragglers.

"I remember seeing a general come up to him and report that he was 'unable to bring up his men again.' Longstreet turned upon him and replied with some sarcasm, 'Very well, never mind, then, General, just let them remain where they are; the enemy's going to advance and it will spare you the trouble.' He asked for something to drink. I gave him some rum out of my silver flask, which I begged he would keep in remembrance of the occasion; he smiled, and to my great satisfaction accepted the memorial.

If Longstreet's conduct was admirable, that of General Lee was perfectly sublime. He was engaged in rallying and encouraging the broken troops, and was riding about a little in front of the wood, quite alone—the whole of his staff being engaged in a similar manner farther to the rear. His face, which is always placid and cheerful, did not show signs of the slightest disappointment, care, or annoyance; and he was addressing every soldier he met, a few words of encouragement, such as: 'All this will come right in the end, we'll talk it over afterwards; but in the mean time all good men must rally. We want all good and true men just now,' etc. He spoke to all the wounded men that passed him, and the slightly wounded he exhorted 'to bind up their hurts and take up a musket in this emergency.' Very few failed to answer his appeal, and I saw many badly wounded men take off their hats and cheer him. He said to me, 'This has been a sad day for us, Colonel, a sad day; but we can't expect always to gain victories.' "